While every care has been taken in the compiling of information contained in this volume, the publishers cannot accept any liability for loss, financial or otherwise, incurred by reliance placed on the information herein.

All prices quoted in this book are obtained from a variety of auctions in various countries during the twelve months prior to publication and are converted to dollars at the rate of exchange prevalent at the time of sale.

The publishers wish to express their sincere thanks to the following for their involvement and assistance in the production of this volume:

NICKY FAIRBURN (Art Director)
EELIN McIVOR (Sub Editor)
ANNETTE CURTIS (Editorial)
CATRIONA DAY (Art Production)
KATE SMITH (Art Production)
FRANK BURRELL (Graphics)
DONNA BONAR
JACQUELINE LEDDY
JAMES BROWN
EILEEN BURRELL
FIONA RUNCIMAN
RICHARD SCOTT
DONNA CRUIKSHANK

British Library Cataloguing in Publication Data

The Lyle Official Arts Review.
 1992

 745.1

 ISBN 0862481384

 ISBN 86248-138-4

Typset by Word Power, Auchencrow, Berwickshire
Printed and bound in Great Britain by
Butler & Tanner Ltd, Frome and London

THE LYLE OFFICIAL ARTS REVIEW 1992

COMPILED & EDITED BY
TONY CURTIS

be guided by

LYLE

Erotic Antiques

1001 Antiques worth a Fortune (which not a lot of ...now about)

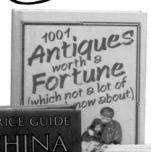

LYLE PRICE GUIDE
CHINA

LYLE PRICE GUIDE
DOLLS & TOYS

LYLE PRICE GUIDE
ART NOUVEAU & DECO

TONY CURTIS

THE **LYLE** OFFICIAL
ARTS REVIEW 1992

The Price Guide to Paintings

Tony Curtis

THE **LYLE** OFFICIAL
ANTIQUES REVIEW 1992

Over 1 million copies sold

The Price Guide to Antiques

Tony Curtis

Introduction

Published annually and containing details of thousands of oil paintings, watercolours and prints, The Lyle Official Arts Review is the most comprehensively illustrated reference work on the subject available at this time.

Each entry is listed alphabetically under the Artist's name for easy reference and includes a description of the picture, its size, medium, auctioneer and the price fetched at auction during the twelve months prior to publication.

As regards authenticity of the works listed, this is often a delicate matter and throughout this book the conventional system has been observed:

The full Christian name(s) and surname of the artist denote that, in the opinion of the auctioneer listed, the work is by that artist.

The initials of the Christian name(s) and the surname denote that, in the opinion of the auctioneer listed, the work is of the period of the artist and may be wholly or partly his work.

The surname only of the artist denotes that, in the opinion of the auctioneer listed, the work is of the school or by one of the followers of the artist or painted in his style.

The word 'after' associated with the surname of the artist denotes that, in the opinion of the auctioneer listed, the picture is a copy of the work of the artist. The word 'signed' associated with the name of the artist denotes that, in the opinion of the auctioneer listed, the work bears a signature which is the signature of the artist.

The words 'bears signature' or 'traces of signature' denote that, in the opinion of the auctioneer listed, the work bears a signature or traces of a signature which may be that of the artist.

The word 'dated' denotes that the work is dated and, in the opinion of the auctioneer listed, was executed at that date.

The words 'bears date' or 'inscribed' (with date) denotes that, in the opinion of the auctioneer listed, the work is so dated and may have been executed at about that date.

All pictures are oil on canvas unless otherwise specified. In the dimensions (sight size) given, the height precedes the breadth.

Although the greatest possible care has been taken to ensure that any statement as to authorship, attribution, origin, date, age, provenance and condition is reliable, all such statements can only be statement of opinion and are not to be taken as statements or representations of fact.

The Lyle Official Arts Review offers a unique opportunity for identification and valuation of paintings by an extremely broad cross section of artists of all periods and schools.

Unless otherwise stated descriptions are placed immediately underneath the relevant illustrations.

We firmly believe that dealers, collectors and investors alike will treasure this and subsequent annual editions of the Lyle Official Arts Review (published in September each year) as changing trends in the fluctuating world of art values are revealed.

Tony Curtis

Auction Acknowledgements

AB Stockholms Auktionsverk, Box 16256, 103 25 Stockholm, Sweden
Allen & Harris, St Johns Place, Whiteladies Road, Clifton, Bristol BS8 2ST
Jean Claude Anaf, Lyon Brotteaux, 13 bis place Jules Ferry, 69456 Lyon, France
Anderson & Garland, Marlborough House, Marlborough Crescent, Newcastle upon Tyne NE1 4EE
Auktionshause Arnold, Bleichstr. 42, 6000 Frankfurt a/M, Germany
Australian Art Auctions, Suite 333, Park Regis, 27 Park Street, Sydney 2000, Australia
Bearnes, Rainbow, Avenue Road, Torquay TQ2 5TG
Biddle & Webb, Ladywood Middleway, Birmingham B16 0PP
Bigwood, The Old School, Tiddington, Stratford upon Avon
Bonhams, Montpelier Street, Knightsbridge, London SW7 1HH
Bonhams Chelsea, 65–69 Lots Road, London SW10 0RN
Michael Bowman, 6 Haccombe House, Near Netherton, Newton Abbot, Devon TQ12 4SJ
Butterfield & Butterfield, 220 San Bruno Avenue, San Francisco CA 94103, USA
Butterfield & Butterfield, 7601 Sunset Boulevard, Los Angeles CA 90046, USA
Christie's International SA, 8 place de la Taconnerie, 1204 Genève, Switzerland
Christie's, 8 King Street, London SW1Y 6QT
Christie's, 502 Park Avenue, New York, NY 10022, USA
Christie's East, 219 East 67th Street, New York, NY 10021, USA
Christie's, Cornelis Schuytstraat 57, 1071 JG Amsterdam, Netherlands
Christie's (Monaco), S.A.M, Park Palace 98000 Monte Carlo, Monaco
Christie's SA Roma, 114 Piazza Navona, 00186 Rome, Italy
Christie's Scotland, 164–166 Bath Street Glasgow G2 4TG
Christie's South Kensington Ltd., 85 Old Brompton Road, London SW7 3LD
Bruce D Collins Fine Art Gallery, Box 113, Denmark, Maine, USA
Du Mouchelles Art Galleries Co., 409 E. Jefferson Avenue, Detroit, Michigan 48226, USA
Duran Sala de Artes y Subastas, Serrano 12, 28001 Madrid, Spain
Eldred's, Box 796, E. Dennis, MA 02641, USA
Finarte, 20121 Milano, Piazzetta Bossi 4, Italy
Galerie Koller, Rämistr. 8, CH 8024 Zürich, Switzerland
Galerie Moderne, 3 rue du Parnasse, 1040 Bruxelles, Belgium
Germann Auktionshaus, CH 8032 Zürich, Zeltweg 67/Ecke Markurstr., Switzerland
Glerum Auctioneers, Westeinde 12, 2512 HD's Gravenhage, Netherlands
Graves Son & Pilcher, 71 Church Road, Hove, East Sussex, BN3 2GL
W R J Greenslade & Co., 13 Hammet Street, Taunton, Somerset, TA1 1RN
Halifax Property Services, 53 High Street, Tenterden, Kent
Hauswedell & Nolte, D-2000 Hamburg 13, Pöseldorfer Weg 1, Germany
Hotel de Ventes Horta, 390 Chaussée de Waterloo (Ma Campagne), 1060 Bruxelles, Belgium
P Herholdt Jensens Auktioner, Rundforbivej 188, 2850 Nerum, Denmark
Hobbs & Chambers, 'At the Sign of the Bell', Market Place, Cirencester, Glos.
G A Key, Aylsham Saleroom, Palmers Lane, Aylsham, Norfolk, NR11 6EH
Kunsthaus am Museum, Drususgasse 1–5, 5000 Köln 1, Germany
Kunsthaus Lempertz, Neumarkt 3, 5000 Köln 1, Germany
W.H. Lane & Son, 64 Morrab Road, Penzance, Cornwall, TR18 2QT
Lawrence Fine Art, South Street, Crewkerne, Somerset TA18 8AB
David Lay, The Penzance Auction House, Alverton, Penzance, Cornwall TA18 4KE
Phillips, Blenstock House, 7 Blenheim Street, New Bond Street, London W1Y 0AS
Phillips, 65 George Street, Edinburgh EH2 2JL
Phillips Marylebone, Hayes Place, Lisson Grove, London NW1 6UA
Pinney's, 5627 Ferrier, Montreal, Quebec, Canada H4P 2M4
Riddetts, Richmond Hill, Bournemouth
Ritchie's, 429 Richmond Street East, Toronto, Canada M5A 1R1
Selkirk's, 4166 Olive Street, St Louis, Missouri 63108, USA
Skinner Inc., Bolton Gallery, Route 117, Bolton MA, USA
Sotheby's, 34–35 New Bond Street, London W1A 2AA
Sotheby's, 1334 York Avenue (at 72nd Street), New York, NY 10021, USA
Sotheby's Monaco, Le Sporting d'Hiver, Place du Casino, 98001 Monte Carlo, Monaco
Henry Spencer, 40 The Square, Retford, Notts. DN22 6DJ
Tennants, 27 Market Place, Leyburn, Yorkshire
Woolley & Wallis, The Castle Auction Mart, Salisbury, Wilts SP1 3SU

ARTS
REVIEW 1992

It is indeed a sign of the times that one needs to be something of a fiscal wizard to understand much of what has been going on in the art market during this past year.

In the Far East, the main story has been the Itoman scandal, which broke in October 1990 in Japan and threatens to become as big as the Recruit scandal which forced the resignation of Prime Minister Takeshita in 1988. In conjunction with the Gulf War, it has brought Japanese corporate art buying as we have known it over the past few years to a virtual halt.

The scandal has effectively revealed how these multi-million dollar purchases of French Impressionist paintings have been used in one of the biggest tax-avoidance scams of all time, assisted of course by the arbitrary and wildly overheated prices paid for the top entries at the New York Impressionist sales. The Itoman company of Osaka deals in land and property (and latterly, of course, in fine art) and it found itself in trouble when the Japanese property market collapsed, with debts of some £4.2 billion, mostly to its partner, the Sumitomo bank. Itoman had used huge loans to acquire paintings, which, it turned out, were worth only a fraction of the money obtained for their purchase. So where had the rest of the loans gone? Well, it seems that the procedure is as follows. An art appraiser is paid to grossly overvalue a work, on the strength of which a loan is obtained. The work is then bought for a lesser sum and the change thus becomes invisibly available for other purposes. Variations on this theme include gifts by buyers to sellers of land by giving or selling them a picture and then buying it back at an inflated price, so the owner keeps the cash and avoids tax; or to use the same procedure to offer bribes to tax officials and politicians, again selling low and buying back high.

Maurice de Vlaminck, Le Printemps au Village, oil on canvas, 65 x 92cm.
(Christie's)

$186,010   £104,500

Moïse Kisling, Portrait of Marguerite Gros, the artist's sister-in-law, oil on canvas, 54.2 x 45cm.
(Christie's)   **$88,110   £49,500**

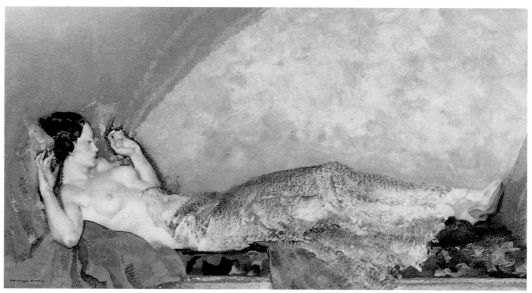

Sir William Russell Flint, Blue and Silver, water and bodycolour, 33 x 60.4cm.
(Bonhams)   **$30,560   £16,000**

Edgard Tytgat, La Petite Ouvrière, oil on canvas, 63.5 x 76.8cm.
(Christie's)   **$106,150   £55,000**

Rafael del Real, View of Madrid, oil on canvas, 73 x 100cm.
(Duran)   **$3,536   £1,832**

Thomas Hart Benton, The Bathers, watercolour, pastel and pencil, 37.8 x 33.3cm.
(Christie's, New York)   **$26,400   £15,312**

Circle of Francesco de Mura, Flora handed a basket of flowers by two putti, oil on panel, 62.2 x 109.2cm.
(Christie's)   **$52,800   £26,400**

So far the scandal has caused the resignations of the President of Itoman and the Chairman of Sumitomo, while Itoman's art buyer committed suicide in December 1990. Mitsubishi is now also tainted by a similar scandal, being unable to account for $11 million of the cheques used to pay for Renoir's Après Le Bain and Jeune Fille Lisant in March 1989.

It seems likely that the taxman's interest in the uses to which the purchase of high priced paintings in Japan are put will make corporations think twice about buying in the foreseeable future, while the collapse of the property market has had the further effect that the banks which relied on the former boom to finance these purchases are no longer able to offer such loans.

If the Japanese are retreating, at any rate from the preserves at the top end of the market, the Italians are advancing, notably in the field of Old Masters. When it is considered, however, that Italy had a negative growth rate in 1990 of 1.5%, it must be asked where the money is coming from? Can we expect future scandals here as well?

William Henry Margetson, Two young women seated, oil on canvas, 73.5 x 91.5cm.
(Bonhams)　　　　　$5,280　£3,000

Wilfred Gabriel De Glehn, 'The Picnic' – Girls on the cliff, Gwendreath, Cornwall oil on canvas, 25 x 30in.
(W.H. Lane & Son)　　　　　$17,280　£9,000

Henry Scott Tuke, The Midday Rest, oil on canvas, 102 x 132cm.
(Christie's)

$90,992   £48,400

Englerth, A reclining nude, oil on canvas, 75.6 x 100.7cm.
(Christie's)

$10,340   £5,500

Attributed to Katherine Clausen, In the fields, oil on canvas, 33.1 x 24.8cm.
(Lawrence)   **$1,575   £900**

Again, a large fly in the ointment seems to be the taxman, with the regime in Italy one of the most stringent in the West. As a result, parallel 'black' and 'white' economies are developing, the former, needless to say, a whole lot healthier than the latter! Art has become one of the main units of currency in the 'black economy', a highly convenient place to store assets which will never pass visibly through any books whatever. Furthermore, Italian law, in an effort to deter the accumulation of funds by drug barons, currently forbids a cash settlement of any transaction over L20 million (£9,000). This has had the effect of throwing out the baby with the bathwater and driven a lot of other transactions underground as well. The fact that much art dealing is done outside Italy is another advantage, as there are always difficulties in getting large cash sums out of the country.

In the UK too, the taxman has been showing an increased interest in works of art. As a cautionary tale, we return to that hardy perennial, Sunflowers. Now the vendors, the beneficiaries of the Helen Gertrude Chester Beatty Will Trust, had had the option of donating the picture to the nation under the Government's 'in lieu' scheme, whereby the government would have returned 25% of the tax deducted. The picture was valued at £10 million, thus after deduction of 60% tax, the family would have received £4 million plus 25% refund of the £6 million tax deducted, i.e. a total of £5.5 million with all liabilities settled. Instead, they opted to send it for auction, where it fetched £24.75 million. All very fine, one might think. Then, however, there was capital gains tax of 30% on the difference between the valuation and the price obtained, and Christie's commission, which together dropped the amount received to £17.17 million. There came a further complication because of an earlier exemption from inheritance tax at the time of a previous death in the family, which incurred a further tax of between 65 and 80%. At the full 80% the family would have taken home a mere £3.43 million, and still have tax to settle on the rest of the estate. After such an experience it is hardly surprising that they subsequently opted to donate a Cezanne to the nation, which now hangs in the National Gallery, and they are now to auction a further batch of pictures, presumably in view of the continuing demands of the taxman.

It is, one supposes, one way of acquiring some works of art for the nation, given the lamentable funding of the national art galleries.

Since 1985 for example, the National Gallery's grant has been frozen at a lower level than that of 1981. It receives a mere £2.75 million, plus the income on J. Paul Getty Jr's £50 million donation. When one considers the average price of an Impressionist or Contemporary painting even in these deflated times, that doesn't leave a lot in the annual kitty.

How much happier things might be all round if we could adopt the method practised by the French, whereby works of art considered of national importance and worthy of acceptance in lieu are completely free of tax liability. The vendor can start bargaining with the state at a price of his choosing, and then has the freedom to agree a sale or not, with both sides having the option to back out. The tax authorities inform the Museums of France of the tax due, and they negotiate accordingly. In short, the scheme operates as a payment of kind, pure and simple.

We might, for example, be able to keep our hands on a few more Old Masters, the new boom area in the art market, and one

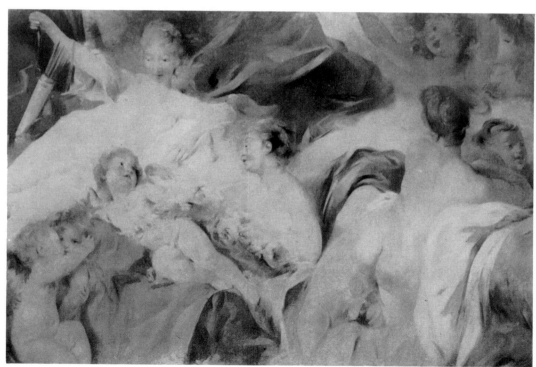

19th century Italian School, Female nudes, oil on canvas, 156 x 250cm. (Finarte)

$11,084   £6,637

El Greco, The Coronation of the Virgin, in a painted oval.
(Christie's, New York)

$2,310,000   £1,210,692

where Italian interest is most noticeable. The Imelda Marcos sale at Christie's in New York was a case in point. No less than 73 of the 93 works on sale were of Italian origin, and though it was the fashionable thing to ridicule Mrs Marcos' taste in pictures with rumours of doubtful authenticity which she had not had the knowledge to distinguish, the Italian contingent turned up in force, and with bulging wallets. On the day it did not seem to matter after all that many pictures were wrecked, heavily restored or so clumsy that no confident attribution could be made.

It proved to be the only Old Masters sale in years to sell out completely, and at crazy prices. The total value amounted to $20.3 million, of which $14.4 million will benefit the Philippines Land Reform programme. (Mrs M., of course, will not see a penny.) Top price was fetched by El Greco's sketch for the 1603 Coronation of the Virgin, which sold to a New York dealer for $2.31 million.

This was but one sale, but Old Masters sales in London and New York throughout the year have seen a strong Italian representation among the bidders. They bid primarily and almost indiscriminately for their own pictures, which means that what one auctioneer described as 'perfectly ghastly' Italian Old Masters are still finding a ready market.

Their Dutch counterparts, however, are not finding things quite so easy, with national buyers bidding much more cautiously and only the best commanding a premium. Nevertheless, a couple of Breughels did quite well. In Christie's sale on January 11 1991, Pieter Breughel the Younger's The Wedding Dance sold for $950,000 and Jan Breughel the Younger's unframed oil of flowers in a blue and white vase leapt above its $400–600,000 estimate to sell for $1 million the previous day at Sotheby's New York.

Pieter Brueghel The Younger, The Wedding Dance.
(Christie's, New York) $950,000

William Weekes, Consulting the Oracle, oil on panel, $7^{1}/_{2}$ x 11in.
(Bearne's)   E

$7,728   £4,600

David James, Penzance Fishing boats off the coast, oil on canvas, 64 x 127cm.
(Bonhams) **$7,011   £3,800**

Vincent Clare, 'Basket of Fruit
Basket of Flowers', pair of oils.
(Greenslades) **$5,180   £2,800**

Isaac Snowman, Two Children on a rocky shoreline, oil on board, 32 x 26cm.
(Phillips)

$4,989   £3,000

British interest centred mainly round Constable's The Lock, auctioned by Sotheby's in November 1990. The last of Constable's 'six footers' in private hands, it was estimated at £10–15 million, not a lot when compared with the estimable Dr Gachet, but then Constable has never really received his due recognition outside his own country. It was hoped, perhaps, that The Lock might change all that. In the event it sold to Baron Thyssen for £10.78 million (£9.8 million plus premium) in rather mysterious circumstances, since the rival bidder dropped out at £9 million and when the hammer fell some thought the picture had fallen below reserve and had not sold. So where had the extra come from? Had Sotheby's bridged the gap between the top bid and the reserve out of their own funds under a clause in (very) small print in their conditions of sale in order to facilitate such a high profile sale? Sotheby's aren't saying, and Constable fails to make headlines again, just as he had when Phillips at much the same time had offered The Entrance to Fen Lane, estimated at £2–3 million. It failed to make the reserve and was withdrawn.

John Frederick Lewis, An Eastern Girl Carrying a Tray, pencil and watercolour, 299 x 203 cm. (Christie's)　　$46,200　£26,400

Helen Allingham, A Surrey cottage, watercolour, 25.4 x 34.2cm.
(Bonhams)   **$31,246 £17,000**

Antoine Bouvard, A Venetian Canal with the Church of SS Giovanni e Paolo, oil on canvas, 64.8 x 91.4cm.
(Bonhams)   **$31,246 £17,000**

Karoly Gyurkovich, Portrait of Franz and Maria Rathauer, oil on canvas, 122 x 95cm. (Finarte) **$7,250 £4,166**

Guiseppe Carelli, The Bay of Naples, oil on board, 33.5 x 51cm. (Christie's) **$11,418 £6,600**

Rene Magritte, Les barricades mysterieuses, oil on canvas, 80.7 x 128cm.
(Christie's, New York) $2,200,000 £1,317,365

Turning to the Impressionist collapse, we have already touched on some possible reasons for this. Certainly in the period October–December 1990, which saw the nadir of Impressionist fortunes on both sides of the Atlantic, the traditional bidders (read Japanese) turned up but did not bid, and with their silence millions of yen/£/$ fell away from the value of the container loads of paintings which had been imported into Japan in the last five years. The fault however lay not so much in the pictures themselves, overvalued as these had been, but the fact that the banks which financed these purchases were in trouble and had pulled the plug on the funds which had previously been made available to buy them.

The auction houses, in contrast to previous recessions, reacted quickly to this disaster and immediately slashed estimates, deeming it better to keep some momentum than no sales at all. Vendors, on the other hand, will understandably take a little time to adjust to the fact that they are no longer going to get such heady sums for their pictures, and the result has been something of a picture famine.

Christie's and Sotheby's have both been determinedly cheerful in the face of this disaster, (though one notes the somewhat fixed nature of the smiles), preferring to refer to it as 'a return to normality', and going on (naturally) to extol the virtues of the indifferent works they have to sell. Faced with very slimmed down entries of very moderate works in New York in May 1991, they would both probably have preferred to drop the razmatazz completely and revert to run of the mill daytime sales. The punters wanted their gala event, however, and duly turned up in their dinner jackets and tiaras, though this time they came as spectators rather than bidders. Top prices were $4.51 million for Matisse's La Robe Persane at Sotheby's and $2.2 million for a Magritte at Christie's. The total value of the sales were $18 million and $23 million compared to $284 and $269 million last year, which really says it all. While it is unlikely that things can get any worse, one wonders how the situation can be turned around sufficiently to tempt potential vendors to trot out their top class Renoirs and Monets once again.

Other collapsing markets have been the 'national' sales which boomed so healthily over the past few years. At Christie's Scandinavian sale in November 1990, for example, under one third of the total lots were sold. The only one of these to top estimate was the first of all, Harald Slott Mullers brooding study of Georg Brandes at the University of Copenhagen, which sold for £36,300. After the fourth lot only one further picture found a buyer. This contrasts strongly with the £1 million which Zorn and Schjerfbeck were attracting last year, but Scandinavian pictures have always relied strongly on interest from their country of origin, and the collapse of the Swedish economy obviously played a major role in their dull performance.

Harald Slott-Møller, Georg Brandes at the University in Copenhagen, oil on canvas, 92 x 81cm. (Christie's, London) **$71,511 £36,300**

Spanish pictures too, which were riding on a high eighteen months or so ago, have similarly moved back. No further specialist sales are planned, and like their Scandinavian counterparts, they have been reincorporated under the European Picture sale umbrella. Their grand nephews, so to speak, or Latin American pictures, are enjoying mixed fortunes. Christie's report that sales have never been better, while Sotheby's have closed down their Latin American department in New York. Time, as usual, will doubtless reveal whose is the more accurate reading of the market. In the meantime, the uncertainty is pardonable, for while there were many casualties at Christie's Latin American sale in New York in May 1991, Frida Kahlo's haunting Self Portrait with Loose Hair achieved $1.65

million, at once a record for a Latin American painting and the lower end of the pre-sale estimate.

A late attempt to catch a rapidly departing bus failed utterly when Christie's auctioned some of the finest Belgian pictures to be seen on the market for a long time in November 1990. Only fourteen lots out of seventy-two found buyers, and the total value of the sale amounted to only a third of the estimate.

Belgian interest was naturally very strong, and it was well attended, but, as is happening so often now, they came to see and not to buy. Quite why this should be so is unclear. Quality, certainly was not lacking, but Christie's first Belgian sale had reportedly caused much resentment over the fact that it was being held

Frida Kahlo, Self portrait with Loose Hair, oil on masonite, 61 x 45cm.
(Christie's, New York) $1,650,000   £970,588

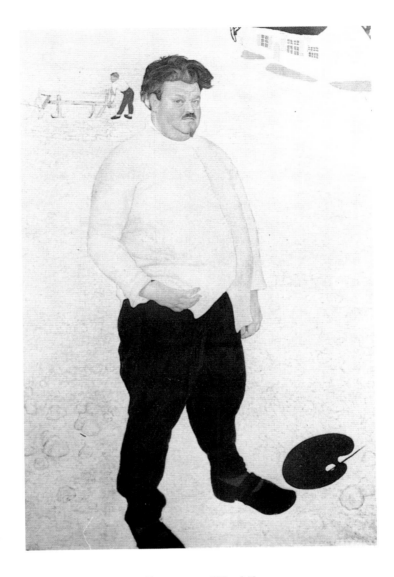

Gustave van de Woestijne, Valerius de Saedeleer, oil on canvas, 220 x 140cm.
(Christie's) $424,600   £220,000

in London rather than Brussels, with a possible inflationary effect upon prices (plus a deflationary effect on national pride?) and it may be that something of this persisted.

Finally, from the nationalistic aspect, the expected flood of art from Russia on behalf of a government starved of hard currency has so far failed to materialise. This year has seen persistent reports of a fabled hoard of Nazi art treasures found in the Soviet Union, but so far nothing specific has emerged. Sotheby's have been wooing the Russians for several years, most lately with a top level delegation to Moscow, and the idea seems to be that the Russians will sell off second rate works, notably from the Tretyakov Gallery, to earn hard currency to buy back some of the first rate pictures sold off under Lenin and Stalin. This, however, is all in direct contravention of the previous Ministry of Culture directives forbidding sales of pre-1945 Russian art except by licence. Possibly the answer is not to hold one's breath – there may yet be any number of U-turns to come.

Valentin Aleksandrovitch Serov (1865-1911), Portrait of Prince Feliks Feliksovitch Iusopov, signed and dated 09, oil on canvas, 90 x 83cm.
(Christie's) **$107,250 £55,000**

Such Russian Imperialist and post-Revolutionary art as has been available in the West has had a mixed reception. The market is still reliant on material coming from Western collections and very little is coming forward. When quality items do appear, such as Valentin Serov's portrait of Prince Feliks Iusopov, they do fetch good prices: the picture in question sold at Christie's for £55,000. Otherwise, the market is dogged and complicated by fakes, which are at the moment the things which *are* finding their way westwards out of the Soviet Union.

Like the Impressionists, contemporary art has taken quite a knock over the last twelve months, for, like the Impressionists, it had enjoyed a period of somewhat indiscriminate popularity in the late 1980s, when people were prepared to pay huge sums for thoroughly second rate pictures just because they were signed by a Warhol or a de Kooning. All this came to an end in the last months of 1990, when both Christie's and Sotheby's Contemporary Art sales saw bought-in rates of 60% or more by value. One of the few to sell at Christie's was Dubuffet's Mr McAdam from the René de Montaigu collection, which went for £800,000, while at Sotheby's Antonio Saura's Crucifixion Triptych confounded the general trend by selling above estimate at £155,000. As elsewhere, the keynote was fewer paintings and poorer quality

February 91 however saw signs of a modest upswing for both houses. While the number of pictures entered was still much fewer than at the same time the previous year, the bought-in rates dropped substantially, and there was strong bidding both from the trade and private collectors for fresh-to-the-market, quality material, with a European interest particularly noticeable.

Andy Warhol, Siberian Tiger, silkscreen print,
96.5 x 96.5cm. (Glerum) **$6,630 £3,788**

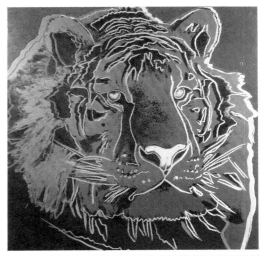

Sir Stanley Spencer, The Crucifixion, oil on canvas, 216 x 216cm.
(Sotheby's) **$2,191,200 £1,320,000**

*Jean Dubuffet, Monsieur
Macadam.
(Christie's, London)*
$1,733,600   £880,000

*Louis Icart, En barque ..., oil on board, 33.5 x 51cm.
(Jean Claude Anaf)*

$57,381   £31,356

Claude Strachan, Two young girls crossing a river with thatched cottages beyond, watercolour, 35.6 x 51.4cm. (Bonhams)   **$5,514   £3,000**

F R Donat, Reading the news, oil on panel, one of a pair, 50.8 x 40.7cm. (Christie's S. Ken.) **$15,170 £7,700**

Sir William Russell Flint, Silver & White, watercolour, 30.5 x 54.7cm.
(Bonhams) $72,580 £38,000

A more realistic approach has emerged too in sales of 19th and 20th century pictures at the more modest end· of the market. Again, sale content has been markedly down, but where vendors have been content with a reasonable reserve, the pictures have 'sold well, especially where they have been chosen to appeal to the private buyer at 'affordable prices'. Within the range, there are signs of a slightly reduced demand for cottage garden and Victorian and Edwardian genre scenes, while good maritime and topographical pictures are finding favour, especially with Continental buyers.

On the other hand, getting down to the really cheap and cheerful, Bonhams report humorously that there is a strong market for Victorian 'tat', for which 'the best that can be said is that it's an original oil painting'. Time, perhaps, to search through the attic again?

Bonhams are continuing with their popular theme sales (doggy pictures for Cruft's week, maritime art for Cowes etc.) and have also given Russell Flint a further two airings. There seems to be a steady flow of material coming forward from private collectors, though the second sale, in May 1991, was much slimmer and the top price fetched was only £8,500 for the watercolour Rendezvous, Ardisa, as against £38,000 the previous December for Silver & White, both nearer the lower than the upper estimates.

Cornelius Krieghoff, A Moccasin Seller and companion piece, oil on board, 15.3 x 12.2cm.
(Bonhams) $9,190 £5,000

William Thornley, A fishing port at dawn, one of a pair, oil on canvas, monogrammed, 11¹/₂ x 9in. (Michael J. Bowman)
$4,250   £2,500

Finally, isn't it strange how these high-selling pictures of the last few years seem to return to haunt us (in the latest case potentially literally!)? There is the Sunflowers saga above, then Alan Bond's embarrassments with the financing for the purchase of Irises, and now Dr Gachet and Au Moulin de la Galette have made front page news in the dailies again just recently, when their purchaser, Mr Saito, head of the Daishowa Paper Co., announced his intention of having them cremated with him on his death. The fact that he is 75 had the effect of concentrating the collective mind of the art world wonderfully on the rights and morals of the case. It turned out to be a hoax, but for 48 hours or so it looked quite serious.

One wonders just what the Japanese taxman would have made of that particular method of disposing of one's assets....

EELIN McIVOR

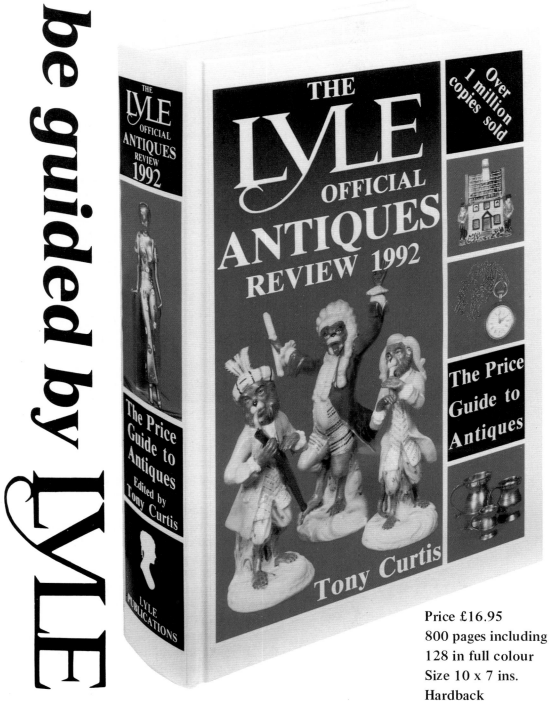

ARTS
REVIEW 1992

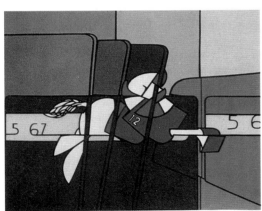

VALERIO ADAMI (b. 1935) – Corsa a ostacoli a Ascot –
signed – acrylic on canvas – 129.5 x 161.7cm.
(Christie's) **$58,740 £33,000**

CHARLES JAMES ADAMS (1859-1931) A Woodland
Road near Farnham, Surrey – signed 'C. J. Adams', and
inscribed as title on the reverse, pencil and watercolour
– 11 x 15½in.
(Christie's) **$980 £605**

JOHN OTTIS ADAMS (1851-1927)|–Spring Along
the Creek – signed J. Ottis Adams and dated 1897,
l.r.–oil on canvas–22 x 32in.
(Christie's) **$17,600 £10,208**

LILIAN ADAMS – Old Gloucester – signed – oil on board
– 12 x 16in.
(Bruce D. Collins) **$770 £416**

ERICH ADAMSON-ERIC – "Serenade" – signed and
dated 24 – oil on canvas – 92 x 65cm.
(AB Stockholms Auktionsverk) **$2,399 £1,256**

33

ALEXANDER ADRIANSSEN (1587–1661) – Still life with cup of fruit and birds on a table – signed - oil on panel – 43.3 x 60.8cm.
(Sotheby's) **\$23,293 £13,387**

After EDMUND ADLER – The pet canary – signed – oil on canvas – 71.3 x 54.9cm.
(Ritchie's) **\$643 £333**

WILLIAM AFFLECK (b. 1869) – An elegant young lady in a country garden – signed – pencil and watercolour – unframed – 11¾ x 16½in.
(Christie's) **\$7,469 £3,850**

GOSTA ADRIAN-NILSSON (1884–1965) – Head in grey – signed and dated -54 – watercolour – 20.5 x 15cm.
(AB Stockholms Auktionsverk) **\$1,243 £651**

ACS AGOSTON (1889–1947) – Fruit picking – signed – oil on canvas – 129 x 95cm.
(Hôtel de Ventes Horta) **\$3,586 £2,049**

A*** AGOSTINI – Reading in front of a fire – signed and indistinctly dated – oil on canvas – 110 x 140cm.
(Sotheby's) **$9,845 £5,500**

CURT AGTHE (20th Century) – 'Dryade' – signed – 113 x 94cm.
(Christie's) **$4,077 £2,420**

IVAN AGUELI (1869–1917) – Southern landscape with trees and water – oil on canvas laid down on board – 32 x 45cm.
(AB Stockholms Auktionsverk) **$13,859 £7,256**

AIVAZOVSKII

IVAN KONSTANTINOVITCH AIVAZOVSKII (1817–1900) – Coastal shipping on the Black Sea – signed in Cyrillic and dated on reverse 1895 – oil on canvas – 36.5 x 59.2cm.
(Christie's)   **$42,900**   **£22,000**

JOHANNES EVERT AKKERINGA (1861–1942) – Women reading in the dunes – signed – 40 x 57.5cm.
(Christie's)   **$12,071**   **£6,035**

FRANCESCO ALBOTTO (1722–1757) – View of the Grand Canal, Venice, with the Fondaco dei Turchi – oil on canvas (unlined) – 41 x 57cm.
(Sotheby's)   **$104,500**   **£55,000**

HELEN ALLINGHAM, R.W.S. (1848–1926) – Cottage near Pinner -- signed – 39 x 28cm.
(Phillips)   **$30,430**   **£17,000**

HELEN ALLINGHAM (1848–1926) – A fruit stall at the base of the Campanile, San Giovanni Elemosinario, near the Rialto, Venice – signed and inscribed on reverse – watercolour – 14³/₄ x 11¹/₂in.
(Christie's)   **$13,587**   **£7,040**

ADRIAN ALLINSON (1890–1959) – Bathers by a river –
oil on canvas – 43 x 61.5cm.
(Christie's) $7,348 £4,400

HELEN ALLINGHAM (1848–1926) – In a Pinner
Garden – signed – pencil and watercolour – 9³/₄ x 7¹/₄in.
(Christie's) **$9,390 £4,840**

HELEN ALLINGHAM (1848–1926) – 'A Dorsetshire
Cottage' – signed – watercolour with scratching out –
29.5 x 24.5cm.
(Phillips) **$17,900 £10,000**

LAURA, LADY ALMA-TADEMA (1852–1909) – A
carol – signed and inscribed – oil on panel –
38.1 x 23.5cm.
(Christie's) **$12,313 £6,380**

ALMA-TADEMA

SIR LAWRENCE ALMA-TADEMA, O.M., R.A.
(English 1836–1912) – Love's jewelled fetter – signed and
inscribed – oil on panel – 63.5 x 44.5cm.
(Sotheby's)   **$517,660   £286,000**

JOSE AMAT (b. 1901) – Café de Barcelona - oil on
board – signed - 76.5 x 58cm.
(Duran)   **$18,188   £9,424**

NICOLAS ALPERIZ (Spanish b. 1869) – Children's games in the kitchen – signed – oil on canvas –
unframed – 110.5 x 150cm.
(Sotheby's)   **$26,169   £14,300**

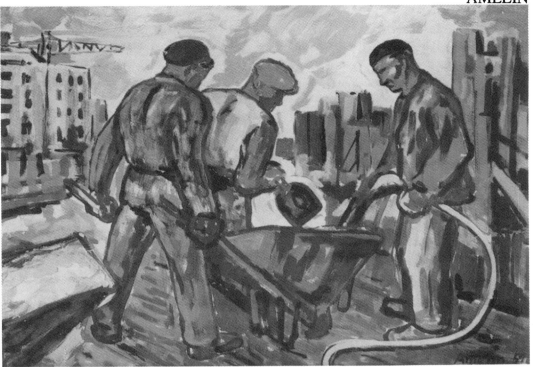

ALBIN AMELIN (1902–75) – Road menders – signed
and dated 59 – gouache – 69 x 98cm.
(AB Stockholms Auktionsverk)   **$3,197   £1,674**

ALBIN AMELIN (1902–75) – Female nude – signed and
dated 35 – gouache – 70 x 54cm.
(AB Stockholms Auktionsverk)   **$1,776   £930**

ALBIN AMELIN (1902–75) – Still life with cut flowers
in a jug – signed and dated -46 – gouache – 99 x 68cm.
(AB Stockholms Auktionsverk)   **$5,686   £2,977**

CUNO AMIET (Swiss, 1868–1961) – Winter landscape
with building site – signed with monogram – oil on canvas
– 38 x 45.5cm.
(Galerie Koller Zürich)   **$26,906   £14,050**

J.A.G. ACKE (ANDERSSON) (1859–1924) – The
prodigal son – signed – oil on canvas – 154 x 111cm.
(AB Stockholms Auktionsverk)   **$1,791   £923**

JACOPO AMIGONI (1682–1752) – Hercules and
Omphale – oil on canvas – 43.5 x 55.5cm.
(Sotheby's)   **$146,300   £77,000**

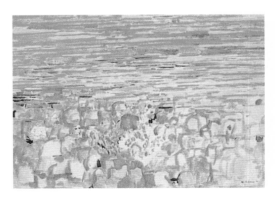

TORSTEN ANDERSSON (b. 1926) – Composition in
yellow – signed and dated 60 – oil on canvas – 74 x 104cm.
(AB Stockholms Auktionsverk)   **$1,280   £670**

FREDERICO ANDREOTTI – Courtship – signed – oil
on canvas – 103 x 77.5cm.
(Sotheby's)   **$25,597   £14,300**

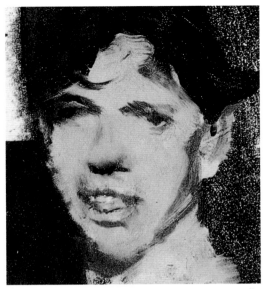

MICHAEL ANDREWS (b. 1928) – Head of a man – oil
on board – unframed – 19.5 x 21cm.
(Christie's)   **$25,608   £13,200**

HERMEN ANGLADA-CAMARASA (Spanish
1873–1959) – Ladies in a box at the theatre – signed – oil
on panel – 23 x 32cm.
(Sotheby's)   **$130,845   £71,500**

ALBERT ANKER (1831–1910) – A still life of two
glasses of red wine, a bottle of wine, a corkscrew and a
plate of biscuits on a tray – signed – oil on canvas –
43.2 x 36.9cm.
(Christie's)   **$140,250   £82,500**

ANKER

ALBERT ANKER (1831–1910) – Portrait of a young boy, possibly Sammeli Niederhüsler – signed – oil on canvas – 45 x 35.6cm.
(Christie's) $205,700   £121,000

ALBERT ANKER (1831–1910) – Girl working in the kitchen – watercolour on pencil – 20.5 x 15.3cm.
(Galerie Koller Zürich) $12,662   £6,612

ALBERT ANKER (1831–1910) – A girl knitting – signed and dated 1908 – watercolour on paper – 34.2 x 24.2cm.
(Christie's) $74,800   £44,000

ALBERT ANKER (1831–1910) – Portrait of a young girl – signed – oil on canvas – 42 x 33cm.
(Christie's) $243,100   £143,000

SCHOOL OF ANTWERP, 1616 – The Sacrifice of Isaac
– signed 'TFs. Ft' and dated 1616 – 81.2 x 85.2cm.
(Christie's) **$2,614 £1,320**

KAREL APPEL (b. 1921) – A Figure – signed and dated
69 – acrylic on cardboard laid down on board –
66 x 50.5cm.
(Christie's) **$24,112 £12,578**

SIEGFRIED ANZINGER (German, b. 1952) – Diver –
signed and dated 1982 – acrylic on paper – 55 x 42cm.
(AB Stockholms Auktionsverk) **$1,421 £744**

FRED APPLEYARD – Spring – signed and dated 1905 –
oil on canvas – 19½ x 15¾in.
(Bearne's) **$6,208 £3,200**

OLOF ARBORELIUS (1842–1915) – Coastal landscape
with figures and boats – signed – oil on canvas –
37 x 60cm.
(AB Stockholms Auktionsverk)   **$5,374   £2,770**

JOSEF M. ARENTZ (1903–69) – Every seventh wave –
oil on board – facsimile signature stamp – 6 x 9in.
(Bruce D. Collins)   **$385   £208**

JOSE JIMENEZ ARANDA (1837–1903) – The picador
– signed – watercolour - 22.5 x 14cm.
(Duran)   **$2,926   £1,528**

OUMBERTOS ARGYROS (Greek 1884–1963) –
Coming ashore – signed – oil on canvas – 68 x 108cm.
(Sotheby's)   **$13,084   £7,150**

EDITH ARKWRIGHT (exh. 1884) – A little Girl with a black Labrador, an English Toy terrier, a Bichon Frise and its puppy – signed with initials – oil on canvas – 128.3 x 87.6cm.
(Christie's)   **$10,450 £5,500**

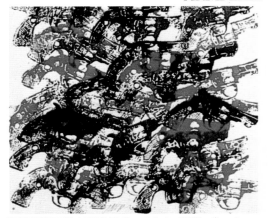

FERNANDEZ ARMAN (Spanish, b. 1928) – Revolver – No 2, 1971 – signed – mixed media on laid paper – 76 x 57cm.
(AB Stockholms Auktionsverk)   **$5,331 £2,791**

GEORGE ARMFIELD (circa 1808–1893) – A Blenheim Cavalier King Charles spaniel and a terrier in a barn – signed and dated 1885 – oil on canvas – 45.7 x 60.9cm.
(Christie's)   **$8,360 £4,400**

ARMAN (Armand Fernandez) (b. 1928) – Gipsy variation – signed and dated 1962 – smashed violin with bow mounted on a painted wooden board – 77 x 63.7cm.
(Christie's)   **$95,348 £48,400**

MAXWELL ASHBY ARMFIELD (1882–1972) – Three Graces – signed with monogram – oil on board – 17 x 17cm.
(Christie's)   **$3,674 £2,200**

ARNAU

FRANCISCO PONS ARNAU (b. 1886) – Mujer en la Nieve – signed and dated 1929 – oil on canvas – unframed – 69.8 x 60.3cm.
(Christie's) **$15,510 £8,250**

J. ATKINSON – 'Stagshaw Bank Horse Fair' – signed – watercolour – 18 x 24in.
(The Auction Galleries Berwick on Tweed) **$3,772 £1,900**

ZO ATTESLANDER (b. 1874) – La Belle Epoque – signed and dated 1900/Paris – pastel and coloured chalks on paper – 65.5 x 50cm.
(Christie's) **$5,174 £2,640**

AUSTRIAN SCHOOL – The story teller – oil on metal panel – 57.5 x 85cm.
(Hôtel de Ventes Horta) $1,366 £704

ALBERT AUBLET (French 1851–1938) – A still life of peonies in a vase – signed and dated 1887 – oil on canvas – 198 x 115cm.
(Sotheby's) $19,123 £10,450

ENRIQUE SERRA AUQUE (1859–1918) – Procession of priests – oil on canvas – signed – 30 x 78cm.
(Duran) $15,156 £7,853

MILTON AVERY (1893–1965) – Turbaned girl – signed and dated 1961 – oil on canvasboard – 25.5 x 20.2cm.
(Christie's) $8,800 £4,664

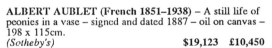

Studio of LUDOLF BACKHUIZEN (1631–1708) - A yacht passing before an East Indiaman and other shipping in choppy seas – oil on canvas – 50 x 82cm.
(Phillips)   **$10,740   £6,000**

MILTON AVERY (1893–1965) – Girl with scarf – signed – dated 1955 and inscribed – oil on canvasboard – 42.2 x 30.4cm.
(Christie's)   **$8,800   £4,664**

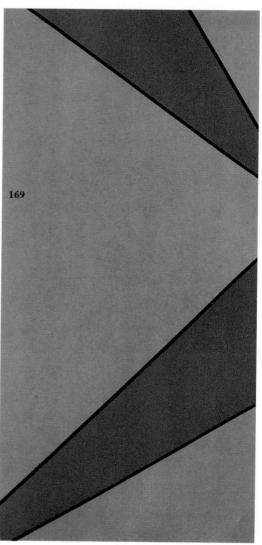

169

JEAN-JACQUES BACHELIER (1724–1806) – The head of a dog – signed and dated 1758 – oil on canvas – 52 x 46cm.
(Sotheby's)   **$17,470   £10,040**

OLLE BAERTLING (1911–81) – "Yoyana" – signed on reverse and dated 1970 – oil on canvas – 180 x 92cm.
(AB Stockholms Auktionsverk)   **$88,838   £46,512**

LEV SAMOILOVICH [ROSENBERG] BAKST
(1866–1924) – Costume design for Cleopatra–a dancer –
signed and dated 1910 – pencil, gouache and gold paint on
paper – 34.8 x 25cm.
(Christie's) **$34,320 £17,600**

OLLE BAERTLING – Polychrome diagonal-composition
– signed and numbered 26/100 – serigraph – 74 x 38cm.
(AB Stockholms Auktionsverk) **$1,567 £808**

C T BALE (19th Century) – Still life – signed – oil on
canvas – 13 x 17in.
(Jacobs & Hunt) **$920 £460**

NATHANIEL HUGHES JOHN BAIRD – Fugitives –
monogrammed – oil on canvas – 22 x 30in.
(Michael Newman) **$2,600 £1,300**

C.T. BALE – Still life with grapes – signed – oil on
canvas – 35.5 x 46cm.
(Hôtel de Ventes Horta) **$4,763 £2,358**

BALLA

GIACOMO BALLA (1871–1958) – Portrait of Signora
Adelaide Cottreau – signed – oil on canvas – 100 x 100cm.
(Christie's) **$411,730 £209,000**

LAILA BALODE – Heritage – signed – watercolour –
73 x 100cm.
(Jean-Claude Anaf) **$197 £103**

FILIPPO BARATTI (late 19th Century) –The
introduction after the bath – signed and dated 1889 – oil on
canvas – 97.2 x 139.1cm.
(Christie's) **$299,200 £176,000**

CHARLES BURTON BARBER (1845–1894) – A girl's
best friend – signed and dated 1882 – oil on canvas –
31.1 x 91.4cm.
(Christie's) **$39,204 £19,800**

E* BARBOT (French 19th Century)** – A village on
the Nile – signed – watercolour – 39 x 76cm.
(Sotheby's) **$2,636 £3,080**

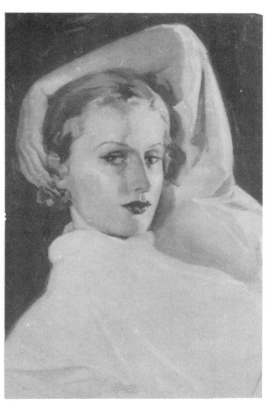

MCCELLAND BARCLAY – Portrait of an Art Deco
period woman – signed – oil on canvas – unframed –
22 x 16in.
(Du Mouchelles) **$2,200 £1,134**

JOHN EDWARD BARKER (1889–1953) – Fishing boats in the harbour, low tide, Fowey – signed – oil on board – 58.5 x 81.5cm.
(Christie's)   **$11,940   £7,150**

WRIGHT BARKER – A fine pack – signed – oil on canvas – 120 x 150cm.
(Sotheby's)   **$25,883   £14,300**

WRIGHT BARKER (fl. 1891–1935, d. 1941) – A mare and her foal at a ford – signed and inscribed on reverse – oil on canvas – 71 x 91.5cm.
(Christie's)   **$11,676   £6,050**

ARTS REVIEW

EDWARD CHARLES BARNES (fl. 1856–1882) – The new breeches – signed – oil on canvas – 71 x 92cm.
(Christie's) $6,369 £3,300

FRANCISCO BARO (b. 1926) (Fran Baró) – Le Pont Marie – oil on canvas – signed and titled on reverse – 54 x 66cm.
(Duran) $3,032 £1,571

FRANCISCO BARO (b. 1926) (Fran Baró) – The dock at Honfleur – oil on canvas – signed and titled on reverse – 50 x 65cm.
(Duran) $4,294 £2,225

Circle of FEDERICO BAROCCI (1526–1612) – The rest on the flight into Egypt – oil on copper – 38 x 28cm.
(Phillips) **$14,320 £8,000**

PAUL BASILIUS BARTH (Swiss, 1881–1955) – Woman at table – signed and dated 1939 – oil on canvas – 81.5 x 65cm.
(germann Auktionshaus) **$15,649 £9,205**

LAUREANO BARRAU Y BUNOL (Spanish b. 1864) – The flower seller – signed – watercolour – 45 x 32cm.
(Sotheby's) **$8,052 £4,400**

EDWARD LE BAS, R.A. (1904–1966) – The terrace, Ischia – signed – inscribed on the frame – oil on canvas – 78 x 55cm.
(Phillips) **$15,798 £9,500**

BASHKIRTSEVA

MARIA KONSTANTINOVNA BASHKIRTSEVA (1860–1884) – Girl reading by a waterfall – signed – pencil and watercolour on paper – 30.5 x 21cm.
(Christie's) **$6,435 £3,300**

NOEL BATAILLE (late 19th Century) – Washing day – signed – oil on canvas – 125.1 x 90.2cm.
(Christie's) **$8,272 £4,400**

H. BASTIEN – The Madonna Annunciate – signed and dated 1622 – 63.4 x 50.7cm.
(Christie's) **$6,565 £3,520**

Follower of POMPEO GIROLAMO BATONI – Portrait of a gentleman, seated three-quarter length on a terrace, in a red coat holding a pinch of snuff – unframed – 106 x 82.5cm.
(Christie's) **$3,944 £1,980**

CARL BAUERLE – Nursery life – signed – oil on canvas
– 93 x 78cm.
(Sotheby's) $49,775 £27,500

EDWARD BAWDEN, R.A. (1903–1990) – Pond at
Beslyns, Great Bardfield, Essex – signed and dated 1955 –
inscribed with title on the reverse – pen and ink,
watercolour and bodycolour – 46 x 58cm.
(Phillips) $9,146 £5,500

ELISABETH JERICHAU BAUMANN (1819–1881) –
The water carrier – signed – oil on canvas – 57.2 x 47.3cm.
(Christie's) $6,204 £3,300

BAWDEN

EDWARD BAWDEN (1903–1989) – English garden delights – signed – oil on nine panels – 211 x 72cm. each panel
(Christie's) $32,147   £19,250

SIR CECIL BEATON – Ascot costumes VIII – signed twice – annotated by the artist, and with attached samples of material – pencil and watercolour heightened with white – 18 x 12in.
(Tennants) $3,000   £1,500

CECILIA BEAUX (1863–1942) – Dressing dolls – signed – oil on canvas – 90.5 x 74cm.
(Christie's) $71,500   £37,180

JEAN BEAUDUIN (Belgian, 1851–1916) – Young girl sitting on a bundle of wheat in a setting overlooking farmland – signed – oil on wood panel – 14½ x 18in.
(Du Mouchelles) $4,000   £2,145

RICHARD BEAVIS – The Thames below Gravesend – signed and dated 1859 – oil on canvas – 21 x 34in.
(G.A. Key) $10,624   £5,200

MILDRED BENDALL (1891–1974) – The green jug – signed – oil on canvas – 56 x 70cm.
(Christie's)   **$4.592 £2,750**

BELGIAN SCHOOL – The painter at his easel – oil on canvas – 70 x 56cm.
(Hôtel de Ventes Horta)   **$6,208 £3,200**

JUAN ANTONIO BENLLIURE Y GIL (Spanish 19th Century) – The basket of flowers – signed – oil on canvas – 61.5 x 50cm.
(Sotheby's)   **$14,091 £7,700**

JAMES BELL (?) (mid/late 19th Century) – Mariana – signed and dated 76 (?) – oil on canvas – 164 x 113cm.
(Christie's)   **$5,577 £3,300**

FRANK MOSS BENNETT – A cardinal at teatime – signed and dated 1931 – oil on canvas – 35.5 x 26cm.
(Sotheby's)   **$7,964 £4,400**

BENSON

FRANK WESTON BENSON (1862–1951) – The leaning tree – signed and dated '22 – watercolour and pencil on paper – 38 x 51cm.
(Christie's)   **$16,500   £8,580**

J. BERARD (1902–1949) – Young country lad – oil on canvas – signed – 45 x 55cm.
(Hôtel de Ventes Horta)   **$2,638   £1,360**

THOMAS HART BENTON (1889–1975) – The Chute-Buffalo River – signed and dated 70 – egg tempera on board – 50.8 x 61cm.
(Christie's)   **$308,000   £160,160**

THOMAS HART BENTON (1889–1975) – Watering the horse – oil on tin – 8 x 10.7cm.
(Christie's)   **$33,000   £17,160**

JEAN BERAUD (1849–1936) – Portrait of a gentleman, standing small full length in morning dress - signed and dated – oil on panel – 46.4 x 25.7cm.
(Christie's)   **$11,220   £6,600**

ADRIAN BERG (b. 1929) – Gloucester Lodge, Regents Park – signed, inscribed and dated on reverse 5.75/76 – oil on canvas – 66 x 86.5cm.
(Christie's) $3,857 £2,310

Manner of NICOLAES BERCHEM – A Levantine scene with an elegant traveller by a quay, a galley and man-of-war beyond – 69.2 x 80cm.
(Christie's) $10,120 £5,060

JEAN BERAUD (1849–1936) – Arrêtez – signed – oil on panel – 40 x 32cm.
(Christie's) $115,940 £68,200

NARCISSE BERCHÈRE (French 1819–91) – The
Caravan's halt – signed – oil on panel – 31 x 41cm.
(Spencer's) **$10,164 £6,050**

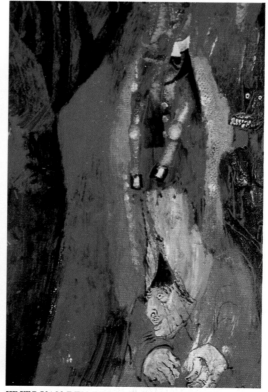

FRANS BERG (1892–1949) – Still life with cut flowers –
signed – oil on canvas – 73 x 61cm.
(AB Stockholms Auktionsverk) **$2,664 £1,395**

FRITS VAN DEN BERGHE (1883–1939) – Masques –
signed – oil on paper laid down on panel – 52 x 35.3cm.
(Christie's) **$89,166 £46,200**

EMILE BERNARD (French, 1868–1941) – Portrait of a lady – signed and dated 40 – oil on panel – 64 x 53cm.
(AB Stockholms Auktionsverk)   **$2,309   £1,209**

OSKAR BERGMAN (1879–1963) – September evening – signed and dated 1936 – watercolour – 33.5 x 24.5cm.
(AB Stockholms Auktionsverk)   **$3,287   £1,721**

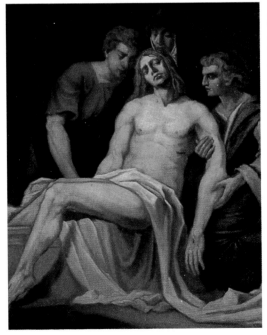

EMILE BERNARD (French, 1868–1941) – The burial of Christ – signed and dated 1912 – oil on canvas – 153 x 129cm.
(AB Stockholms Auktionsverk)   **$3,020   £1,581**

GUNNAR FREDERIK BERNDTSON (Finnish 1854–95) – Cooling the feet – signed and inscribed – oil on panel – 21 x 15cm.
(Sotheby's)   **$36,234   £19,800**

BEROUD

EMILE BERTIN (1878–1957) – Beach scene with bathers – signed – oil on canvas – 56 x 75cm.
(Lempertz)   **$10,779**   **£5,556**

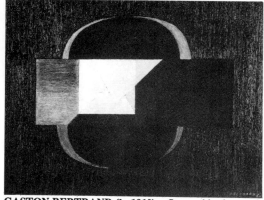

LOUIS BEROUD (1852–1930) – Sainte Clotilde Square, Paris – signed and dated – oil on canvas – 55 x 46cm.
(Christie's)   **$28,952**   **£15,400**

GASTON BERTRAND (b. 1910) – On a red background – signed and dated 60 – oil on panel – 27 x 35cm.
(Christie's)   **$17,706**   **£9,174**

PIERRE DE BERROETA – Composition – oil on canvas – signed and dated 89 – 120 x 89cm.
(Jean-Claude Anaf)   **$6,466**   **£3,350**

Attributed to BALTHASAR BESCHEY (1708–1776), after Sir Peter Paul Rubens – The Madonna and Child with Saint Elisabeth and the Infant Saint John the Baptist – on panel – unframed – 43.4 x 39cm.
(Christie's)   **$8,712**   **£4,400**

WILLIAM ROXBY BEVERLY (1811–1889) – Lugger driven on shore – signed and dated 1870 – pencil and watercolour on Whatman paper - 30½ x 51½in.
(Christie's)   **$8,860 £4,950**

BO BESKOW (1906–89) – Woman seated at a table with fruit, flowers and a bottle of wine – signed and dated 29 – oil on canvas – 98 x 68cm.
(AB Stockholms Auktionsverk)   **$3,197 £1,674**

MOSE' BIANCHI (1840–1904) – Countryside in Verona – pastel on charcoal – signed – 65.5 x 91cm.
(Finarte Casa d'Aste)   **$8,958 £4,673**

JAN VAN BIJLERT (1597/8–1671) – Ulysses and Circe – signed – oil on panel – 50 x 81cm.
(Sotheby's)   **$121,220 £63,800**

BILLET

SAMUEL JOHN LAMORNA BIRCH (1869–1955) –
Painting in the woods, Lamorna – oil on board – signed
and dated 1908 – 9 x 4in.
(David Lay)   **$8,418**   **£4,600**

PIERRE BILLET – Gazing out to sea – signed and dated
– oil on canvas – 33 x 44.5cm.
(Sotheby's)   **$4,922**   **£2,750**

Manner of BARTOLOMMEO BIMBI – An upturned
basket of cherries – 94 x 129.6cm.
(Christie's)   **$13,200**   **£6,600**

SAMUEL C. BIRD (fl. 1865–1893) – Snooding hooks –
signed and dated 1877 – oil on canvas – 142.2 x 111.8cm.
(Christie's)   **$28,660**   **£14,850**

SAMUEL JOHN LAMORNA BIRCH (1869–1955) –
Old Lamorna Quay – oil on board – signed – 13 x 16in.
(David Lay)   **$10,431**   **£5,700**

BIRGER E BIRGER: Jr (b. 1904) – Geese for slaughter –
signed and dated 1981 on reverse – oil on panel – 121 x
121cm.
(AB Stockholms Auktionsverk)   **$2,577**   **£1,349**

ROGER BISSIERE – Sleeping woman with map –
signed – oil on canvas – 38 x 55.5cm.
(Jean-Claude Anaf)   **$22,438**   **£11,626**

TOR BJURSTROM (1888–1966) – 'Quite a normal day'
– landscape with trees and white houses – signed – oil on
panel – 53 x 64cm.
(AB Stockholms Auktionsverk)   **$3,730**   **£1,953**

WILLIAM KAY BLACKLOCK (fl. 1897–1922) –
Fishing from the bridge – signed – oil on canvas –
61 x 51.2cm.
(Christie's)   **$22,308**   **£13,200**

JULIUS VON BLAAS (b. 1845) – The Circus – signed
and dated 1896 – oil on canvas – 83.5 x 143.5cm.
(Christie's)   **$26,004**   **£13,200**

JULIUS VON BLAAS – Colonel Kuser in a trotting race –
signed and dated – oil on canvas – 84 x 100cm.
(Sotheby's)   **$19,690**   **£11,000**

WILLIAM KAY BLACKLOCK (born 1872) – Picking
May Blossom – signed – oil on canvas laid down on panel
– 40.3 x 32cm.
(Christie's)   **$6,794   £3,520**

ANTOINE BLANCHARD (mid 20th Century) –
L'Opéra, Paris; Porte St. Denis, Grands Boulevards, Paris –
both signed – oil on canvas – 45.5 x 46.2cm.
(Christie's)   **$8,686   £4,620**

MAURICE BLIECK (1876–1922) – Riding on the beach
– signed – oil on canvas – 61 x 40cm.
(Hôtel de Ventes Horta)   **$4,763   £2,358**

THOMAS BLINKS (1860–1912) – Hounds in Full Cry – signed and dated 89 – oil on canvas – 81.2 x 27cm.
(Christie's) **$14,630 £7,700**

ROBERT FREDERICK BLUM (1857–1903) – Watching the election returns – signed – grey brush and black ink on board – 22.8 x 29.4cm.
(Christie's) **$7,150 £4,243**

ABRAHAM BLOEMAERT (Dutch 1564–1651) – Manner of – The four Evangelists – oil on panel – 83 x 113cm.
(AB Stockholms Auktionsverk) **$7,345 £3,786**

PIETER BOEL (1622–1674), Attributed to – An eagle and a fox in a landscape – oil on canvas – 162 x 226cm.
(Sotheby's) **$13,588 £7,809**

PIETER VAN BLOEMEN (1657–1720) – Soldiers and peasants on the outskirts of a village, a cannon to the right – signed with initials – oil on canvas – 75 x 98.5cm.
(Phillips) **$30,876 £15,500**

JACOB BOGDANY, Circle of – Exotic birds, ducks and fowl by a fountain in an ornamental park – 152.3 x 182.8cm.
(Christie's) **$21,025 £10,450**

BOILLY

LOUIS-LEOPOLD BOILLY (1761–1845) – A mother and child – oil on copper – circular – 8cm. diameter
(Sotheby's)   **$16,720 £8,800**

CHRISTIAN LUDWIG BOKELMANN (1844–1894) – In the anteroom of the court – signed and dated 1883 – oil on canvas – 84 x 121cm.
(Lempertz)   **$37,665 £21,523**

GIOVANNI BOLDINI (Italian 1845–1931) – A portrait of Madame Georges Victor-Hugo – oil on panel – 31 x 21cm.
(Sotheby's)   **$109,505 £60,500**

G. BOLDINI (Italian, 1842–1931) – The spinner – signed – oil on panel – 35.5 x 25cm.
(Hôtel de Ventes Horta)   **$18,934 £9,836**

BLANCHE BOLDUC (b. 1907) – The general store – signed – oil on board – 36.2 x 51.5cm.
(Pinney's)   **$893 £533**

DAVID BOMBERG (1890–1957) – The Hospital of the Knights of St. John, Bethlehem Road, Jerusalem; Moonlight – signed and dated 23 – oil on canvas – 41 x 51cm.
(Christie's)   **$58,784   £35,200**

ROSA BONHEUR (French 1822–99) – The old monarch – signed – watercolour – 24.5 x 33cm.
(Sotheby's)   **$16,104   £8,800**

DAVID BOMBERG (1890–1957) – Theatre players – charcoal, watercolour and bodycolour – 48 x 54cm.
(Christie's)   **$7,682   £3,960**

SUZANNE BONHIVERS – Lady - oil on canvas – signed and dated 43 – 116 x 82cm.
(Duran)   **$3,536   £1,832**

SERGEI BONGART (1918–1985) – The Artist's studio – signed and dated 1973 – oil on canvas – 91.5 x 107cm.
(Butterfield & Butterfield)   **$7,700   £3,774**

PIERRE BONNARD (French, 1867–1947) – Three women in a landscape – signed – oil on canvas – 36.5 x 57cm.
(Galerie Koller Zürich)   **$284,875   £148,760**

BONNARD

PIERRE BONNARD – La Seine à Vernon – signed – oil on canvas – 33.2 x 37.5cm.
(Sotheby's)   **$149,600**   **£88,000**

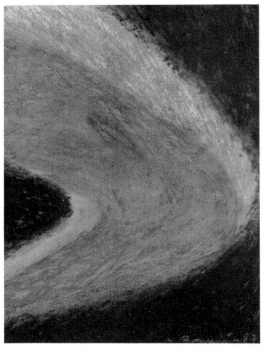

PIERRE BONNARD (1876–1947) – Woman undressing – signed – oil on canvas – 56.2 x 66cm.
(Christie's)   **$853,600**   **£440,000**

OLLE BONNIER (b. 1925) – Composition in violet – signed and dated 87 – pastel – 35 x 28cm.
(AB Stockholms Auktionsverk)   **$1,776**   **£930**

PIERRE BONNARD (1867–1947) – Woman in a red dressing gown – with studio stamp – oil on canvas – 50.5 x 34cm.
(Christie's)   **$498,410**   **£253,000**

CARLO BONONI, Circle of – Saint Sebastian – oil on copper – unframed – 15.8 x 11.7cm.
(Christie's)   **$1,948**   **£968**

FRANÇOIS BONVIN (1817–1887) – A Platter of oysters, sliced lemons and a glass of red wine on a draped table – signed – oil on canvas – 38.4 x 46.3cm.
(Christie's)   **$9,702   £4,950**

T*** LUCENA Y BORRARAS – Two brothers – signed and dated – oil on canvas – 34 x 46cm.
(Sotheby's)   **$8,860   £4,950**

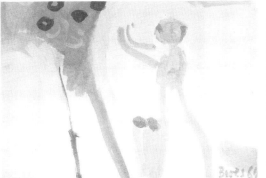

FRANCISCO BORES (1898–1972) – Figure in a landscape – gouache – signed and dated 64 – 25 x 31cm.
(Duran)   **$3,789   £1,963**

AMBROSIUS BOSSCHAERT THE ELDER (1573–1621) – A still life of flowers, in a 'Waanli Kraak' porcelain vase with shells – bears monogram – oil on copper – 28.5 x 19.5cm.
(Sotheby's)   **$668,800   £352,000**

After VLADIMIR LUKICH BOROVIKOVSKII – Portrait of Ekaterina Aleksandrovna Novosil'tseva – oil on canvas – 69.5 x 55cm.
(Christie's)   **$5,148   £2,640**

C. BOTHE (Circa 1800) – Still life with raspberries, grapes and peaches – signed and dated 1835 – oil on canvas – 26 x 31cm.
(AB Stockholms Auktionsverk)   **$2,328   £1,200**

FRANCESCO BOTTI (Active 17th Century) – Flora –
on canvas – 87.2 x 72cm.
(Phillips) $10,740 £6,000

EUGENE BOUDIN (1824–1898) – Bordeaux, Bacalan.
View from the quay – signed and dated 74 – oil on canvas
– 40.5 x 65cm.
(Christie's) $195,030 £99,000

EUGENE-LOUIS BOUDIN (1824–1898) – Berck, the
fishing boats sailing – signed and dated 1879 – oil on
canvas – 65.4 x 90.8cm.
(Galerie Koller Zürich) $197,831 £103,306

FRANCOIS BOUCHER (1703–1770) – The young
archer – oil on panel – oval – 69 x 50.5cm.
(Sotheby's) $69,880 £40,161

EUGENE BOUDIN (1824–1898) – Trouville, The jetties,
high tide – signed and dated 94 – oil on panel –
26.7 x 34.9cm.
(Christie's) $151,690 £77,000

EUGENE BOUDIN (1824–1898) – Figures on the beach
at Trouville – the studio stamp lower right (L.828) – dated
1869 – watercolour and pencil on paper – 13.3 x 25.7cm.
(Christie's) $45,507   £23,100

LUCIEN BOULIER – Bathers – signed – oil on canvas –
116 x 145cm.
(Jean-Claude Anaf) $7,140   £3,719

Manner of SEBASTIAN BOURDON – Abraham
presented by his sons with Joseph's bloodstained coat – oil
on canvas laid down on panel – 43.2 x 53.9cm.
(Christie's) $2,178   £1,100

HENRI-JACQUES BOURCE (Belgian 1826–99)
–Manner of – Shore scene with women mending nets – oil
on canvas – 87 x 136cm.
(AB Stockholms Auktionsverk) $6,449   £3,324

Manner of SEBASTIAN BOURDON – An Arcadian
scene – 91.4 x 144.7cm.
(Christie's) $9,801   £4,950

BOUT

Attributed to PIERRE BOUT, (Flemish School) – The
halt – oil on canvas – 37 x 45cm.
(Hôtel de Ventes Horta)   **$8,691   £4,480**

ANTOINE BOUVARD (d. 1956) – Gondolas on the
Grand Canal with La Salute and Punta della Dogana,
Venice – signed – oil on canvas – 50.2 x 66cm.
(Christie's)   **$17,248   £8,800**

ANTOINE BOUVARD (d. 1956) – The Grand Canal,
Venice – signed – oil on canvas – 50.5 x 65.4cm.
(Christie's)   **$8,686   £4,620**

ANTOINE BOUVARD (d. 1956) – Venetian backwaters
– both signed – 26.7 x 34.3cm.: a pair, one illustrated.
(Christie's)   **$3,521   £2,090**

ANTOINE BOUVARD (d. 1956) – The Bacino of St.
Mark's, Venice – signed – oil on canvas – 50.8 x 64.8cm.
(Christie's)   **$12,936   £6,600**

AUGUSTUS JULES BOUVIER (1837–1881) – The
harem favourite – signed with monogram – 29.3 x 39.4cm.
(Christie's)   **$4,819   £2,860**

WILLIAM BOWYER, R.A. (b. 1926) – Barnes Pond –
signed and dated 89 – oil on canvas – 63.5 x 89cm.
(Christie's)   **$6,429   £3,850**

GEORGE PRICE BOYCE (1826–1897) – Head study of
Ellen Smith – oil on panel – 19 x 14.1cm.
(Christie's)   **$6,098   £3,080**

FRANK BRAMLEY, R.A. (1857–1915) – Simplicitia –
signed and dated '87 – also signed, inscribed and dated on
the reverse – oil on canvas – 18 x 15cm.
(Phillips)   **$11,641   £7,000**

HELEN BRADLEY (1900–1979) – Little girl, you say your mother's been eaten by a tiger – signed with a fly
– oil on canvasboard - 40 x 50cm.
(Phillips)   **$17,461   £10,500**

BRANDEIS

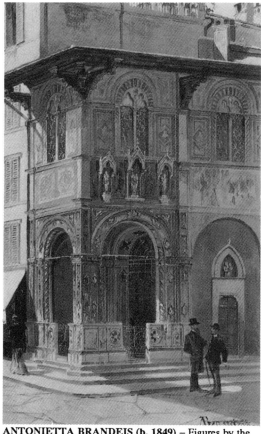

ANTONIETTA BRANDEIS (b. 1849) – A Neapolitan
street scene – signed – oil on panel – 24 x 15.3cm.
(Christie's) **$8,624 £4,400**

SIR FRANK BRANGWYN, R.A. (1864–1956) – The
Printed Word - signed with initials – oil on canvas –
376 x 549cm. – lunette
(Christie's) **$27,555 £16,500**

ANTONIETTA BRANDEIS (b. 1849) – Figures by the
Loggia del Bigallo, Florence – signed – oil on panel –
24 x 13.5cm.
(Christie's) **$3,881 £1,980**

SIR FRANK BRANGWYN, R.A. (1864–1956) – Venus
– signed with initials and dated 92 – oil on canvas –
198 x 98cm.
(Christie's) $6,429   £3,850

NORMUND BRASLINS (b. 1962) – The two sisters –
signed and dated 90 – oil on canvas
(Jean-Claude Anaf) $668   £349

VICTOR BRAUNER – Autoenroulement – signed –
titled and dated IV 1961 – oil on canvas – 79.5 x 63.5cm.
(Sotheby's) $224,400   £132,000

ALFRED DE BREANSKI (1852–1928) – Coniston Lake
and Old Man – signed – oil on canvas – 40.7 x 55.9cm.
(Christie's) $7,629   £4,180

Circle of JAN PIETER BREDAEL (1683–1735) – An
extensive landscape with travellers on a wooded track, a
town with a chateau on a lake beyond – oil on copper –
38.8 x 49.4cm.
(Christie's) $21,780   £11,000

BREDAEL

Follower of PIETER VAN BREDAEL – A winter
landscape with sledges and skaters near a castle – signed
with initials 'M. H.' – 57.8 x 65.4cm.
(Christie's)   **$5,500 £2,750**

GEORGE HENDRIK BREITNER (1857–1923) – An
elegant lady sitting at a table – signed – oil on board –
37 x 27.5cm.
(Christie's)   **$11,023 £5,750**

GEORGE HENDRIK BREITNER (1857–1923) – A
maid – and a sketch of a nude by a mirror on the reverse –
signed – black charcoal and pastel on paper – 42.5 x 28cm.
(Christie's)   **$6,200 £3,234**

**QUIRYN GERRITSZ. VAN BREKELENKAM (after
1620–1668)** – Portrait of a lady, bust length, in a black
dress and lace collar – oil on panel – 67.2 x 54.2cm.
(Christie's)   **$4,356 £2,200**

RUDOLF BREMMER (born 1900) – A view of glasshouses, Loosduinen, a church in the distance – signed with initials and dated '35 – oil on board – 28 x 39.5cm.
(Christie's)   **$4,478   £2,336**

HANS ANDERSEN BRENDEKILDE (Danish 1857–1920) – Village street with woman at a fence – signed – oil on canvas – 48 x 50cm.
(AB Stockholms Auktionsverk)   **$7,345   £3,786**

MAURICE BRIANCHON – Le Pont – signed – oil on canvas – 92 x 73cm.
(Sotheby's)   **$84,150   £49,500**

JORG BREU, the elder (active 1475/80–1537) – Portrait of a man before a landscape – oil on panel – 53.2 x 43cm.
(Phillips)   **$59,760   £30,000**

W. SMITHSON BROADHEAD – Portrait of Steve Donoghue, three-quarter length, in racing silks, seated with a crop – signed – inscribed "Steve Donoghue 1924" on the stretcher – oil on canvas – 101.5 x 76cm.
(Phillips)   **$7,483   £4,500**

BROECK

J.P. VAN DEN BROECK – The awakening – signed - oil on canvas – 90 x 60cm.
(Hôtel de Ventes Horta)   **$260   £129**

HARRY BROOKER (1848–1940) – The tea party; and Homework – one signed and dated 1907, and one signed and dated 1908 – both oil on canvas – 30.5 x 38.1cm. - a pair
(Christie's)   **$22,308   £13,200**

ALFRED BROGE – A woman and child playing shadow puppets – signed and dated – oil on canvas – 64 x 53.5cm.
(Sotheby's)   **$9,845   £5,500**

HARRY BROOKER (1848–1940) – Playing school - signed and dated 1893 – oil on canvas – 70.8 x 91.5cm.
(Christie's)   **$13,799   £7,150**

HENRY JAMYN BROOKS – Windsor from "Rafts" –
signed – oil on canvas – 61 x 91cm.
(Sotheby's)   **$21,901   £12,100**

FORD MADOX BROWN (English, 1821–1893) – Italian
fisherboy – signed on reverse – oil on paper laid down on
panel – 18.4 x 16.5cm.
(Bonhams)   **$10,110   £5,000**

SIR JOHN ARNESBY BROWN, R.A. (1866–1955) –
The coming day (Second version) – signed – oil on canvas
– 56 x 81cm.

ADRIAEN BROUWER (1605/6–1638) — Village gossip
– signed with monogram – oil on wood – 23 x 27.2cm.
(Kunsthaus am Museum)   **$22,190   £11,438**   *(Phillips)*   **$59,868   £36,000**

BROWN

JOHN GEORGE BROWN (1831–1913) – Shoeshine
Boy – signed J.G. Brown, N.A., l.l. – oil on canvas –
66 x 46cm.
(Christie's)   **$35,200**   **£18,656**

JOHN GEORGE BROWN (1831–1913) – That's me
pumpkin – signed and dated 1879 – oil on canvas –
46 x 30.5cm.
(Christie's)   **$30,800**   **£16,016**

JOHN GEORGE BROWN (1831–1913) – Watching the train – signed and dated 1881 – oil on canvas –
71 x 112cm.
(Christie's)   **$297,000**   **£154,440**

WILLIAM MASON BROWN (1828–1898) – Still life
with peaches and melon – signed with initials – oil on
canvas – 51 x 41cm.
(Christie's)   **$6,600**   **£3,432**

WILLIAM MASON BROWN (1828–1898) – Fruits of
Autumn – signed with conjoined initials – oil on canvas –
40.5 x 50.6cm.
(Christie's)   **$18,700**   **£9,971**

BYRON BROWNE (1907–1961) – Cataclysm – signed –
dated 1949 and inscribed on the reverse – oil on canvas –
76.5 x 97cm.
(Christie's)   **$15,400**   **£8,162**

COLLEEN BROWNING – Interior scene – signed –
pastel on board – 79 x 56cm.
(Christie's)   **$110**   **£58**

S W BROWNLOW – The basket weaver's family –
signed – oil on canvas – 25 x 62cm.
(Allen & Harris)   **$9,486**   **£5,100**

BRUEGHEL

JAN BRUEGHEL the Younger, (1601–1678) Circle of –
Bowl of flowers – oil on panel – 43.5 x 60cm.
(Sotheby's)   **$81,526**   **£46,854**

PIETER BRUEGHEL II called Brueghel d'Enfer (circa
1564–1638), (Attributed to) – The faggot gatherers - oil on
panel – round – 17.5cm. diam.
(Sotheby's)   **$38,823**   **£22,312**

**Manner of PIETER BRUEGHEL the younger
(1564–1637)** – A wedding dance in an interior – oil on
panel – 58.5 x 83.2cm.
(Phillips)   **$23,904**   **£12,000**

GUILLAUME CHARLES BRUN (1825–1908) – The
little flower-seller – signed and dated 1873 – 80.5 x 46cm.
(Christie's)   **$7,376**   **£3,688**

LEON BRUNIN (1861–1949) – A still life with herrings on a plate, a pewter jug, a glass of wine and a pipe on a draped table – signed and inscribed Antwerpen 1888 – oil on panel – 58 x 77.5cm.
(Christie's) **$7,376 £3,688**

FRANÇOIS BRUNERY (late 19th Century) – Love's duty – signed and dated – oil on panel – 32.4 x 24.1cm.
(Christie's) **$6,204 £3,300**

JEAN BRUSSELMANS (1884–1953) – North Sea dunes – signed – oil on canvas – 54.5 x 76cm.
(Hôtel de Ventes Horta) **$43,032 £24,590**

FRANÇOIS BRUNERY (Italian 19th Century) – Lighting a shrine on the Venetian Lagoon; selling water melons on the Piazzetta, Venice – a pair – both signed – oil on canvas – each 43 x 25cm.
(Sotheby's) **$14,091 £7,700**

BARTHOLOMAUS BRUYN the Elder (1493–1555) – Portrait of a bearded man – half length – oil on wood – oval – 29 x 22cm.
(Lempertz) **$31,291 £17,880**

BRUYN

JOHANNES CORNELIS DE BRUYN, Attributed to – A peach, bunches of grapes, berries and flowers on a marble ledge, woodland beyond – with signature P.T. van Brussel – oil on panel – unframed – 20.9 x 15.9cm.
(Christie's) $7,746 £3,850

BERNARD BUFFET (b. 1928) - Portrait de femme – signed and dated – oil on canvas – 100 x 81cm.
(Christie's) $84,645 £49,500

FRANK BUCHSER (1828–1890) – A groom meeting young women before an Andalucian farmstead – signed and dated 1858 – oil on canvas – 69 x 54cm.
(Galerie Koller Zürich) $31,653 £16,529

BERNARD BUFFET (b. 1928) – La Place de la Bastille et le Génie – signed and dated – inscribed on reverse – oil on canvas – 146.7 x 114.3cm.
(Christie's) $526,680 £308,000

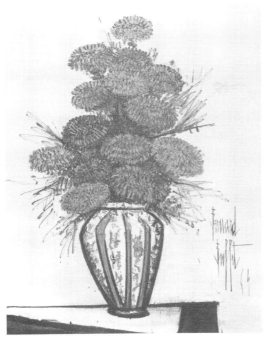

BERNARD BUFFET (b. 1928) – Bouquet de Dahlias – signed and dated lower right Bernard Buffet 64 – oil on canvas – 146 x 115cm.
(Christie's)   **$489,060**   **£286,000**

BERNARD BUFFET – The circus, musical clowns – oil on canvas – signed and dated 55 – 195 x 300cm.
(Jean Claude Anaf)   **$996,875**   **£572,917**

BERNARD BUFFET (b. 1928) – Tête de clown – signed and dated – oil on canvas – 100 x 60cm.
(Christie's)   **$206,910**   **£121,000**

BERNARD BUFFET – Le Canal – signed and dated 1982 – oil on canvas – 81 x 130cm.
(Sotheby's)   **$108,460**   **£63,800**

BERNARD BUFFET – St Marc la Mare et le Lavoir - (Eure) – signed and dated 1975 - oil on canvas – 88 x 128cm.
(Sotheby's)   **$168,300**   **£99,000**

BUFFET

EDGAR BUNDY (1862–1922) – Visiting the Physician –
signed – oil on canvas – 101.9 x 137.2cm.
(Christie's)   **$5,621**   **£3,080**

BERNARD BUFFET (b. 1928) – Clown au Fond jaune –
signed and dated 55 – watercolour, brush and black ink on
paper – 108 x 75cm.
(Christie's)   **$244,530**   **£143,000**

LOUIS BUISSERET (1888–1956) – Orvieto – signed –
oil on canvas – 38 x 55cm.
(Hôtel de Ventes Horta)   **$1,496**   **£741**

CHARLES EPHRAIM BURCHFIELD (1893–1967) –
Maytime – signed and dated 1917 – watercolour and pencil
on paper laid down on board – 45.5 x 55.5cm.
(Christie's)   **$30,800**   **£16,016**

J.G. BUISSON – The wig – oil on panel – signed –
31 x 37cm.
(Hôtel de Ventes Horta)   **$6,208**   **£3,200**

ARTHUR JAMES WETHERALL BURGESS – In tow
on the flowing tide – signed – oil on canvas –
29¼in x 39½in.
(Bearne's)   **$3,880**   **£2,000**

JOHN BAGNOLD BURGESS, R.A. – Going to the ball – signed with initials and dated 1875 – oil on canvas – 83 x 64cm.
(Sotheby's) $8,960   £4,950

CHARLES H.H. BURLEIGH (–1956) – The maid – signed – oil on canvas – 51 x 41cm.
(Phillips) $4,989   £3,000

EMERSON C. BURKHARDT (1905–1969) – Fragmentary history of the Iron Age – oil on canvas – 77.5 x 99cm.
(Christie's) $8,250   £4,372

BURLEIGH

CHARLES H.H. BURLEIGH (–1956) – Veronica –
inscribed with title and dated 1918 – oil on canvas –
unframed – 76 x 56cm.
(Phillips) $6,984   £4,200

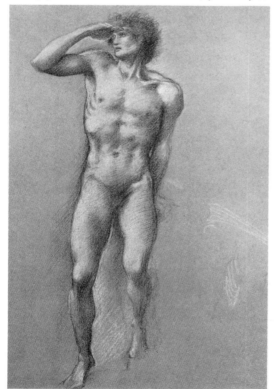

SIR EDWARD COLEY BURNE-JONES, Bt., A.R.A.
(English 1833–98) – Study for "The call of Perseus" –
black and white chalk on buff paper – 48 x 32.5cm.
(Sotheby's) $63,712   £35,200

SIR EDWARD COLEY BURNE-JONES (English
1833–98) – King Cophetua and the beggar maid – signed
with initials and dated – gouache and gum arabic –
72.5 x 36.5cm.
(Sotheby's) $438,020   £242,000

EDWARD BURRA (1905–1976) – Birdman and pots in a
landscape – watercolour and bodycolour – 56.5 x 78.5cm.
(Christie's) $107,250   £55,000

MILDRED ANNE BUTLER – An interior at Kilmurry –
watercolour – signed and dated 1920 – 19.7 x 24.8cm.
(Bonhams) $400 £200

EDWARD BURRA (1905–1976) – Approaching storm –
signed – watercolour, bodycolour and pencil – 135 x 80cm.
(Christie's) $60,621 £36,300

THEODORE EARL BUTLER (1861–1936) – The
Lieutenance, Honfleur – signed – oil on canvas –
65.2 x 81.3cm.
(Christie's) $17,600 £9,152

VALDIS BUSS (b. 1924) – Sloka – signed and dated - oil
on canvas – 50 x 70cm.
(Jean-Claude Anaf) $255 £133

JAMES E. BUTTERSWORTH (1817–1894) – New
York Bay – signed – oil on board – 15.2 x 25.3cm.
(Christie's) $17,600 £9,328

91

BUZZI

A*** BUZZI (Italian 19th/20th Century) – The harem –
signed – watercolour over traces of pencil – 53.5 x 75cm.
(Sotheby's)   **$10,065   £5,500**

**LOUIS SIMON CABAILLOT called Louis Lassalle
(French, b. 1810)** – Children Walking Through a Snowy
Landscape – signed – oil on paper – 9³/₄ x 8in.
(Skinner)   **$300   £155**

JOSE CABALLERO (b. 1916) – Garcia Lorca – oil on
canvas - signed – 100 x 73cm.
(Duran)   **$15,156   £7,853**

MAXIMO CABALLERO – You've lost – signed and
dated 1900 – oil on canvas – 82 x 102cm.
(Jean-Claude Anaf) **$25,786 £13,430**

RICARDO LOPEZ CABRERA (Spanish, 19th
Century) – Spanish mountain landscape – signed – oil on
board – 14 x 23cm.
(Kunsthaus am Museum) **$2,353 £1,213**

ALEXANDRE CABANEL (1824–1889) – Paolo and
Francesca – signed and dated 1870 – oil on canvas –
91 x 129cm.
(Sotheby's) **$31,236 £17,849**

RICARDO LOPEZ CABRERA (c. 1900) – An old lady
sewing – signed and inscribed – unframed –
35.6 x 48.9cm.
(Christie's) **$2,224 £1,320**

ADRIAEN VAN DER CABEL, Circle of — A rocky
Mediterranean Coastline with Dutch shipping and a
landing party greeted on the shore — 43.2 x 61.6cm.
(Christie's) **$9,296 £4,620**

RICARDO LOPEZ CABRERA (1864–1950) – Resting
in the evening sun – oil on canvas – signed and dated 92 –
32.5 x 67cm.
(Duran) **$13,136 £6,806**

HECTOR CAFFIERI – Mother and child looking out to sea – signed – watercolour – 33 x 50.2cm.
(Bonhams) $3,618 £1,800

HECTOR CAFFIERI (British, 1847–1932) – Lady and her dog in a punt – signed – watercolour heightened with bodycolour – 35 x 25cm.
(Phillips) $4,596 £2,400

HECTOR CAFFIERI – Children in a courtyard – watercolour heightened with bodycolour – signed – 13³/₄ x 9³/₄in.
(Bearne's) $3,820 £2,000

RALPH CAHOON – Sailor and a mermaid on shore – signed – oil on panel – 21 x 26in.
(Eldred's)   **$2,000**   **£995**

HECTOR CAFFIERI – In the walled garden – signed – watercolour and bodycolour – 25.3 x 35.6cm.
(Bonhams)   **$6,834**   **£3,400**

GUSTAVE CAILLEBOTTE (1840–1897) – Bord de Sene à Argenteuil – signed lower left G. Caillebotte – oil on canvas – 54 x 65cm.
(Christie's)   **$1,370,600**   **£770,000**

CAILLEBOTTE

GUSTAVE CAILLEBOTTE (1840–1894) – Portrait
d'Eugène Lamy, en buste – oil on canvas – 65 x 54.5cm.
(Christie's)   **$65,835 £38,500**

GUSTAVE CAILLEBOTTE (1848–1894) – Normandy
landscape – signed – oil on canvas – 63 x 73cm.
(Galerie Koller Zürich)   **$735,930 £384,298**

After FRANCESCO DEL CAIRO – A Sybil, head and
shoulders – unframed – 74 x 58.5cm.
(Christie's)   **$3,267 £1,650**

After JACQUES CALLOT – The Mocking of Christ; and Christ being presented to the People – oil on paper laid down on panel – 10.1 x 28.8cm. – a pair – one illustrated
(Christie's)   **$2,069   £1,045**

G.W. CALLOW (British, 19th Century) – On the Dutch coast – watercolour heightened with white – 22.5 x 48cm. – and a companion, Evening on Devonshire coast – a pair
(Phillips)   **$843   £440**

WILLIAM CALLOW (1812–1908) – Bruges – signed and dated 1853 – watercolour – 26.5 x 35.5cm.
(Phillips)   **$5,656   £2,800**

Follower of FRANCESCO DEL CAIRO – The Mater Dolorosa – unframed – 74.8 x 62.5cm.
(Christie's)   **$4,400   £2,200**

ALEXANDER CALDER (American, 1898–1976) – Two Acrobats – edition of 150 - signed and numbered 123/150 – lithograph on paper – 24¼ x 13in.
(Skinner Inc.)   **$550   £295**

ALDOLPHE FELIX CALS (1810–1880) – Still life with a cucumber and sandstone pot – signed and dated 1847 – oil on panel - 16 x 19cm.
(Sotheby's)   **$11,713   £6,693**

CALVAERT

STEVEN CAMPBELL (b. 1953) – Two men with a Carriage Royale to catch a Queen Bee – oil on canvas – unframed – 284 x 274cm.
(Christie's)   **$22,407 £11,550**

Attributed to ANTONIO CALZA (1653–1725) – A cavalry skirmish on a broad plain at the foot of a mountain range – oil on canvas – 97.5 x 134.5cm.
(Phillips)   **$37,848 £19,000**

DENYS CALVAERT (1540–1619) – The Madonna Della Ghiara – oil on panel – 60.5 x 44.5cm.
(Sotheby's)   **$21,945 £11,550**

HEINRICH CAMPENDONK – Two girls – gouache
(Hauswedell & Nolte) **$53,464 £30,464**

GIACOMO CAMPI – Young man in Renaissance
costume – signed – watercolour – 35 x 26cm.
(Ritchie's) **$207 £107**

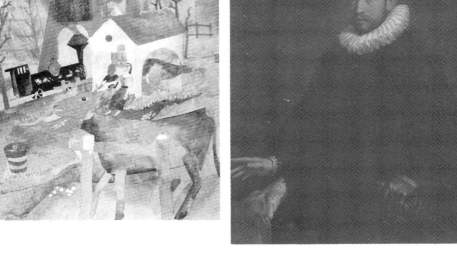

HEINRICH CAMPENDONK (1889–1957) – The
Barbara mine, Penzberg – signed and dated 1919 –
watercolour and pencil on paper – 37.5 x 31.5cm.
(Christie's) **$260,040 £132,000**

GIULIO CAMPI (c. 1500–1572) –Portrait of a gentleman
– bears inscription – oil on canvas – 110 x 99cm.
(Sotheby's) **$22,990 £12,100**

CAMPIGLI

MASSIMO CAMPIGLI – Due donne al piano – signed and dated '48 – oil on canvas – 60 x 66.5cm.
(Sotheby's) **$224,400   £132,000**

Follower of ANTONIO CANALE, IL CANALETTO – The Entrance of the Grand Canal, Venice, with Santa Maria della Salute; and The Bacino di San Marco seen from the Grand Canal – 54.7 x 91.5cm. – a pair
(Christie's) **$39,204   £19,800**

JOSE CANAVERAL (1833–1894) – Andalucian courtyard – oil on panel – indistinctly signed – 18 x 27cm.
(Duran) **$11,150   £5,759**

GIORGIO CANELLA (19th Century) – Piazza San Marco, Venice – signed – 66.1 x 104.2cm.
(Christie's) **$12,974   £7,700**

NICCOLO CANNICCI (Italian 1846–1906) – The midday meal – signed and dated 1881 – oil on canvas – 95 x 76cm.
(Sotheby's) **$119,460   £66,000**

Attributed to SIMONE CANTARINI (1612–1648) – Portrait of Cardinal Antonio Barberini – oil on canvas – 64 x 80cm.
(Sotheby's) **$20,900   £11,000**

V.* CAPESSIERO (Italian, 19th century) – Figures by beached fishing boats – signed – oil on board – unframed – 15.5 x 29.3cm.
(Bonhams)   **$1,011**   **£500**

ULISSE CAPUTO (1872–1948) – La Liseuse – signed – oil on board – 36.8 x 44.5cm.
(Christie's)   **$10,780**   **£5,500**

JOSEPH CARAUD (1821–1905) – Feeding the Pigeons – signed – oil on canvas – 98.8 x 66.7cm.
(Christie's)   **$26,004**   **£13,200**

Follower of VINCENTE CARDUCHO – Christ on the road to Calvary – unframed – 132.1 x 170.8cm.
(Christie's)   **$3,960**   **£1,980**

JEAN PHILIPPE ROBERT CAREENEN called JEAN RAINE (Belgium, b. 1927) – Place de la Concorde, Paris – signed – oil on canvas – 12 x 16in.
(Skinner Inc.)   **$600**   **£322**

GIUSEPPE CARELLI (1858–1921) – Near Naples – signed – oil on panel – 25.4 x 45.7cm.
(Christie's)   **$9,918**   **£5,060**

CARELLI

GIUSEPPE CARELLI – Fishing boats in a bay – signed
– oil on canvas – 14¹/₂ x 25¹/₂in. – unframed
(Bearne's)   **$10,476   £5,400**

ALOIS CARIGIET (1902–85) – Ballet dancers – signed
and dated 1958 and inscribed 'Epreuve d'artiste' – colour
lithograph – 54 x 47cm.
(AB Stockholms Auktionsverk)   **$1,567   £808**

ALOIS CARIGIET (Swiss, 1902–1985) – Ballet girls –
signed and dated 1982 – colour lithograph –
49.5 x 66.5cm.
(germann Auktionshaus)   **$3,921   £2,016**

WILLIAM CARLAW (1847–1889) – Shore scene with
figures loading seaweed into horsedrawn cart – signed –
watercolour – 17 x 28in.
(Russell, Baldwin & Bright)   **$561   £300**

JOHN WILSON CARMICHAEL – 'Port of the Brill' –
signed and dated 1860 – 31.5 x 49.5cm.
(Anderson & Garland)   **$25,258   £14,600**

JULIUS SCHNORR VON CAROLSFELD (1794–1872)
– The Madonna and Child – signed with monogram and
dated 1855 – oil on canvas – 69.2 x 47cm.
(Christie's)   **$32,505   £16,500**

GIULIO CARPIONI (1613–1679) – Head of a woman wearing an elaborate turban headdress decorated with jewels – oil on canvas – 50 x 39cm.
(Phillips) $12,948   £6,500

EMILE AUGUSTE CAROLUS-DURAN (1838–1917) – Spring – signed and dated 1882 – oil on canvas – 150.5 x 92.1cm.
(Christie's) $24,310   £14,300

HENRI JOSEPH GOMMARUS CARPENTERO (1820–1874) – Peasants merrymaking in an inn – signed and dated 1850 – oil on panel – 41 x 48cm.
(Christie's) $8,046   £4,023

AGOSTINO CARRACCI (1557–1602) – Portrait of an old man – oil on paper laid down on wood – 25.5 x 22cm.
(Sotheby's) $250,800   £132,000

CARRACCI

Attributed to ANNIBALE CARRACCI (1560–1609) –
A youth, half length, holding a flute – in a painted oval –
on panel – 59 x 41cm.
(Phillips) $46,540 £26,000

PIERRE CARRIER-BELLEUSE (1851–1932) – Devant
la Vague – signed and dated 1910 – pastel on canvas –
114.3 x 146.4cm.
(Christie's) $5,170 £2,750

PIERRE CARRIER-BELLEUSE (1851–1932) –
Columbine – signed – pastel – 105 x 50cm.
(Christie's) $8,624 £4,400

PIERRE CARRIER-BELLEUSE (1851–1932) – Les Danseuses – signed and dated 1928 – pastel on canvas – 116.9 x 75cm.
(Christie's)　　　　　　　　　　$12,826　£6,820

PIERRE CARRIER-BELLEUSE (1851–1932) – Pierrot – signed – pastel – 105 x 50cm.
(Christie's)　　　　　　$8,624　£4,400

EUGENE CARRIERE – The art lover – signed and dated 1874 – oil on canvas – 53.5 x 43cm.
(Jean-Claude Anaf)　　　　　$7,221　£3,703

CARROLL

HENRY WILLIAM CARTER (Exh. 1880–95) – "Cat and dog life" – four studies – oil on board – each signed and dated 1882 – each 4¼ x 5½in.
(David Lay) **$1,240 £620**

W.J. CARROLL – Portrait of a young girl – signed – watercolour – 60 x 50cm.
(Phillips) **$1,200 £600**

MARY CASSATT – La jeune femme à la toque or Susan in a toque trimmed with two roses – oil on canvas – 65 x 54cm.
(Sotheby's) **$1,402,500 £825,000**

ANTO CARTE (1886–1954) – Saint Christophe – signed – oil on canvas – 120 x 100.4cm.
(Christie's) **$53,075 £27,500**

MARY CASSATT – Girl with a banjo – signed – pastel on paper laid down on canvas – 60 x 73cm.
(Sotheby's) **$561,000 £330,000**

PATRICK CAULFIELD (b. 1936) – Pool, 1975 – with stitching signature – wool tapestry – 248.9 x 198.2cm.
(Christie's) **$3,887 £2,090**

H. CASSIERS (Belgian, 1858–1944) – Amsterdam – signed – gouache on board – 27 x 37cm.
(Hôtel de Ventes Horta) **$2,052 £1,066**

HENRY CASSIERS (Belgian, 1858–1944) – Street at Katuyk – signed – gouache heightened with oil and gum arabic on grey paper – 6³/₈ x 8¹/₄in.
(Skinner) **$450 £231**

CATERINA – Seated man and mannequin – signed – mixed media on paper – 168 x 124cm.
(Galerie Moderne) **$2,926 £1,532**

LOUIS DE CAULLERY (Active circa 1598) – (a) An elegant couple standing on a hill above an encampment; and companion (b) Elegant figures standing on a hill above a town where travelling musicians play - oil on panel – a pair – 26 x 21.5cm.
(Phillips) **$12,948 £6,500**

CAVALLINO

Follower of BERNARDO CAVALLINO – Venus and
Adonis – circular – 38.1cm. diameter
(Christie's) **$1,966 £990**

MICHEL-J* CAZABON (b. 1814)** – Brazilians –
signed – watercolour heightened with gouache –
275 x 215mm.
(Sotheby's) **$2,677 £1,339**

EUGENIO CECCONI (1842–1903) – Leading the dogs –
signed – 45.5 x 70cm.
(Christie's) **$38,892 £19,446**

HIPOLITO HIDALGO DE CAVIEDES (b. 1901) – Girl
with doll – signed and dated 1948 – oil on canvas –
69 x 53cm.
(Duran) **$2,128 £1,111**

INTA CELMINA (b. 1946) – Girl with light – signed –
oil on canvas – 100 x 81cm.
(Jean-Claude Anaf) **$530 £277**

EDMOND CERIA – Pont de Seine – signed – oil on panel – 26.5 x 40cm.
(Jean-Claude Anaf)   **$3,422   £1,773**

GUANDALLINI CENTENTA – The Dance of Cupid – Venus and Cupid in the Clouds – signed and dated 1838 – circular 61cm. diameter
(Spencer's)   **$3,820   £2,000**

GIULIO CERVI (late 19th Century) – Il Sonetto – signed – inscribed and dated 1873 – oil on canvas – 62.2 x 45.7cm.
(Christie's)   **$12,408   £6,600**

Follower of CARLO CERESA – Portrait of a young girl, standing three quarter length, in a red dress – 101 x 78.1cm.
(Christie's)   **$15,682   £7,920**

MARC CHAGALL (1887–1985) – Vue sur Paris – signed – gouache and oil on paper – 54.5 x 71cm.
(Christie's)   **$677,160   £396,000**

CHAGALL

MARC CHAGALL – Soleil au cheval rouge – signed and
dated 1977 – oil on canvas – 89 x 116cm.
(Sotheby's)   **$3,366,000   £1,980,000**

MARC CHAGALL (1887–1985) – Les Amoureux au
Clair de Lune – signed – gouache on board –
64.2 x 48.8cm.
(Christie's)   **$376,200   £220,000**

MARC CHAGALL (Russian/French, 1887–1985) –
Rabbiner - from the series Mein Leben – signed and
numbered 31/110" – etching and drypoint on laid paper –
9³/₄ x 7³/₈in.
(Skinner Inc.)   **$3,750   £2,011**

MARC CHAGALL – The artist with orange cockerel – coloured pencil drawing – signed and dated - 31 x 48cm.
(Jean Claude Anaf) $87,436   £50,251

MARC CHAGALL (1887–1985) – Vase de fleurs et la Tour Eiffel – signed and dated 1965 – watercolour, brush and black ink on paper – 63.5 x 48cm.
(Christie's) $244,530   £143,000

FRANK TOLLES CHAMBERLAIN (1873–1961) – Rome, 1910 – signed with monogram – oil on canvas – 81 x 53cm.
(Butterfield & Butterfield) $1,980   £970

MARC CHAGALL – Le violoniste – signed – oil on canvas – 81.5 x 60cm.
(Sotheby's) $1,683,000   £990,000

FRANK TOLLES CHAMBERLAIN (1873–1961) – Still life with fruit and jug – signed with monogram and dated 1931 – oil on canvas – 51 x 61cm.
(Butterfield & Butterfield) $2,750   £1,348

CHAMPAIGNE

PHILIPPE DE CHAMPAIGNE (1602–1674) – The Annunciation – oil on canvas – 95 x 129cm.
(Christie's) **$154,258 £79,286**

Follower of JEAN BAPTISTE SIMON CHARDIN – Portrait of Auguste-Gabriel Godefroy (1728–1813) watching a top spin – oil on canvas – 66 x 53cm.
(Phillips) **$3,386 £1,700**

A.* CHANETIE (Continental, 19th century) – The New Doll – signed and dated '73 – oil on canvas – 45.7 x 35.6cm.
(Bonhams) **$3,235 £1,600**

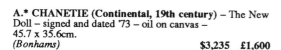

CONRAD WISE CHAPMAN (1842–1910) – The trump card – oil on canvas – 53 x 65cm.
(Christie's) **$7,700 £4,004**

CONSTANCE-MARIE CHARPENTIER (1767–1849) – A mother and her daughter – oil on canvas – unframed – 81 x 103cm.
(Christie's) **$33,055 £16,990**

CONSTANCE-MARIE CHARPENTIER (1767–1849)
– The five senses – oil on canvas – 90 x 120cm.
(Christie's)   **$22,037   £11,327**

WILLIAM MERRITT CHASE (1849–1916) – Portrait
of a German boy – oil on board – 45.7 x 38cm.
(Christie's)   **$16,500   £8,580**

WILLIAM MERRITT CHASE (1849–1916) –
Shinnecock Hills (A view of Shinnecock) – signed and
dated 1891 – oil on panel – 45.5 x 61cm.
(Christie's)   **$286,000   £148,720**

HENRI JEAN SAINT ANGE CHASSELAT (French, 1813–1880) – Playing at soldiers – oil on canvas – signed – 54 x 76.2cm.
(Bonhams)   **$3,861   £2,200**

JOSE CHAVEZ (19th Century) – Maja – oil on canvas – signed – 57 x 30cm.
(Duran)   **$2,526   £1,309**

GERARDO CHAVEZ (Peruvian, b. 1937) – The watchman of Ancient Chaos – signed and dated 74 – pastel on canvas – 130 x 97cm.
(AB Stockholms Auktionsverk)   **$1,243   £651**

JOSE CHAVEZ (19th Century) – Waiting in the Calle de la Sopa – oil on canvas – signed – 57 x 30cm.
(Duran)   **$3.032   £1,571**

ULPIANO CHECA (1860–1916) – Talking in a classical amphitheatre - oil on canvas – signed – 59 x 92cm.
(Duran)   **$10,105   £5,236**

JULES CHERET (French, 1836–1932) – Harlequin
figure – signed – oil on canvas – 21¹/₄ x 14³/₄in.
(Du Mouchelles)   **$4,750   £2,547**

JAN VAN CHELMINSKI (1851–1925) – A despatch
from Napoleon – signed – oil on panel – 30.5 x 22.9cm.
(Christie's)   **$1,861   £990**

JAN CHELMINSKI – Afternoon ride – on panel – signed
– 9 x 10³/₄in.
(Tennants)   **$4,400   £2,200**

LILIAN CHEVIOT (exh. 1894–1902) – Royal, a
tricolour working Springer spaniel – signed – oil on canvas
– 76.2 x 63.5cm.
(Christie's)   **$25,080   £13,200**

CHEVIOT

LILIAN CHEVIOT (exh. 1894–1902) – Silver Persian kittens playing – signed – oil on canvas – 50.8 x 60.9cm.
(Christie's) **$3,135 £1,650**

GIORGIO DE CHIRICO (1888–1978) – Natura morta – signed – oil on canvas – 46.3 x 35cm.
(Christie's) **$90,288 £52,800**

GAETANO CHIERICI – Welcome Alms – signed and dated 1875 – oil on canvas – 22 x 31in.
(Michael Newman) **$50,000 £25,000**

GIORGIO DE CHIRICO – Gli Archeologi – signed – charcoal and wash heightened with white gouache on paper laid down on canvas – 98 x 80cm.
(Sotheby's) **$523,600 £308,000**

JAMES WARREN CHILDE – A full length portrait of a lady with a King Charles Spaniel at her feet – and a full length portrait of a gentleman – a pair – signed and dated 1839 – watercolour heightened with white – one illustrated 43.2 x 32.4cm.
(Bonhams) **$1,464 £850**

GIORGIO DE CHIRICO (1888–1978) – Lampo – signed – oil on canvas – 39.7 x 49.5cm.
(Christie's) **$91,014 £46,200**

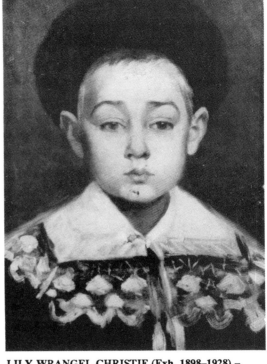

RENE-LOUIS CHRETIEN (French, 1867–1942) – An interior genre scene – signed – oil on canvas – 28 x 21½in. *(Skinner Inc.)* **$1,100 £590**

CHRISTIAN – Hunting scene – oil on wood panel – 12 x 16in. *(Du Mouchelles)* **$500 £268**

LILY WRANGEL CHRISTIE (Exh. 1898–1928) – Portrait of a boy – signed – oil on canvas – 15½ x 14in. *(David Lay)* **$95 £50**

CHRISTO

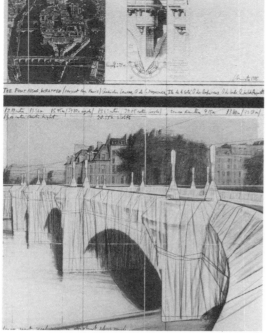

CHRISTO (b. 1935) – The Pont Neuf wrapped (project for Pont Neuf, Paris) – signed – inscribed and dated 1985 – collage with fabric, string, coloured crayon, pencil, gouache and photograph on cardboard –
Top panel: 31 x 78.7cm – Bottom panel: 67.3 x 78.7cm.
(Christie's) **$113,520 £66,000**

HOWARD CHANDLER CHRISTY (1872–1952) – Bill of Rights – signed – dated 1942 and inscribed – oil on canvas – 52.3 x 101cm.
(Christie's) **$33,000 £17,490**

HOWARD CHANDLER CHRISTY – Portrait of a sea captain – signed – oil on millboard – 58.7 x 49.5cm.
(Ritchie's) **$551 £285**

HOWARD CHANDLER CHRISTY – Portrait of a young woman seated in a wicker chair – signed and dated 1902 – oil on canvas – 100.3 x 85.6cm.
(Ritchie's) **$2,527 £1,310**

ANTONIO CIRINO (1889–1983) – Lobsterman's
rendezvous – oil on canvas – signed – 25 x 30in.
(Bruce D. Collins) $11,000   £5,986

GIACOMO FRANCESCO CIPPER called Il
Todeschini (1670–1738) - A peasant drinking from an
earthenware jug at a table spread with bread and sausage
meat – oil on canvas – 68.5 x 52cm.
(Phillips) $27,888   £14,000

ANTONIO CIRINO (1889–1983) – Fisherman tending
his gear – oil on board – signed – $12^{1}/_{2}$ x $17^{1}/_{2}$in.
(Bruce D. Collins) $4,070   £2,200

GIACOMO FRANCESCO CIPPER, IL
TODESCHINI, Attributed to – A shepherd boy –
132.1 x 94.6cm.
(Christie's) $7,968   £3,960

ANTONIO CIRINO (1889–1983) – Covered bridge,
Autumn – oil on canvas – signed – 20 x 24in.
(Bruce D. Collins) $3,025   £1,635

C.L.

C.L. (active 1698) – A portrait of a gentleman, aged 73, wearing a black coat with white stock, by a window – signed with initials and dated 1698 – oval – 91.5 x 76cm.
(Christie's)   **$3,920**   **£1,980**

OLIVER CLARE – Still life of plums – signed – 9^{1}/$_{2}$ x 7^{1}/$_{2}$in.
(Bearne's)   **$1,241**   **£656**

OLIVER CLARE (English, 19th Century) – A still life of fruit – oil on canvas – signed – and companion piece – a pair – one illustrated – 18.7 x 23.7cm.
(Bonhams)   **$3,510**   **£2,000**

WILLIAM HENRY CLAPP (1879–1954) – Shirley – oil on canvas – 45.6 x 38cm.
(Pinney's)   **$2,381**   **£1,421**

ALBERT CLARK – 'Penbroke', horse study in a stable – signed and dated 1886 – oil on canvas – 19^{1}/$_{4}$ x 23^{1}/$_{2}$in.
(Hobbs & Chambers)   **$1,206**   **£620**

ALBERT CLARK – 'Cicero', study of race horse and jockey – signed and dated 1909 – oil on canvas – 18³/₄ x 23³/₄in.
(Hobbs & Chambers) $2,723   £1,400

W.A. CLARK – Faithful friends – signed – oil on canvas – 15 x 18in.
(G.A. Key) $411   £210

SAMUEL BARLING CLARKE (English, fl. 1852–1878) – Flower of Scotland – signed – oil on board – 28 x 21.6cm.
(Bonhams) $768   £380

WILLIAM ALBERT CLARK – Mr. Charles Henry Simmons in a buggy drawn by the carriage horses, 'Burleigh Meh-Met Boy and Maidstone Viscount', on a track in a landscape – signed and dated 1917 – 51 x 61cm.
(Christie's) $3,068   £1,540

EMILE CLAUS (Belgian 1849–1924) – A young girl seated in a corn field – signed – oil on canvas – 40 x 50cm.
(Sotheby's) $123,442   £68,200

121

SIR GEORGE CLAUSEN, R.A. (1852–1944) –
Elizabeth, aged six – signed – pastel and pencil –
30.5 x 23.5cm.
(Christie's)   **$7,715 £4,620**

FRANCESCO RODRIGUEZ SAN CLEMENT
(1861–1956) – A flamenco dancer with a black hat –
signed – 55.8 x 45.7cm.
(Christie's)   **$2,224 £1,320**

FRANCISCO RODRIGUEZ SAN CLEMENT
(1861–1956) – Sleeping beauty – signed – 59.7 x 71.8cm.
(Duran)   **$3,192 £1,667**

FRANCISCO RODRIGUEZ SAN CLEMENT
(1861–1956) – At the bull fight – oil on canvas – signed –
129 x 96cm.
(Duran)   **$6,568 £3,403**

ROBERT CLEMINSON (English, 19th Century) –
'Duck and Ducklings' – oil on canvas – signed and dated –
and companion piece – a pair – one illustrated –
25.3 x 35.6cm.
(Bonhams)   **$1,667 £950**

ROBERT CLEMINSON (fl. 1865–1868) – A Chamoise Cocker spaniel with a pheasant – signed and dated 1868 – oil on board – 61 x 45.7cm.
(Christie's)   **$1,463**   **£770**

Manner of FRANÇOIS CLOUET – Portrait of a Lady as Diana, small bust length, wearing a gold embroidered dress and an elaborate headdress – on panel – 26.8 x 20.2cm.
(Christie's)   **$1,430**   **£715**

FRANCOIS CLOUET (c. 1522–1572) – Attributed to – Portrait of a young knight – bust length – oil on wood – 27 x 13cm.
(Lempertz)   **$22,020**   **£12,583**

PRUNELLA CLOUGH (b. 1919) – Fisherman with scales, Lowestoft Harbour – signed – oil on canvas – 71.5 x 49cm.
(Christie's)   **$17,451**   **£10,450**

COATES

A. H. COATES (20th Century) – Clicquot, a French Bulldog – signed and inscribed – oil on canvas – 35.6 x 27.9cm.
(Christie's) **$1,254** **£660**

Circle of **BENEDETTO COFFRE (d. 1722)** – A young woman in a night cap and wrap writing a letter – signed and dated 1796 – on panel – 33.5 x 24.5cm.
(Phillips) **$1,600** **£800**

DAVID COB – The Cutty Sark passing the Royal Yacht Britannia – oil on canvas – 18 x 26in.
(G.E. Sworder & Sons) **$2,069** **£1,050**

FREDERICK SIMPSON COBURN (1871–1960) – Loading wood in Quebec – signed and dated '27 – oil on canvas – 51.3 x 71.2cm.
(Christie's) **$15,400** **£8,162**

ALPHONSE COLAS (1818–1887) – Portrait of the musician Lavaud and his family – signed and dated 1862 – oil on canvas – 144 x 112cm.
(Sotheby's) **$5,622** **£3,346**

JAMES COLE (fl. 1856–1885) – The model boy – signed and dated 1880 – oil on canvas – 40.7 x 55.8cm.
(Christie's)   **$3,011   £1,650**

Follower of **WILLIAM COLLINS, R.A.** – Wayside gossips; and The pet hamster – 35.6 x 50.8cm. – a pair – one illustrated
(Christie's)   **$3,011   £1,650**

JEAN COLIN (1881–1961) – Gipsy – signed – oil on canvas – 125.5 x 100.5cm.
(Hôtel de Ventes Horta)   **$3,155   £1,803**

ROI CLARKSON COLMAN (1884–1945) – Changing tide – signed – oil on board – 35.5 x 51cm.
(Butterfield & Butterfield)   **$2,200   £1,078**

The Hon. **JOHN COLLIER** (1850–1934) – Circe – signed and dated 1885 – oil on canvas – 132.7 x 220cm.
(Christie's)   **$71,060   £41,800**

ITHELL COLQUHOUN – 'Tendrils of sleep (I)' – signed and dated 1944 – on panel – 57.1 x 29.2cm.
(Christie's)   **$1,540   £770**

ROBERT COMBAS – Geneviève – oil on canvas – signed and dated 87 – 160 x 128cm.
(Jean Claude Anaf)   **$43,717   £25,125**

Follower of SEBASTIANO CONCA – The Madonna and Child – oil on copper – 27.8 x 20.7cm.
(Christie's)   **$3,703   £1,870**

LEON FRANÇOIS COMERRE (1850–1916) – After the bath – signed - oil on canvas – 55 x 53cm.
(Christie's)   **$28,985   £17,050**

Follower of NICHOLAS CONDY – Children making a model boat on the beach – 35.5 x 20.5cm.
(Christie's)   **$1,222   £605**

PHILIP CONNARD, R.A. – Bayswater, on the Serpentine – signed with monogram – also inscribed on a label on the reverse – oil on canvas – 51 x 61cm.
(Phillips) $34,923   £21,000

A. CONNELLY (British 19th/20th Century) – Still life of chrysanthemums – signed – watercolour and bodycolour – 49.5 x 29cm. and a companion
(Phillips) $575   £300

CONSTANT (born 1920) – Bathers – signed – oil on canvas – 50 x 65cm.
(Christie's) $6,200   £3,234

TITO CONTI (1842–1924) – The suitor spurned – signed – oil on canvas – 96.4 x 70.5cm.
(Christie's) $41,140   £24,200

CONTI

TITO CONTI (1842–1924) – A good book – signed – oil on canvas – 61.9 x 48.3cm.
(Christie's) $12,821   £6,820

CONTINENTAL SCHOOL – Full length portrait of a gentleman wearing a scarlet cloak, seated at a writing table – 66 x 53cm.
(Spencer's) $764   £400

TITO CONTI (1842–1924) – The Introduction – signed – oil on canvas – 78 x 103cm.
(Christie's) $43,340   £22,000

CONTINENTAL SCHOOL, 19th Century – The Shepherd – unsigned – oil on canvas – unframed – 23 x 32in.
(Skinner) $550   £284

CONTINENTAL SCHOOL (20th Century) – Miniature Pinchers – signed with initials and dated 'P S 39' – pastel – 47 x 49.9cm.
(Christie's) $627   £330

CONTINENTAL SCHOOL

CONTINENTAL SCHOOL, 19th century – A busy
town scene – oil on board – 61 x 45.7cm.
(Bonhams)   **$1,618   £800**

CONTINENTAL SCHOOL (19th Century) – Portrait of
a lady, seated three-quarter length, in a black dress with
lace cuffs - signed with initials E.M and dated '52 –
108 x 86cm.
(Christie's)   **$7,414   £4,400**

CONTINENTAL SCHOOL (19th Century) – A
reclining female nude – 88 x 70cm.
(Christie's)   **$3,707   £2,200**

CONTINENTAL SCHOOL (20th Century) – Two
Gascony Grande Bleu de Gascoignes – signed with initials
and dated 'P S 39' – pastel – 58.4 x 46.9cm.
(Christie's)   **$627   £330**

BERYL COOK – Ladies' bowling team – signed and inscribed on the reverse – on board – 38.1 x 57.1cm.
(Christie's)   **$7,315   £3,850**

EBENEZER WAKE COOK (1843–1926) – Girls feeding pigeons by the bronze well head (Vera da Pozzo) in the Doges' Courtyard, Venice – signed – pencil and watercolour – 11¼ x 15¼in.
(Christie's)   **$975   £495**

BERYL COOK (b. 1926) – The lion tamer – signed – oil on panel – 53.5 x 53.5cm.
(Christie's)   **$12,859   £7,700**

EBENEZER WAKE COOK (British, 1843–1926) – Old Palace, Florence – signed – watercolour over pencil – 24 x 12.5cm.
(Phillips)   **$1,532   £800**

ALFRED EGERTON COOPER – Country village – oil on board – signed with initials – 30.5 x 45.5cm.
(Bonhams) $900 £450

MAY LOUISE GREVILLE COOKSEY (English, b. 1878) – The house at Bethany – signed and dated 1906 – oil on canvas – 122 x 152.4cm.
(Bonhams) $2,224 £1,100

COLIN CAMPBELL COOPER (1856–1937) – Building at San Diego Fair, 1916 – signed – gouache on board – 27 x 35.5cm.
(Butterfield & Butterfield) $7,700 £3,774

ALEXANDER DAVIS COOPER (fl. 1837–1888) – A Golden Retriever – signed with monogram and dated 1881 – oil on canvas – 50.8 x 40.7cm.
(Christie's) $3,344 £1,760

ALEXANDER DAVIS COOPER (fl. 1837–1888) – A Cairn terrier and a Norfolk terrier near a Highland loch – signed with monogram and dated 1878 – oil on canvas
(Christie's) $6,270 £3,300

J SIDNEY COOPER – Group of six sheep under a cloudy sky – watercolour – signed and dated 1873 – 20 x 31cm.
(Allen & Harris) $2,697 £1,450

THOMAS SIDNEY COOPER, R.A. (1803–1902) –
Cattle and sheep in an open landscape – signed and dated
1888 – pencil and watercolour – 9³/₄ x 13³/₄in.
(Christie's) $3,792   £1,925

WILLIAM SIDNEY COOPER (1854–1927) – View of
Herne Mill with flock of sheep to foreground – signed and
dated 1914 – oil on canvas – 13 x 15in.
(GA Canterbury Auction Galleries) $4,202   £2,200

THOMAS SIDNEY COOPER (1803–1902) – On the
Banks of the Medway – signed and dated 1858 – oil on
board – 26.5 x 39.4cm.
(Pinney's) $5,527   £3,299

J. COORENS (Belgian, 1814–1907) – The model –
signed and dated 1863 – oil on panel – 32 x 27cm.
(Hôtel de Ventes Horta) $1,072   £557

WILLIAM SIDNEY COOPER – Near Littleburn, Kent –
signed and dated 1909 – watercolour heightened with
white – 8 x 11in.
(Christie's) $890   £506

FERN COPPEDGE (1888–1951) – Rigatta (sic.) at
Gloucester, ME. – oil on canvas – signed – hand carved
gilded frame – 18 x 20in.
(Bruce D. Collins) $11,000   £5,946

AUGUSTE CORKOLE – Pair of sweethearts – signed – oil on wood – 55 x 42cm.
(Galerie Moderne)   **$5,852**   **£3,064**

EDITH CORBET née ELLENBOROUGH (1850–c. 1920) – The sleeping girl – signed – oil on canvas – unframed – 91.7 x 55.2cm.
(Christie's)   **$10,782**   **£6,380**

LOVIS CORINTH (1858–1925) – Das Homerische Gelachter II – signed and dated 1919 – oil on paper laid on panel – 60 x 72cm.
(Christie's)   **$84,513**   **£42,900**

JEAN-BAPTISTE-CAMILLE COROT (French 1796–1875) – Vénus au bain – signed – oil on canvas – 116 x 90cm.
(Sotheby's)   **$2,986,500**   **£1,650,000**

CORRADINI

F. CORRADINI (Italian, late 19th century) – Flirtation – signed – oil on canvas – 82 x 62.3cm.
(Christie's)   **$4,096 £2,090**

HERMANN DAVID SALOMON CORRODI – A woman and child in the Roman campagna – signed and inscribed – oil on canvas – 56.5 x 44.5cm.
(Sotheby's)   **$5,907 £3,300**

EDOUARD CORTES (1882–1969) – L'Arc de Triomphe, Paris – signed – oil on canvas – 33 x 45.8cm.
(Christie's)   **$28,028 £14,300**

ANTONIO ALLEGRI IL CORREGGIO, After – St. Catherine, half length – oil on canvas – 79 x 61cm.
(Phillips)   **$1,656 £920**

EDOUARD CORTES (French, 1882–1969) – View of Paris in the rain from the Champs Elysées with the Arc de Triomphe – signed – oil on canvas – 33 x 46cm.
(AB Stockholms Auktionsverk)   **$7,285 £3,814**

EDOUARD CORTES – La Porte St. Denis – oil on canvas – signed – unframed – 46 x 56cm.
(Bonhams)   **$27,000 £13,500**

HERMAN COSSMANN (1821–1890) – The introduction – signed – oil on canvas – 66 x 53cm.
(Hôtel de Ventes Horta)   **$6,353 £3,145**

EDOUARD CORTES (1882–1969) – Les Champs Elysées, Paris – signed – oil on canvas – unframed – 26 x 35cm.
(Christie's)   **$18,612 £9,900**

EDOUARD CORTES (1882–1969) – Evening, Paris – signed – oil on canvas – 33 x 45.8cm.
(Pinney's)   **$15,305 £9,137**

G.* COSTA (Italian, 19th Century) – The basket of cherries – oil on board – signed – 39.4 x 25.4cm.
(Bonhams)   **$1,316 £750**

COSTA

GIOVANI COSTA (c. 1900) – Monks sharing a repast – signed – 25.4 x 38.2cm.
(Christie's)   **$834   £495**

JOHN E. COSTIGAN (1888–1972) – Mother and children – signed – oil on canvas – 109.2 x 127.3cm.
(Christie's)   **$10,450   £5,539**

Circle of FRANCIS COTES, R.A. (circa 1725–1770) – Portrait of a lady, standing half length, in a white satin dress, holding a branch of apple blossom – 88.8 x 69.2cm.
(Christie's)   **$1,606   £880**

JOHN JOSEPH COTMAN (1814–1878) – A faggot gatherer on a country lane – signed and dated 1870 – pencil and watercolour – 16³/₈ x 26in.
(Christie's)   **$1,842   £935**

HORATIO HENRY COULDERY – The age of innocence – bears another signature – inscribed with title – oil on canvas – unframed – 45.5 x 60.5cm.
(Sotheby's)   **$7,168   £3,960**

WILLIAM ALEXANDER COULTER (1849–1936) – Ship in the arctic – signed and dated 1881 – oil on canvas – 46 x 79cm.
(Butterfield & Butterfield)   **$4,675   £2,292**

EANGER IRVING COUSE (1866–1936) – The badger
skin – signed – oil on canvas – 30.7 x 40.7cm.
(Christie's)   **$19,800   £10,296**

ANGELO DE COURTEN (Italian, 19th Century) – 'It's
a bargain' – signed – oil on canvas – 131 x 86cm.
(Duran)   **$11,703   £6,111**

CHRISTIAN COUWENBERG (1604–1667) – The
happy toper – oil on canvas – 90 x 83cm.
(Sotheby's)   **$46,587   £26,774**

HERMANN COURTENS (1884–1956) – Final
preparations – signed and inscribed – oil on panel –
unframed – 46 x 38.5cm.
(Christie's)   **$5,029   £2,514**

SIR NOËL COWARD (1900–1973) – On the Jamaican
coast – signed – oil on canvas – 56 x 71cm.
(Christie's)   **$9,821   £5,280**

COWARD

SIR NOEL COWARD (1900–1973) – Houseboy on the terrace, Firefly, Jamaica – signed – oil on canvas – 44.5 x 34cm.
(Christie's)   **$6,429**   **£3,850**

SIR NOEL COWARD – The fruit market – signed – on canvas-board - 29.9 x 20.3cm.
(Christie's)   **$8,360**   **£4,400**

SIR NOEL COWARD (1900–1973) – On a beach in Jamaica – signed – oil on board – 51 x 41cm.
(Christie's)   **$7,775**   **£4,180**

SIR NOEL COWARD – Theatrical design – Woman on a terrace – watercolour – 26.6 x 22.3cm.
(Christie's)   **$2,090**   **£1,100**

DAVID COX – Going to the hayfield – watercolour – signed – 8½ x 12in.
(Riddetts) $5,835 £3,000

ALLEN GILBERT CRAM (1886–1947) – A gathering, Santa Barbara Fiesta – signed – oil on canvas – 61 x 71cm.
(Butterfield & Butterfield) $3,575 £1,752

LUCAS CRANACH, (Manner of) – Portrait of a man, half length – bears signature device and dated 1543 – oil on panel – 36 x 23cm.
(Phillips) $1,800 £1,000

LUCAS CRANACH, the younger (1515–1586) – The Madonna and child with St. Anne, seated in a landscape – oil on panel – 42.5 x 27.5cm.
(Phillips) $67,728 £34,000

THOMAS CRAWSHAW (19th century) – Harvest Time – signed and dated 1864 – 60.9 x 91.5cm.
(Christie's) $4,015 £2,200

CREIXXAMS

PIERRE-LOUIS CRETEY (1645–1690) – The vision of
Saint Jerome – on canvas – 150 x 127cm.
(Phillips) $53,700 £30,000

PERE CREIXAMS (1893–1965) – Flower painting –
signed – oil on panel – 44 x 31cm.
(Duran) $2,926 £1,528

PERE CREIXAMS (1893–1965) – Albaicín, Granada –
signed and dated 1956 – oil on canvas – 114 x 113cm.
(Duran) $10,640 £5,556

THEODORE MORROW CRILEY (American,
1880–1930) – Figure By a Stream – estate monogram – oil
on canvas – 16 x 12³/₄in.
(Skinner) $800 £412

CUMBERLAND MARKET GROUP

GERTRUDE CROMPTON (Exh. 1897–1927) –
Preparing fishing boats – watercolour – signed – 11 x 15in.
(David Lay) $580 £290

LENA CRONQVIST (b. 1938) – Storm, Kalvö – signed
and dated 88 – oil on canvas – 39 x 44cm.
(AB Stockholms Auktionsverk) **$2,044 £1,070**

EDWARD CUCUEL (1875–1951) – Woman by the sea –
signed – dated and inscribed – watercolour and gouache on
paper – 48 x 43.7cm.
(Christie's) **$2,090 £1,108**

DOMINGO MUNOZ Y CUESTA (1850–1912) – Tavern
brawl - oil on canvas – 72 x 137cm.
(Duran) **$10,105 £5,236**

WILLIAM CROSBY (English, fl. 1859–1873) – 'Tired
out' – oil on board – signed and dated 1862 – 24.1 x 19cm.
(Bonhams) **$7,020 £4,000**

CUMBERLAND MARKET GROUP – Hay carts,
Cumberland market – oil on canvas – inscribed with title
on reverse – 25 x 33.5cm.
(Bonhams) **$1,360 £680**

CUNAEUS

CONRADIJN CUNAEUS (1828–1895) – Portrait of the borzoi dog *Fairy* – signed – oil on panel – 43.5 x 61.5cm.
(Christie's)   **$3,017**   **£1,509**

JENNY C. CURTIS – Hat full of cherries – signed and dated 1874 – oil on canvas laid down on board – 21³/₄ x 26³/₄in.
(Du Mouchelles)   **$2,700**   **£1,392**

RINALDO CUNEO (1877–1939) – Fort Point, San Francisco Bay – signed – oil on canvas laid down – 28 x 32cm.
(Butterfield & Butterfield)   **$2,750**   **£1,348**

PETER CURLING – The steeplechasers – signed – 101.5 x 153.5cm.
(Christie's)   **$6,600**   **£3,300**

JOSEP CUSACHS (1851–1908) – Equestrian portrait of Alfonso XIII – oil on canvas – signed and dated 1906 – 210 x 124cm.
(Duran)   **$90,942**   **£47,120**

ELEANOR P. CUSTIS (1897–1983) – Marketplace –
gouache – signed – 19 x 25in.
(Bruce D. Collins)   **$2,310   £1,249**

LADISLAS VON CZACHORSKI –An Italian beauty by
a North Italian lake – signed – oil on canvas –
41 x 63.5cm.
(Sotheby's)   **$15,752   £8,800**

AELBERT CUYP (1620–1691) – Landscape with three
windmills – signed – oil on panel – 61 x 82cm.
(Christie's)   **$219,734   £113,265**

ALBERT CUYP (1605–1691) – View of Dordrecht with
fishing boat in foreground – traces of signature – oil on
canvas – 60.5 x 82.5cm.
(Hôtel de Ventes Horta)   **$9,467   £4,918**

RICHARD DADD (1817–1886) – The death of Richard II
– signed, inscribed and dated 1852 - watercolour –
14^1/$_8$ x 10^1/$_8$in.
(Christie's)   **$16,984   £8,800**

DAFFINGER

MORITZ MICHAEL DAFFINGER – Tokens of love – a pair – both signed and dated 1818 – pencil and watercolour heightened with white – 9½ x 7¼in.: one illustrated.
(Christie's) $5,129   £2,750

HANS DAHL (Norwegian 1849–1937) – Country girl – signed and dated 80 – oil on canvas – 51 x 33cm.
(AB Stockholms Auktionsverk) $11,644   £6,002

HANS DAHL (1849–1937) – A Summer's Day in Norway – signed – 83 x 117cm.
(Christie's) $19,070   £9,680

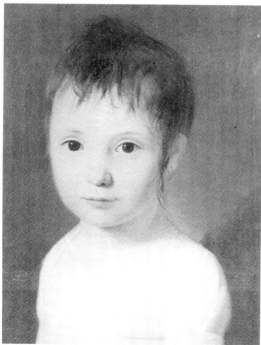

PIERRE EDOUARD DAGOTY (Active c. 1800) – Portrait of a small girl, bust length, in a white dress – with inscription and dated 1802, on the stretcher – oil on canvas – 37.5 x 28cm.
(Phillips) $7,296   £3,800

HANS ANDREAS DAHL (Norwegian 1881–1919) – A young girl by a fjord – signed – watercolour and bodycolour – 46.5 x 31cm.
(Sotheby's) $5,233   £2,860

PETER DAHL – Drinking festival – signed and dated
1978 and numbered 66/260 – colour litho – 44 x 57.5cm.
(AB Stockholms Auktionsverk)   **$1,387**   **£714**

SALVADOR DALI (Spanish, 1904–1989) – Untitled –
signed and dated 1963 – etching over collotype on paper –
unframed – 15^1/$_2$ x 19^3/$_8$in.
(Skinner Inc.)   **$500**   **£268**

SALVADOR DALI (Spanish, 1904–1989) – Homage to
Millet – signed – colour lithograph – 65 x 50cm.
(germann Auktionshaus)   **$220**   **£115**

SALVADOR DALI (1904–1989) – "Femme Tulipe" –
watercolour (sepia ink wash on woodcut paper) – signed -
26 x 16cm.
(Duran)   **$12,126**   **£6,283**

SALVADOR DALI (Spanish, 1904–1989) – (after a
painting) – Dream caused by the flight of a bee round a
pomegranate, one second before awakening – colour
lithograph – 76 x 56cm.
(germann Auktionshaus)   **$256**   **£151**

DAMSCHROEDER

JAN JAC MATTHYS DAMSCHROEDER (German 1825-1905) – Interior with a peasant consoling his weeping wife – signed – oil on canvas – 100 x 125cm.
(AB Stockholms Auktionsverk)   **$3,762**   **£1,939**

JAN JACOBUS MATTHIJS DAMSCHROEDER (1825–1905) – Preparing the meal – signed – 63.5 x 76.2cm.
(Christie's)   **$3,521**   **£2,090**

Follower of CESARE DANDINI – A young woman warming her hands over a brazier – in a painted oval – 65.1 x 50.1cm.
(Christie's)   **$3,267**   **£1,650**

GEORGE DANCE, R.A. (1741–1825) – Portrait of Thomas King, half-length, seated, facing to the left – signed and dated 1797 – pencil – 10 x 7½in.
(Christie's)   **$1,287**   **£660**

JOSEPH DANHAUSER (1805–1845) – Portrait of a lady of Quality – oil on canvas – 92 x 74.5cm.
(Christie's)   **$5,509**   **£2,832**

FELIX OCTAVIUS CARR DARLEY (1822–1888) –
Civil War – signed – pencil and grey washes heightened
with white on paper – 30.5 x 38.1cm.
(Christie's)   **$6,050**   **£3,590**

SARA KOLB DANNER (1894–1969) – Bathers – signed
– oil on canvas – 86 x 91.5cm.
(Butterfield & Butterfield)   **$4,400**   **£2,157**

WILDER M. DARLING (American, 1855/56–1933) –
Dutch Market Scene – estate stamp of the artist – oil on
canvas – 12 x 18in.
(Skinner)   **$400**   **£206**

NILS DARDEL (1888–1943) – View from the studio
across the Nybroplan – watercolour – 48 x 36cm.
(AB Stockholms Auktionsverk)   **$6,574**   **£3,442**

ANDRÉ-HENRI DARGELAS (French, 1828–1906) –
Girl with broom – signed – oil on canvas – 48 x 36cm.
(Auktionshaus Arnold)   **$1,700**   **£909**

WILLIAM DARLING (1882–1963) – Ghost Town,
Bodie, California – signed – oil on canvas laid down –
46 x 56cm.
(Butterfield & Butterfield)   **$1,650**   **£809**

DAUCHOT

GABRIEL DAUCHOT – The paddock – signed –
81.5 x 99.5cm.
(Christie's)   **$2,926   £1,540**

THOMAS DAVIDSON (fl. 1863–1893) – Caractacus
being paraded by the Emperor Claudius, A.D. 50 – signed
– oil on canvas – unframed – 128 x 102.5cm.
(Christie's)   **$7,430   £3,850**

ARTHUR BOWEN DAVIES (1862–1928) – Aspiration
– signed – oil on canvas – 35.7 x 28cm.
(Christie's)   **$10,450   £5,434**

ARTHUR BOWEN DAVIES (1862–1928) – Two standing female nudes and study for "Strewing of Star Dust" – Two pastels – both signed with initials - both pastel on paper – the first 42.6 x 29.2cm. – the second 40 x 27.3cm.: one illustrated.
(Christie's)   **$5,500   £3,264**

JOSEPH LUCIEN DAVIS (1860–1951) - A woman in elegant costume beside a stream - signed and dated 96 – watercolour heightened with white – $10^5/8$ x $7^3/8$in.
(Christie's)   **$2,757   £1,540**

JOHN SCARLETT DAVIS (1804–1845) – Figures at prayer in the Church of Saint Sulpice, Paris – signed with initials, inscribed and dated 1836 – pencil and watercolour – $9^5/8$ x $6^1/2$in.
(Christie's)   **$6,864   £3,520**

LUCIEN DAVIS – A reflective moment – signed – watercolour and bodycolour – 59 x 38.7cm.
(Bonhams)   **$3,216   £1,600**

DAWANT

ALBERT-PIERRE DAWANT (1852–1923) – Scene in the Assembly – signed – oil on canvas – 90 x 72cm.
(Sotheby's) **$7,496 £4,462**

MONTAGUE DAWSON – The South Australian, built 1868, 1040 tons – signed – watercolour and bodycolour – 21½ x 29½in.
(Hy. Duke & Son) **$21,240 £12,000**

MONTAGUE DAWSON (English, 1895–1973) – 'British destroyers in northern waters' – oil on board – 25.4 x 48.2cm.
(Bonhams) **$1,011 £500**

BRIAN C DAY – 'Twilight, Baby Barn Owl' – signed – watercolour – 9 x 7in.
(G.A. Key) **$735 £360**

JAMES FRANCIS DAY (1863–1942) – Storytime – signed – oil on canvas – 101.6 x 76.2cm.
(Christie's) **$7,700 £4,081**

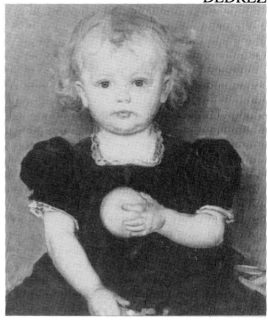

MARC DECOSTER (Continental, 19th Century) – The orange – oil on panel – signed and dated 1889 – 53.3 x 43.2cm.
(Bonhams)   **$3,510   £2,000**

EDWIN DEAKIN (1838–1923) – Church interior Westminster Abbey – signed and dated 1877 – oil on canvas – 61 x 41cm.
(Butterfield & Butterfield)   **$1,650   £809**

WALTER LOFTHOUSE DEAN (American, 1854–1912) – Old Fish Tales – signed – oil on canvas – unframed – 30 x 40in.
(Skinner)   **$1,600   £825**

ALEXANDRE-GABRIEL DECAMPS (1803–1860) – The sentries – signed – oil on canvas – 32.5 x 40.5cm.
(Sotheby's)   **$15,618   £8,925**

D. DEDREZ (Circa 1800) – Officer on horseback – signed – oil on panel – 36 x 26cm.
(AB Stockholms Auktionsverk)   **$1,434   £739**

DEGAS

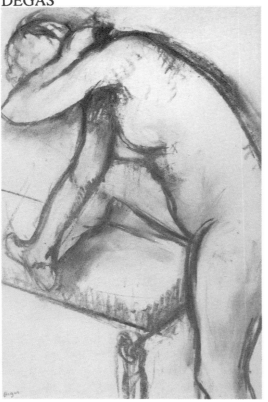

EDGAR DEGAS (1834–1917) – Etude de Danseuse en
Maillot – bears studio stamp – charcoal on paper –
52 x 34cm.
(Christie's)   **$169,290   £99,000**

EDGAR DEGAS (1834–1917) – Trois Danseuses (Jupes
jaunes, Corsages bleus) – studio stamp – pastel on board –
55 x 50cm.
(Christie's)   **$3,328,600   £1,870,000**

J. DEGREEF – Carts in the forest – signed – oil on
canvas – 43 x 62cm.
(Galerie Moderne)   **$1,820   £939**

EDGAR DEGAS (1834–1917) – Dancer at the barre –
signed with studio stamp lower left (L.657) – pencil on
paper laid down on card – 30.7 x 20cm.
(Christie's)   **$125,686   £63,800**

JEAN DEGREEF (Belgian, 1852–1894) – Village street
at Woluwe-St-Pierre – signed – oil on canvas –
98 x 130cm.
(Hôtel de Ventes Horta)   **$10,730   £5,574**

VICTOR DELACROIX (Flemish, 19th Century) – The
morning toilet – signed and dated 1882 – oil on canvas –
24 x 20cm.
(Duran)   **$7,980   £4,167**

HIPPOLYTE called PAUL DELAROCHE (1797–1856)
- Portrait of the artist Horace Vernet – oil on canvas –
47 x 38cm.
(Sotheby's)   **$25,379   £14,502**

PAUL DELAROCHE (1797–1856) – Children in a park –
the children on Madame Morel Deville – with inscription
on the reverse – on panel – 26.7 x 20.3cm.
(Christie's)   **$1,668   £990**

Circle of ALBERT DELERIVE (late 18th century) – A
man helping a woman dismount outside a booth – oil on
panel – 32.3 x 26.8cm.
(Christie's)   **$1,634   £825**

DELORME

PAUL DELVAUX – Two young nude girls – signed and dated – 36 x 44cm.
(Hôtel de Ventes Horta) **$38,729 £22,131**

RAPHAEL DELORME (French, 1890–1962) – Woman with pink flamingo – signed – gouache – 50 x 30.8cm.
(germann Auktionshaus) **$2,846 £1,674**

PAUL DELVAUX (b. 1897) – Sitting girl – signed and numbered 19/75 – serigraph – 60.5 x 41.5cm.
(AB Stockholms Auktionsverk) **$1,891 £974**

PAUL DELVAUX (b. 1898) – Femmes et Lampes – signed and dated – watercolour and pen and black ink on paper laid down on board – 48.2 x 64.5cm.
(Christie's) **$225,720 £132,000**

PAUL DELVAUX – Reclining nude – signed and dated 1947 – brush and indian ink and gouache on paper laid down on board – 17.8 x 26.7cm.
(Sotheby's) **$18,700 £11,000**

Z. DEMJEN (1860–1927) – The corn harvest – signed –
oil on canvas – 40 x27cm.
(Hôtel de Ventes Horta)   **$1,032**   **£590**

CHARLES HENRY DEMUTH (1883–1935) – Ta Nana
– signed with initials – dated 1916 – watercolour and
pencil on paper – 20.3 x 25.5cm.
(Christie's)   **$22,000**   **£11,440**

PAUL DELVAUX – Three girls – signed and numbered
3/75 – serigraph – 59.5 x 43cm.
(AB Stockholms Auktionsverk)   **$1,801**   **£929**

DEMUTH

CHARLES HENRY DEMUTH (1883–1935) – Spray of flowers – signed – watercolour on paper – 46 x 30.4cm.
(Christie's) $38,500 £20,020

BALTHASAR DENNER (1685–1749) – Portrait of a man, bust length, wearing an open jacket – oil on panel – 41.5 x 36cm.
(Phillips) $2,112 £1,100

DENIS – Coming out of Mass – signed – watercolour – 24 x 18cm.
(Duran) $821 £421

STEPHEN POYNTZ DENNING (1795–1864) – Portrait of a young girl, seated full length, in a green dress, holding a posy of flowers, in a landscape – signed and dated 1859 on reverse – oil on panel – 26.7 x 21.6cm. – and two other portraits of children by the same hand
(Christie's) $2,008 £1,100

ANDRE DERAIN (1880–1954) – Vase of zinnias – signed – oil on canvas – 55.3 x 46.4cm.
(Christie's)   **$73,678**   **£37,400**

ANDRE DERAIN – Bouquet de fleurs – signed – oil on canvas – 61 x 50cm.
(Sotheby's)   **$130,900**   **£77,000**

AMELIE DESCHAMPS (French, 19th century) – Mother's Pride – watercolour heightened with white – signed – 13.3 x 18.4cm.
(Bonhams)   **$506**   **£250**

ANDRE DERAIN (1880–1954) – Bouquet of flowers in a vase – signed and numbered – coloured woodcut – 28 x 17.4cm.
(Galerie Koller Zürich)   **$3,562**   **£1,860**

CHARLES MELCHIOR DESCOURTIS – "Paul et Virginie" – set of four – watercolour – 39.5 x 45.5cm.
(AB Stockholms Auktionsverket)   **$840**   **£442**

DESHAYES

CHARLES FELIX EDOUARD DESHAYES (b. 1831)
– Watering the horses – signed and dated 1890 – oil on
canvas - 130 x 90cm.
(Christie's)   **$6,037   £3,080**

GEORGES D'ESPAGNAT – Petit jardin sicilien –
signed; titled on the reverse – oil on canvas – 65 x 110cm.
(Sotheby's)   **$56,100   £33,000**

JEAN-BAPTISTE-EDOUARD DETAILLE
(1848–1912) – French Cuirassiers proceeding to battle –
signed and dated 1900 – pencil and watercolour –
33 x 22.9cm.
(Christie's)   **$3,722   £1,980**

CESARE AUGUSTE DETTI (Italian 1847–1914) –
Elegant company in a boat – signed and dated Paris '81 –
oil on canvas – 33 x 55cm.
(Sotheby's)   **$14,091   £7,700**

LUDWIG DEUTSCH (1855–1935) – La toilette – signed
and dated 1918 – oval – oil on board – 46 x 36.5cm.
(Christie's)   **$11,374   £6,050**

LUDWIG DEUTSCH (1855–1935) – The Milk Seller,
Cairo – signed, inscribed and dated 1886 – oil on panel –
53.2 x 45.8cm.
(Christie's)   **$130,020   £66,000**

ANDRE DEVAMBEZ – At the Montmartre theatre –
signed – watercolour and bodycolour – 23 x 29cm.
(Jean-Claude Anaf)   **$417   £214**

LUDWIG DEUTSCH (1855–1935) – Les Fumeurs de
Narguile – signed – oil on panel – 23.8 x 28.6cm.
(Christie's)   **$44,880   £26,400**

ANTHONY DEVAS (b. 1911) –Camilla and Mark Sykes
– signed lower left – oil on canvas – 49 x 58.5cm.
(Christie's)   **$16,368   £8,800**

DEVEDEUX

DANIEL VAZQUEZ DIAZ (1882-1969) – A stylish wedding – oil on canvas - signed – 69 x 87cm.
(Duran) **$27,788 £14,398**

LOUIS DEVEDEUX (1820–1874) – A Fête Champêtre – signed – oil on canvas laid down on panel – 55.6 x 42.6cm.
(Christie's) **$8,272 £4,400**

NARCISSE-VIRGILE DIAZ DE LA PENA (French 1807–76) – A wood gatherer in a forest – signed – oil on panel – 35 x 46cm.
(Sotheby's) **$22,143 £12,100**

Attributed to GIACINTO DIANA – Tobias and the Angel – on copper – oval – 26.7 x 18.9cm.
(Christie's) **$3,267 £1,650**

SIR FRANK DICKSEE, P.R.A. (English 1853–1928) – Elsa, daughter of William Hall Esq. – signed and dated 1927 – oil on canvas – 108 x 81cm.
(Sotheby's) **$139,370 £77,000**

THOMAS FRANCIS DICKSEE (English, 1819–1895) –
Sketch of Ophelia – signed with monogram – oil on board
– oval – 10.3 x 7.8cm.
(Bonhams) **$809 £400**

JOHAN DIJKSTRA (1896–1978) – Oogsten in
Groningen – signed – oil on canvas – 60 x 90cm.
(Christie's) **$9,644 £5,031**

FRANK DILLON (1823–1909) – Eavesdropping – signed
– 69.9 x 94.6cm.
(Christie's) **$41,140 £24,200**

THOMAS FRANCIS DICKSEE – Ann Page – signed
with monogram – oil on panel – 52 x 42cm.
(Sotheby's) **$20,905 £11,550**

B. DINATUE (Munich School) – Jovial tavern scene –
indistinct remains of signature – oil on canvas –
36.8 x 55.8cm.
(Ritchie's) **$781 £405**

DINE

JIM DINE – Dorian Gray at opium den – signed – colour
etching – 42 x 28.5cm.
(AB Stockholms Auktionsverk)   **$630**   **£325**

OTTO DIX – Lady with fans – watercolour
(Hauswedell & Nolte)   **$145,281**   **£82,781**

OTTO DIX – Picture of Paula Köhler – signed with
monogram and dated 1938 – mixed media on wood –
84.5 x 65cm.
(Lempertz)   **$53,889**   **£27,778**

OTTO DIX (1891–1969) – Head of a girl – signed and
dated 1922 – watercolour on indian ink and pencil –
33.5 x 28cm.
(Galerie Koller Zürich)   **$63,306**   **£33,058**

OTTO DIX (1891–1969) – The Deep – signed and dated
55 – watercolour – 51 x 69.5cm.
(Lempertz)   **$21,555**   **£11,111**

ANNA DIXON (d. 1959) – Evening on the beach at
Portobello, Edinburgh – signed – oil on canvas –
29.9 x 40.2cm.
(Lawrence)   **$2,300**   **£1,200**

CHARLES DIXON – A British Man-Of-War under sail –
signed and dated '15 – watercolour and bodycolour –
30 x 19.75cm.
(Woolley & Wallis)   **$1,052**   **£560**

MAYNARD DIXON (1875–1946) – The Palominos – signed and dated 1941 – gouache on paper –
42 x 98cm.
(Butterfield & Butterfield)   **$10,450**   **£5,122**

DOBRAJA

INTA DOBRAJA (b. 1940) – Autumn flowers – signed with monogram and dated 90 – signed – oil on canvas
(Jean-Claude Anaf) **$944 £493**

ARTHUR CHARLES DODD (English, fl. 1878–1890) – On the scent – oil on canvas – signed – 45.7 x 61cm.
(Bonhams) **$2,808 £1,600**

ARTHUR CHARLES DODD – A playmate – signed – oil on canvas – 46 x 61cm.
(Sotheby's) **$7,964 £4,400**

FRANK DOBSON (1888–1963) – Portrait of Rollo Peters – unframed – oil on canvas – 45.7 x 40.6cm.
(Lawrence) **$670 £350**

STEVAN DOHANOS (1907–) – Bookbinder's saloon, Philadelphia – signed – brush and black ink and gouache en grisaille on board – 60.3 x 127.7cm.
(Christie's) $6,050   £3,207

After CARLO DOLCI – The Mater Dolorosa – painted surface originally oval – 82.5 x 67cm.
(Christie's) $3,049   £1,540

ROBERTO DOMINGO Y FALLOLA (Spanish b. 1867) – La Capea – signed – gouache – 35.5 x 50.5cm.
(Sotheby's) $5,636   £3,080

JEAN-GABRIEL DOMERGUE – Couple at the races – oil on isorel – signed – 54 x 45cm.
(Jean-Claude Anaf) $26,620   £13,793

OSCAR DOMINGUEZ – Composition – oil on isorel – signed – 60 x 50cm.
(Jean-Claude Anaf) $10,459   £5,419

DOMMERSEN

PIETER CORNELIS DOMMERSEN (born 1834) – Off
Pampus, on the Zuiderzee – signed and dated 1887 –
27.5 x 38cm.
(Christie's)   **$6,035   £3,017**

CORNELIS CHRISTIAN DOMMERSEN (1842–1928)
–Abbeville – signed – on panel – 35.5 x 30cm.
(Christie's)   **$2,038   £1,210**

WILLIAM DOMMERSON (d. 1927) – The Light House
at Violen-on-the-Schelett, Holland; and On the River
Amstel, Amsterdam, Holland – both signed, and inscribed
on reverse – unframed – 40.7 x 60.9cm. – a pair – one
illustrated.
(Christie's)   **$3,707   £2,200**

MARTHA TOUR DONAS (1885–1967) – La musique –
signed – oil and collage on board in the artist's original
frame – 77 x 52.5cm.
(Christie's)   **$191,070   £99,000**

F. R. DONAT – An indiscreet question – signed – oil on
wood – 53 x 41.5cm.
(Auktionshaus Arnold)   **$447   £269**

KEES VAN DONGEN (1877–1968) – Young girl in a red
dress (Dolly van Dongen) – signed – oil on canvas –
99.7 x 80.6cm.
(Christie's)   **$975,150   £495,000**

KEES VAN DONGEN (1877–1968) – Femme Fatale –
signed – oil on canvas – 82 x 61cm.
(Christie's)   **$2,817,100   £1,430,000**

KEES VAN DONGEN (1877–1968) – Nu blond au
Ruban vert – signed – oil on canvas – 100 x 81cm.
(Christie's)   **$685,300   £385,000**

KEES VAN DONGEN (1877–1968) – Picture of a woman
– signed – oil on canvas
(Lempertz)   **$24,923   £12,847**

DONGEN

KEES VAN DONGEN – Deux silhouettes au bois –
signed and inscribed – oil on canvas – 41 x 33cm.
(Sotheby's)   **$168,300**   **£99,000**

MICHEL DORIGNY (1617–1685) – Mercury seated,
with Venus and Cupid – oil on canvas – 152.4 x 119.4cm.
(Phillips)   **$25,896**   **£13,000**

KEES VAN DONGEN – La Fontaine – signed; signed on
the stretcher – oil on canvas – 46 x 33cm.
(Sotheby's)   **$74,800**   **£44,000**

Follower of GERARD DOU – A man at a niche holding a
pipe – oil on copper – 25.7 x 19.9cm.
(Christie's)   **$3,920**   **£1,980**

GERARD DOU, Follower of – An Alchemist in his laboratory – on panel – 45.4 x 35.2cm.
(Christie's) $3,984 £1,980

MARGARET DOVASTON – The new venture – signed – 50.8 x 68.6cm.
(Christie's) **$3,944 £1,980**

SYBIL M. DOWIE (fl. 1893-1904) – A young girl with a blue sash – signed with initials – oil on canvas – 101.9 x 76.6cm.
(Christie's) **$4,090 £2,420**

JOHN DOWNMAN, A.R.A. (1750–1824) – Portrait of Mrs Siddons, small half length, in a white dress with a white fichue and mob cap – signed and dated 1787 – pencil, stump and watercolour – 7½ x 6in.
(Christie's) $4,380 £2,420

PATRICK DOWNIE – Sorting the catch – oil on board – signed – 25.5 x 35.5cm.
(Bonhams) $2,000 £1,000

DOYLE

MICHEL-MARTIN DROLLING (French 1786–1851)
– A portrait of a writer – signed and dated 1819 l.l. – oil on
canvas – 110 x 82cm.
(Sotheby's) $139,370   £77,000

CHARLES ALTAMONT DOYLE (1832–1893) – Girl
being serenaded on a snow covered branch – pen and ink
and watercolour – 40 x 25.5cm.
(Phillips) $2,727   £1,350

ALFRED DE DREUX (1810–1860), Attributed to –
Trumpeter and Municipal Guard – a pair – monogrammed
and dated 1832 and 1833 – oil on panel – 35 x 25cm.
(Sotheby's) $4,123   £2,454

JOOST CORNELIS DROOGSLOOT (1586–1666) –
Peasants merrymaking around a table – oil on panel –
47.5 x 70cm.
(Phillips)   **$10,956   £5,500**

In the manner of **FRANCOIS HUBERT DROUAIS** –
Portrait of a young boy, half length, wearing a brown
jacket with a lace collar and a broad brimmed hat – oil on
canvas – an oval – 65 x 53cm.
(Phillips)   **$1,610   £805**

ADOLPHE HENRI DUBASTY (French, 1814–1884) –
A half-length portrait of a young woman in an interior –
signed and dated 1884 – oil on panel – 35.6 x 26.7cm.
(Bonhams)   **$1,314   £650**

DUBUFE

CLAUDE-MARIE DUBUFE (1790–1864) – Slumber –
signed – oil on canvas – 59 x 72.5cm.
(Sotheby's) **$21,475 £12,271**

CHARLES DUFRESNE (1876–1938) – The bathers –
signed and dated 30 – gouache and watercolour on paper –
33 x 27cm.
(Christie's) **$4,425 £2,293**

ROBERT DUDLEY (Exh. 1880–1893) – The Bridge of
the Dance of Death at Lucerne – signed and dated 1875 –
watercolour – 34 x 44.5cm.
(Phillips) **$2,020 £1,000**

LOUIS DUFFY – The Cable Layers – signed and
inscribed on reverse – oil on canvas – 76 x 101.5cm.
(Christie's) **$8,266 £4,950**

RAOUL DUFY – Le Guéridon, Rue Seguier – signed – oil
on canvas – 55 x 46cm.
(Sotheby's) **$224,400 £132,000**

RAOUL DUFY (1877–1953) – Hommage à Claude
Lorrain – signed – watercolour, pen and black ink on paper
laid down on card – 50.5 x 66cm.
(Christie's)   **$97,812   £57,200**

RAOUL DUFY – Still life – signed – watercolour over
pencil – 51 x 66cm.
(Sotheby's)   **$56,100   £33,000**

A. DUKE – Hunting scene with pack of hounds jumping a
hedge followed by huntsmen – signed – oil on canvas –
16 x 11½in.
(Russell, Baldwin & Bright)   **$1,758   £950**

RAOUL DUFY – La maison rouge sur la côte Normande –
signed - oil on canvas – 54 x 65cm.
(Sotheby's)   **$280,500   £165,000**

HEYMAN DULLAERT (1636–1684) – A young
philosopher in his study – oil on canvas – 66 x 51cm.
(Sotheby's)   **$10,032   £5,280**

173

DUNCAN

WALTER DUNCAN – The Faggot Gatherers; and The Cabbage Harvest – both signed – pencil, watercolour and bodycolour – 7 x 10in. – a pair
(Christie's) **$1,156 £605**

LOUIS DUPRE (French 1789–1837) – Ali Trebelen, Pasha of Janina in a barge – oil on canvas – 61 x 74.5cm.
(Sotheby's) **$30,195 £16,500**

ROBERT SPEAR DUNNING (1829–1905) – Roses, peaches and cherries – signed and dated 1891 – oil on canvas – 33 x 22cm.
(Christie's) **$8,250 £4,290**

A. DURAN (active 1886–1900) – Time is Money – signed and dated indistinctly – oil on canvas – 41 x 51.5cm.
(Christie's) **$20,900 £11,077**

JOHN WARD DUNSMORE (fl. 1884–1888) – The recital – signed and dated 1885 – 30.4 x 38.1cm.
(Christie's) **$2,208 £1,210**

CHARLES-EMILE-AUGUSTE DURAND called CAROLUS-DURAN (1838–1917) – Portrait of Prince Michel Orsini, aged 8 – signed and dated 1885 – 53.5 x 45cm.
(Sotheby's) **$29,987 £17,849**

GEORGE HENRY DURRIE (1820–1863) – Winter at Jones Inn – signed with initials – oil on canvas – 45.7 x 61cm.
(Christie's)   **$74,800   £38,896**

DUTCH SCHOOL (19th Century) – A serving girl with a plate of lobster – 44.4 x 36.2cm.
(Christie's)   **$1,853   £1,100**

DUTCH SCHOOL, 16th Century – The Adoration of the Magi – oil on wood – 77 x 58cm.
(Lempertz)   **$27,815   £15,894**

DUTCH SCHOOL, 18th century – Hephaistos and Aphrodite – oil on canvas – 70 x 105cm.
(Auktionshaus Arnold)   **$1,786   £1,076**

DUTCH SCHOOL, 17th Century – Vanite aux Coquiliages – oil on copper – 17.2 x 13.2cm.
(Sotheby's)   **$19,411   £11,156**

175

DUTCH SCHOOL

DUTCH SCHOOL, 18th Century – Portrait of a man ,said to be Tsar Peter the Great as a ship's carpenter in Zaandam, 1697 – oil on canvas – 73.7 x 59.5cm.
(Christie's)   **$8,151**   **£4,180**

THEOPHILE EMMANUEL DUVERGER (b. 1821) – Backstage – signed – oil on panel – 46 x 37.8cm.
(Christie's)   **$8,272**   **£4,400**

DUTCH SCHOOL, 18th century – In camp – oil on board – 24 x 33cm.
(Auktionshaus Arnold)   **$2,233**   **£1,345**

DUTCH SCHOOL, 19th century – Winter scene – oil on canvas – 64 x 85cm.
(Hôtel de Ventes Horta)   **$4,418**   **£2,295**

WILLEM CORNELISZ DUYSTER (1599–1635) – A man seated, holding a wine glass – oil on panel – 43.8 x 31.4cm.
(Phillips)   **$11,554**   **£5,800**

Circle of SIR ANTHONY VAN DYCK (1599–1641) –
Studies of the head of a bearded man – oil on canvas –
49 x 65cm.
(Phillips)   **$4,800   £2,500**

MAUD EARL (d. 1943) – A brindle and a brindle and
white Greyhound in a landscape – signed – oil on canvas –
102.8 x 129.5cm.
(Christie's)   **$28,215   £14,850**

SCHOOL OF VAN DYCK (circa 1650) – Equestrian
portrait of a gentleman with his page and his dog – oil on
canvas – 280 x 160cm.
(Christie's)   **$92,555   £47,571**

GEORGE EARL (fl. 1856–1883) – Perth Station, going
South – signed and dated 1895 – oil on canvas – 122.9 x
213.4cm.
(Christie's)   **$523,600   £308,000**

EARL

PERCY EARL – '1930's Grand National' having inscriptions of horses names to foreground – signed – 27¹/₂ x 35¹/₂in.
(Hobbs & Chambers)   **$2,876   £1,500**

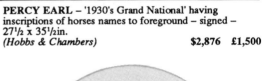

THOMAS EARL (fl. 1836–1885) – The head of a West Highland terrier – oil on board laid down on panel – 25.3 x 8.1cm.
(Christie's)   **$1,778   £935**

EDWIN EARP – Figures and sailing craft in the shallows of a lake with mountains in the distance – watercolour – 16¹/₂ x 13in. – and companion picture
(Hy. Duke & Son)   **$496   £280**

SIR ALFRED EAST, R.A. (1849–1913) – September
sunshine – signed – oil on canvas – 101.6 x 152.4cm.
(Christie's) $13,068 £6,600

**Attributed to CHRISTOFFER WILHELM
ECKERSBERG (1783–1853)** – Portrait of John Daniel
Clemens, seated half length – oil on canvas – 32 x 25cm.
(Christie's) $24,310 £14,300

ALBERT EDELFELT (Finnish 1854–1905) – The pilot –
signed and dated 1894 – oil on canvas – 66 x 54cm.
(AB Stockholms Auktionsverk) $62,697 £32,318

EDEN UPTON EDDIS (English, 1812–1901) – A
portrait of a brother and sister with their pet dog in a
wooded landscape – oil on canvas – 147.3 x 115.5cm.
(Bonhams) $16,176 £8,000

BASH EDIT –The models – signed – oil on canvas –
130 x 98cm.
(Hôtel de Ventes Horta) $2,438 £1,393

EDMUNDS

K. G. EDMUNDS (20th Century) – A brindle Great
Dane bitch – signed – oil on canvas – 60.9 x 50.8cm.
(Christie's) **$878   £462**

LIONEL EDWARDS – Rounding the bend, Pontefract
Races – signed – inscribed and dated 1944 – 20 x 30in.
(Tennants) **$30,000   £15,000**

LIONEL EDWARDS – "Lady Electra" with a groom in
an open landscape, other horses and grooms nearby –
signed – inscribed and dated 1944 - 20 x 30in.
(Tennants) **$25,000   £12,500**

LIONEL EDWARDS – A portrait of a Bay thoroughbred
- Argonaut, in a stable interior - signed and dated '05 –
watercolour over traces of pencil, heightened with
bodycolour and stopping out – 37 x 53.25cm.
(Woolley & Wallis) **$2,914   £1,550**

LIONEL EDWARDS (1878–1966) – October evening,
Glen Garry – signed – pencil, watercolour and bodycolour
– 33 x 53.5cm.
(Christie's) **$2,134   £1,100**

LIONEL DALHOUSIE ROBERTSON EDWARDS
(1878–1966) – A Pekingese – pencil, pen and black ink, on
scraperboard – 14.6 x 12.1cm.
(Christie's) **$627   £330**

OTTO EERELMAN (1839–1926) – A view in a town in winter with an elegant lady in a horse-drawn sledge – signed – 60 x 90cm.
(Christie's)   **$30,174   £15,087**

HERMANN EFFENBERGER (1842–1911) – The young flower seller – signed and dated 83 – 90 x 60cm.
(Christie's)   **$3,336   £1,980**

SUZANNE EISENDIECK – Clown – signed – inscribed on the reverse – 22.9 x 14.6cm.
(Christie's)   **$1,254   £660**

MAURICE ELIOT (b. 1864) – Sur la Barrière – signed and dated 87 – oil on canvas – 50.5 x 66.7cm.
(Christie's) **$5,790   £3,080**

JOHN EMMS (1843–1912) – 'Sharp', an Irish terrier – signed, inscribed and dated 1897 – oil on canvas – 53.3 x 66.1cm.
(Christie's) **$6,897   £3,630**

JOHN ELWYN (b. 1916) – Wood dyers – signed – oil on canvas – 51 x 76cm.
(Christie's) **$1,707   £880**

EDOUARD ENDER (1822–1883) – The inheritance – signed and dated 1851 – oil on panel – 55.3 x 44.4cm.
(Christie's) **$7,546   £3,850**

JOHN ELWYN (b. 1916) – Conversation – signed and dated '54 – oil on canvas – 70 x 90cm.
(Christie's) **$1,323   £682**

ENGLERTH (early 20th Century) – A reclining nude – signed – inscribed and dated 1920 – oil on canvas – 75.6 x 100.7cm.
(Christie's) **$10,340   £5,500**

ENGLISH SCHOOL, 19th century – The Ruins of
Kenilworth Castle – oil on canvas –25 x 48in.
(Bigwood)   **$1,649   £850**

ENGLISH SCHOOL, 18th century – Portrait of a lady,
half length, in a red dress with a brown silk wrap – in a
painted cartouche – 71.1 x 60.9cm.
(Christie's)   **$642   £352**

ENGLISH SCHOOL – Portrait of a gentleman, three-
quarter length, in a scarlet coat and a silver wrap, a view to
a seascape with a galleon beyond – unframed –
127 x 104.2cm.
(Christie's)   **$2,810   £1,540**

ENGLISH SCHOOL 19th Century – Return to
Plymouth – water colour on paper – monogrammed RM –
25 x 54cm.
(Hôtel de Ventes Horta)   **$1,204   £688**

ENGLISH SCHOOL, 19th Century – Portrait of a
young girl, half length in a brown dress holding a doll –
unframed – 43 x 35.5cm.
(Christie's)   **$1,271   £638**

ENGLISH SCHOOL

19th Century ENGLISH SCHOOL – Leaving on the Sunday ride – traces of monogram DG – oil on canvas – 58 x 89cm.
(Hôtel de Ventes Horta) **$4,763 £2,358**

ENGLISH SCHOOL, (18th Century) – Portrait of an officer – oil on canvas – 16½ x 13½in.
(David Lay) **$480 £240**

ENGLISH SCHOOL, circa 1760 – The interior of an inn with figures playing backgammon – pencil, watercolour and bodycolour – 4⅞ x 6½in.
(Christie's) **$4,778 £2,640**

ENGLISH SCHOOL – Portrait of a lady, three-quarter length, in a blue dress and a gold wrap, a view to a garden beyond – unframed – 127 x 104.2cm.
(Christie's) **$2,610 £1,430**

ENGLISH SCHOOL, circa 1830 – Portrait of a little boy, seated full length, in a dark blue dress holding a wild rose, with a Spitz, in a landscape – on canvas laid down on board – 76.2 x 95.3cm.
(Christie's) **$4,180 £2,200**

ENGLISH SCHOOL (19th Century) – A Staffordshire Bull Terrier and an English Toy Terrier – signed with initials and dated 68 – oil on canvas – 20.2 x 25.4cm.
(Christie's) **$732 £385**

ENGLISH SCHOOL, 19th century – The pink rose – 60.9 x 50.8cm.
(Christie's) **$6,424 £3,520**

ENGLISH SCHOOL, 19th century – The Young Highlander – unframed – 25.4 x 35.6cm.
(Christie's) **$1,305 £715**

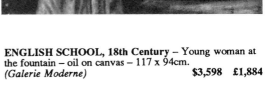

ENGLISH SCHOOL (19th Century) – Bloodhounds outside a stable – oil on canvas – 71.2 x 91.4cm.
(Christie's) **$1,003 £528**

ENGLISH SCHOOL, 18th Century – Young woman at the fountain – oil on canvas – 117 x 94cm.
(Galerie Moderne) **$3,598 £1,884**

ENGSTROM

ALBERT ENGSTROM (1869–1940) – Sailor Mattson with picture of a ship – signed – pastel – 57 x 70cm.
(AB Stockholms Auktionsverk) **$4,478 £2,308**

DELPHIN ENJOLRAS (b. 1857) – The reader - signed – pastel – 540 x 370mm.
(Sotheby's) **$6,693 £3,347**

JOHN JOSEPH ENNEKING (1841–1916) – Evening glow – signed and dated 91 – oil on canvas – 107 x 159cm.
(Christie's) **$33,000 £17,160**

JOHN JOSEPH ENNEKING (American, 1841–1916) – The Potato Harvesters – signed and dated 77 – oil on canvas – 18 x 26in.
(Skinner) **$6,500 £3,351**

JAMES ENSOR (Belgian School) – Still life with Japanese fan – signed – oil on canvas – 47 x 66cm.
(Galerie Moderne) **$163,955 £85,616**

SIR JACOB EPSTEIN – Portrait of the artist's son, Jackie – signed – pencil – 58.5 x 44.5cm.
(Christie's) **$1,980 £990**

SVEN ERIXSON (1899–1970) – Landscape with road
and white house, evening – signed and dated 1930 – oil on
canvas – 73 x 92cm.
(AB Stockholms Auktionsverk) **$7,818 £4,093**

HANS ERNI (Swiss, b. 1909) – Centaur, 1959 – signed –
colour lithograph – 66 x 49cm.
(germann Auktionshaus) **$782 £460**

SIR JACOB EPSTEIN (1886–1959) – Reclining nude –
signed – watercolour, bodycolour and pencil – 57 x 43cm.
(Christie's) **$5,511 £3,300**

VIGILIUS ERIKSEN (1722–1782), Attributed to –
Portrait of Catherine the Great, wearing the Sash and
Diamond Star of the Order of St. Andrew – oil on canvas –
66.3 x 51.8cm.
(Christie's) **$34,320 £17,600**

RUDOLPH ERNST – The tambourine player – signed –
oil on panel – 30 x 17cm.
(Hôtel de Ventes Horta) **$20,081 £11,475**

ESBENS

EMILE ETIENNE ESBENS (French, b. 1821) – The Guitarist – signed – watercolour, gouache and graphite on paper – 8¹/₂ x 6³/₄in.
(Skinner) **$150 £77**

Attributed to WILLIAM ETTY – The bather – oil on canvas – 45.7 x 35.6cm.
(Duran) **$638 £333**

MAURITS CORNELIS ESCHER (Dutch, 1892–1972) – Fish and Frogs – monogrammed – wood engraving on paper – unframed – 3¹/₈ x 2³/₄in.
(Skinner Inc.) **$550 £294**

ADRIANUS EVERSEN (Dutch, 1818–1897) – A Dutch street scene – signed – oil on panel – 22.9 x 18.1cm.
(Bonhams) **$3,842 £1,900**

ADRIANUS EVERSEN (1818–1889) – A view in a town with a peasant selling vegetables near the entrance of a church – signed – 44 x 36cm.
(Christie's) **$7,376 £3,688**

VAN DEN EYCKEN – Portrait of a dog – signed and dated 1885 – oil on canvas – 51 x 42cm.
(Galerie Moderne) **$2,290 £1,199**

JULIUS EXTER (German, 1863–1939) – Summer river landscape with bathers – signed – oil on canvas – 198 x 160cm.
(Auktionshaus Arnold) **$6,072 £3,247**

CHARLES VAN DER EYCKEN (1859–1923) – The overturned bowl – signed – oil on board – 35 x 27.5cm.
(Hôtel de Ventes Horta) **$2,858 £1,415**

EYCKEN

CHARLES VAN DEN EYCKEN (1899–1923) – Kittens playing in a sewing basket – signed and dated 1905 – oil on canvas – unframed – 34.7 x 45.2cm.
(Christie's) **$9,196 £4,840**

FABBIO FABBI – Arabian village festival – signed – oil on canvas – 121.2 x 160.3cm.
(Ritchie's) **$15,624 £8,095**

Circle of PIETRO FABRIS (active 1768–1778) – Figures in a grotto on the coast – oil on canvas – 52.7 x 86.3cm.
(Phillips) **$23,904 £12,000**

FABIO FABBI (1861–1946) – The slave market – signed – oil on canvas – 209.6 x 99.4cm.
(Christie's) **$24,310 £14,300**

RAFFAELE FACCIOLI (b. 1846) – On the beach – signed and dedicated – 43.2 x 22.8cm.
(Christie's) **$4,448 £2,640**

JOHN PHILIP FALTER (1910–1982) - The Fair –
signed – oil on canvas – 61 x 91.5cm.
(Christie's) **$18,700 £9,724**

OYVIND FAHLSTROM (1928–76) – "Orage-Cadre" –
signed and dated 1960 – mixed media – 49 x 64.5cm.
(AB Stockholms Auktionsverk) **$66,628 £34,884**

HENRI FANTIN-LATOUR (1836–1904) – Sortie de
Bain – signed – oil on canvas – 57.5 x 48cm.
(Christie's) **$131,670 £77,000**

LUIS RICCARDO FALERO (1851–1896) – La
Coquette – signed and dated 1879 – oil on canvas –
160.7 x 83.8cm.
(Christie's) **$28,171 £14,300**

ARTHUR CECIL FARE (1876–1958) – A country house
with figures and ducks on lane lined by pollarded trees –
signed – watercolour over pencil – 30.5 x 50.5cm.
(Allen & Harris) **$414 £210**

FARE

JOSEPH FARQUHARSON, R.A. (1846–1935) – The
joyless winter Day – signed – oil on canvas –
61 x 106.7cm.
(Christie's) $30,880 £16,000

ARTHUR CECIL FARE (1876-1958) – The Lord
Mayor's Chapel, Bristol – signed – watercolour over pencil
– 41 x 26cm.
(Allen & Harris) **$709 £360**

JOSEPH FARQUHARSON (1846–1935) – In the garden
– signed – oil on canvas – 46 x 30.5cm.
(Christie's) **$7,623 £3,850**

EMILY FARMER – The daisy chain – signed and dated
1873 – watercolour heightened with white – 21³/₄ x 14in.
(Christie's) **$1,477 £792**

MARY FEDDEN (born 1915) – Anna's lilies – signed
and dated 1978 – oil on board – 91 x 117cm.
(Phillips) **$10,809 £6,500**

MARY FEDDEN (b. 1915) – Cat on a harbour wall –
signed and dated 1981 – watercolour and bodycolour –
21 x 16cm.
(Christie's)   **$2,027   £1,045**

MARY FEDDEN – Stormy weather – signed and dated
1983 – 40 x 29cm.
(Christie's)   **$1,983   £1,045**

MARY FEDDEN (b. 1915) – Still life with fruit – signed
and dated 1984 – oil on canvas – 61 x 50cm.
(Christie's)   **$6,429   £3,850**

MARY FEDDEN (b. 1915) – Lulu – signed and dated –
oil on board – 50 x 40.5cm.
(Christie's)   **$6,547   £3,520**

JOSEPH FERRARI (Italian? 19th Century) – Greek figures in a coastal landscape – oil on board – signed and dated 1851 – 24.2 x 31.1cm.
(Bonhams) $1,229   £700

PAVEL ANDREEVICH FEDOTOV (1815–1852) – Portrait of a young man – signed on reverse – oil on card – 25.3 x 20.4cm.
(Christie's) $12,870   £6,600

CIRO FERRI, Attributed to – The Madonna and Child with the Infant Saint John the Baptist – unframed – 97.8 x 118.7cm.
(Christie's) $5,312   £2,640

HARRY FENN (1845–1911) – House of Samuel Colman, Newport – signed with monogrammed initials – pen and brush and black ink, and pencil heightened with white en grisaille on paper – 30.5 x 45.6cm.
(Christie's) $990   £515

ELOI-FIRMIN FERON (1802–1896) – The ambush – signed and dated – oil on canvas – 33 x 41.2cm.
(Christie's) $7,858   £4,180

ANSELM FEUERBACH (German 1829–80) – A mother and child – signed and dated – charcoal and watercolour heightened with white bodycolour – unframed – 41 x 27.5cm.
(Sotheby's) $12,078   £6,600

JACQUES EUGENE FEYEN (1815–1908) – Les
Ramasseuses de Coquillages – signed – oil on canvas –
61 x 97.8cm.
(Christie's) $6,204 £3,300

Follower of PAOLO FIAMMINGO – Saint John the
Baptist in the Wilderness – oil on panel – unframed –
81.3 x 63.7cm.
(Christie's) $7,040 £3,520

BENJAMIN-EUGENE FICHEL (1826–1895) – The
musical party; and The card party – one signed and dated
1862, the other signed and dated 1856 – both oil on panel –
21.3 x 27.4cm. – a pair
(Christie's) $11,994 £6,380

FICHERELLI

After FELICE FICHERELLI, called Il Riposo – Tarquin and Lucretia – oil on canvas – 118 x 149cm.
(Phillips)   **$4,992**   **£2,600**

ANTON FILKUKA (1888–1947) – Ice breakers in a winter landscape – signed – oil on canvas – unframed – 205.5 x 300.4cm.
(Christie's)   **$13,435**   **£6,820**

WALTER FIRLE (1859–1929) – Dutch girls taking tea – 60.9 x 88.8cm.
(Christie's)   **$10,194**   **£6,050**

LYDIA FIELD-EMMETT (1866–1952) – Portrait of a boy seated full length in a chair – signed – oil on canvas – 157.5 x 106.5cm.
(Christie's)   **$21,230**   **£11,000**

G. FIELDING – Gipsy encampment with horses in a wood – signed – oil on canvas – 24 x 35in.
(Spencer's)   **$1,373**   **£750**

PAUL FISCHER (Danish 1860–1934) – Winter scene with horse drawn vehicles at the Freedom monument, Copenhagen – signed – oil on panel – 20 x 25cm.
(AB Stockholms Auktionsverk)   **$6,449**   **£3,324**

PAUL FISCHER (Danish 1860–1934) – Fisherman in Copenhagen – signed – oil on panel – 43 x 21cm.
(AB Stockholms Auktionsverk)   **$4,656   £2,400**

PAUL FISCHER – Prepared for the rain – signed – oil on canvas – 36.5 x 14.5cm.
(Sotheby's)   **$17,327   £9,680**

PAUL FISCHER – Sunbathing on the dunes – signed – oil on canvas - 38 x 54cm.
(Sotheby's)   **$27,566   £15,400**

FISHER

MARK FISHER (1841-1923) – Sheep shearing in a barn
– signed – oil on canvas – 43 x 62.5cm.
(Christie's) $3,841   £1,980

HARRISON FISHER (1875–1934) – A gentleman
helping a lady – signed and dated 1906 – watercolour,
gouache and black chalk on board – 63 x 47cm.
(Christie's) $8,800   £5,222

PERCY HARLAND FISHER – Girl in a straw hat –
signed – oil on canvas – unframed – 90.5 x 78cm.
(Sotheby's) $8,362   £4,620

HARRISON FISHER (American, b. 1875) – A romantic
dinner – signed and dated 1911 – watercolour and
bodycolour over pencil – 72.5 x 52.5cm.
(Phillips) $6,060   £3,000

PERCY HARLAND FISHER (b. 1867) – The telegram –
signed – unframed – 31 x 36in.
(W.H. Lane & Son) $4,032   £2,100

PERCY HARLAND FISHER (1865–1944) – Best of
friends – signed – oil on canvas – unframed – 76 x 63.5cm.
(Christie's) $4,671   £2,420

FLORENCE FITZGERALD (fl. 1887–1900) – The
daisy chain – oil on canvas – 18 x 12in.
(GA Canterbury Auction Galleries) $1,910   £1,000

PERCY HARLAND FISHER (1865–1944) – A young
student – oil on canvas – unframed – 76 x 63.5cm.
(Christie's) $3,397   £1,760

JOHN AUSTEN FITZGERALD (1832–1906) –
Christmas – signed – oil on canvas – 40 x 35cm.
(Christie's) $10,615   £5,500

FLAXMAN

JOHN FLAXMAN, R.A. (1755–1826) – Mercury uniting the hands of Britain and France – inscribed – pencil, pen and grey ink, grey wash, on Whatman paper – 10¹/₈ x 12³/₄in.
(Christie's) $6,435   £3,300

JOHN FLAXMAN, R.A. (1755–1826) – Prometheus attacked by Jupiter – pencil, pen and grey ink – 9¹/₄ x 9³/₈in. – and a drawing of Achilles, also by Flaxman
(Christie's) $3,647   £1,870

GEORG FLEGEL (1563–1638) – A still life of birds, with insects, fruit, seed and nuts on a table – signed – oil on canvas – 52.5 x 54.5cm.
(Sotheby's) $637,450   £335,500

FLEMISH(?) SCHOOL, Circa 1650 – Portrait of Maria …, bust length, wearing a bejewelled black costume trimmed with ermine, behind a parapet – 72 x 56.3cm.
(Christie's) $2,640   £1,320

FLEMISH SCHOOL, 19th Century – Rubens showing his portrait of the Archduke to the Archduke and the Infanta Isabella – bears signature T.P. Thys – oil on panel – 53 x 68.5cm.
(Phillips) $3,420   £1,900

FLEMISH SCHOOL, 17th Century – The Entombment – 47 x 64.7cm.
(Christie's) $2,051   £1,100

FLEMISH SCHOOL, 18th Century – Peasants playing boules – oil on canvas – 87 x 114cm.
(Phillips) **$6,200 £3,100**

FLEMISH SCHOOL – A peeled orange, plums, peaches on a silver platter, with grapes and wine glasses – 48.3 x 38.1cm.
(Christie's) **$6,534 £3,300**

FLEMISH SCHOOL – Cherubs heads amongst clouds – oil on panel – 20.3 x 30.5cm.
(Christie's) **$1,096 £550**

FLEMISH SCHOOL, 17th Century – Portrait of a cavalry officer over-looking a field of battle – indistinctly signed – black chalk on vellum – 440 x 296mm.
(Phillips) **$379 £220**

BLANDFORD FLETCHER – Sunday evening – signed – pencil and watercolour – $8^3/4$ x 12in.
(Christie's) **$1,549 £880**

SIR WILLIAM RUSSELL FLINT, R.A., P.R.W.S. (1880–1969) – Three idle daughters – signed – watercolour – 49 x 67cm.
(Phillips) **$29,934 £18,000**

FLINT

SIR WILLIAM RUSSELL FLINT, R.A. (1880–1969) –
Cecilia – signed and dated 1961 – watercolour – 27 x 37cm.
(Christie's) **$36,465 £18,700**

SIR WILLIAM RUSSELL FLINT, R.A. (1880–1969) –
Evangeline – signed – red chalk – 29 x 16cm.
(Christie's) **$6,402 £3,300**

SIR WILLIAM RUSSELL FLINT, R.A., P.R.W.S.
(1880–1969) – The little terrace, Vaunavey – signed – also
signed, inscribed with title and dated 1959–60 on the
reverse - watercolour – 51 x 69cm.
(Phillips) **$41,575 £25,000**

SIR WILLIAM RUSSELL FLINT, R.A. (1880–1969) -
Nude rolling a hoop– signed – pencil and watercolour –
32 x 43cm.
(Christie's) **$3,628 £1,870**

FLORENTINE SCHOOL – The Annunciation –
93.9 x 114.3cm.
(Christie's) **$2,213 £1,100**

FLORENTINE SCHOOL, 16th Century – Portrait of Dante – oil on panel – 58 x 44.5cm.
(Phillips)   **$864   £450**

Follower of FRANS FLORIS – The Last Supper – oil on copper – unframed – 61.6 x 84.2cm.
(Christie's)   **$3,267   £1,650**

HENRY FOLEY – Venetian capriccio – signed – 45.8 x 81.3cm.
(Christie's)   **$1,643   £825**

PEDRO VICTOR FLORES (1897–1968) – Bull fighter and maja – oil on canvas – signed - 46 x 38cm.
(Duran)   **$5,053   £2,618**

LAVINIA FONTANA, (1552-1614), Circle of – Portrait of a child – oil on canvas – 49 x 42cm.
(Sotheby's)   **$27,175   £15,618**

FONTANA

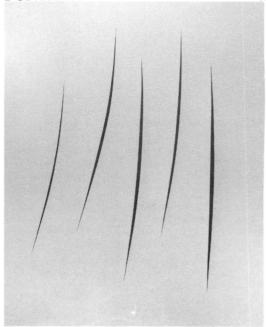

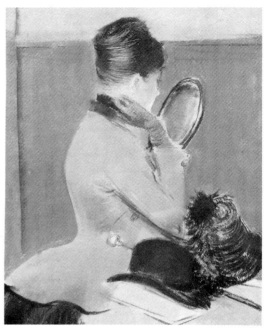

LUCIO FONTANA (1899–1968) – Concetto spaziale – signed and inscribed – water-based paint on canvas – 65 x 54.5cm.
(Christie's)   **$283,800 £165,000**

JEAN LOUIS FORAIN (1852–1931) – At the milliner's – pastel on paper laid on board – 54.6 x 46cm.
(Christie's)   **$69,344 £35,200**

Manner of GIROLAMO FORABOSCO – Head of a young woman with a laurel wreath in her hair – oil on panel – 43 x 36.1cm.
(Christie's)   **$11,000 £5,500**

EDWIN FORBES (1839–1895) – Drummer boy, Rappahannock Station, Va. - signed with initials and inscribed – brush and pen and black ink and black crayon on paper – 50.2 x 34.9cm.
(Christie's)   **$12,100 £7,180**

HELEN FORBES (1891–1945) – Wells Fargo ruin – oil
on canvas – 86 x 102cm.
(Butterfield & Butterfield) **$1,100 £539**

STANHOPE ALEXANDER FORBES, R.A.
(1857–1947) – The walk way – Chateaudun – signed and
inscribed "Chateaudun" – also signed and titled on a label
on the reverse – oil on canvas laid down on board –
49.5 x 33cm.
(Phillips) **$7,483 £4,500**

STANHOPE ALEXANDER FORBES (1857–1947) –
Cutting hay – signed – oil on canvas – 11 x 16in.
(David Lay) **$2,850 £1,500**

STANHOPE ALEXANDER FORBES (1857–1947) –
Children playing on the old quay – oil on canvas – signed
and dated 1931 – 24 x 30in.
(David Lay) **$35,000 £17,500**

STANHOPE ALEXANDER FORBES (1857–1947) –
Head of an old woman – oil on canvas – signed –
19 x 17in.
(David Lay) **$4,625 £2,500**

FORBES

ELEANOR FORTESCUE-BRICKDALE (English, 1871–1945) – The World's Travesties – signed with initials and dated 1900 – watercolour and gouache on board – 35.6 x 42.5cm.
(Christie's)   **$6,600 £3,916**

STANHOPE ALEXANDER FORBES (1857–1947) – The Story Book – oil on canvas – signed and dated 1888 – 31 x 24in.
(W.H. Lane & Son)   **$9,500 £5,000**

STANHOPE ALEXANDER FORBES (1857–1947) – The Old Weighing House, Penzance, Cornwall – oil on canvas – signed – 24 x 30in.
(W.H. Lane & Son)   **$422 £220**

ERIK FORSMAN – Christmas mood – signed – gouache and watercolour – 39 x 69cm.
(AB Stockholms Auktionsverk)   **$2,792 £1,439**

ELEANOR FORTESCUE-BRICKDALE (English 1871–1945) – Love and adversity – signed with initials and dated 1900 – watercolour on board – 52.1 x 34.3cm.
(Christie's)   **$4,950 £2,937**

HERBERT WILSON FOSTER – The village green –
signed and dated 1914 – watercolour – 38.2 x 54.7cm.
(Bonhams) **$1,809 £900**

WILLIAM BANKS FORTESCUE – Winter draweth
nigh – signed – signed and inscribed on the reverse –
91.5 x 71cm.
(Christie's) **$6,688 £3,520**

J*** FOSTER - 'Near Haddon Hall'; A garden terrace by
moonlight – a pair – both signed and dated '78 – oil on
board – each 15½ x 11¾in.
(Tennants) **$1,200 £600**

M. FORTUNY – At the inn – signed – oil on panel –
29 x 18cm.
(Duran) **$1,861 £972**

MYLES BIRKET FOSTER (1825–1899) – Feeding the
geese – signed with monogram – watercolour heightened
with bodycolour – 22.5 x 31cm.
(Phillips) **$8,080 £4,000**

MYLES BIRKET FOSTER (1825–1899) – A Highland
cottage – signed – pencil and watercolour heightened with
white – 6³/₄ x 9¹/₄in.
(Christie's) $10,402   £5,280

TSUGUHARU FOUJITA – Fillete aux oiseaux – signed
and dated 1956 – oil on canvas – 27 x 19cm.
(Sotheby's) $261,800   £154,000

MYLES BIRKET FOSTER (1825–1899) – The Bridge
of Sighs, Venice – signed with monogram – pencil and
watercolour heightened with white – 11⁵/₈ x 8⁷/₈in.
(Christie's) $26,004   £13,200

ARVID FOUGSTEDT (1888–1949) – In evening lamp
light – signed and dated 1935 – watercolour and gouache –
35.5 x 50cm.
(AB Stockholms Auktionsverk) $883   £454

TSUGUHARU FOUJITA – Young girl carrying a cat,
recto, Cat, verso – signed and dated Paris 1951 – pen and
indian ink and watercolour, recto – pen and ink, verso -
22.5 x 16cm.
(Sotheby's) $56,100   £33,000

TSUGUHARU FOUJITA – Les deux enfants portant le pain et le lait – signed and dated Paris 1951 – oil on panel – 34.6 x 26.8cm.
(Sotheby's)   **$486,200   £286,000**

TSUGUHARU FOUJITA – Femme pensive – signed and dated 1926 – oil on canvas – 33 x 41cm.
(Sotheby's)   **$158,950   £93,500**

TSUGUJI FOUJITA (1886–1968) – Rue à Paris avec Tramway – signed and dated 1925 – watercolour, pen and ink on paper – 25 x 32cm.
(Christie's)   **$75,240   £44,000**

A* MOULTON FOWERAKER – Figures in a Spanish square – signed – watercolour – 22.8 x 28cm.
(Bonhams)   **$1,507   £750**

HENRY CHARLES FOX – A shepherd returning with his flock; and Cart horses at a pool – signed and dated 1926 – pencil and watercolour with white – 15 x 10¼in. – a pair
(Christie's)   **$1,646   £935**

HENRY CHARLES FOX (1860–circa 1930) – Horses and a cart in a lane beside a farm; and Cattle watering, a farm among trees beyond – both signed and dated 1911 – watercolour heightened with white – a pair – 14³/₈in x 21¼in.
(Christie's)   **$5,201   £2,640**

FRAGONARD

HONORE FRAGONARD (1732–1806) – Head of a
young girl – oil on canvas – 45.9 x 37.8cm.
(Galerie Koller Zürich)   **$221,569   £115,702**

SAM FRANCIS (b. 1923) – Untitled – signed and dated
1965 on reverse – gouache on paper – 56 x 76cm.
(Christie's)   **$136,224   £79,200**

GUSTAVE FRAIPONT – At the carnival – signed –
pencil and watercolour heightened with white – 7¹/₂ x 5in.
– and three others by the same hand
(Christie's)   **$329   £187**

LUCIEN FRANCK (1857–1920) – Promenade – signed –
oil on panel – 32 x 40cm.
(Christie's)   **$8,113**   **£4,204**

Follower of AMBROSIUS FRANCKEN – Christ bound
– oil on panel – 106 x 74cm.
(Phillips)   **$3,800**   **£1,900**

Follower of FRANS FRANCKEN II – Noli me Tangere -
oil on panel – 62.5 x 48.5cm.
(Phillips)   **$2,500**   **£1,250**

FRANCKEN

HIERONYMUS FRANCKEN (b. 1611) – Portrait of
Agripine d'Aubigné aged 69 – oil on canvas –
55 x 47.5cm.
(Hôtel de Ventes Horta) $3,259 £1,680

ILIO FRANNACCINI? – Nude bathers by a pool –
indistinctly signed - 19½ x 27½in.
(Tennants) $1,200   £600

**Studio of INNOCENZO FRANCUCCI, called
Innocenzo da Imola (circa 1494–circa 1550)** – The Holy
Family with Saint Elizabeth and the infant Saint John the
Baptist – oil on panel – 65.5 x 51.2cm.
(Christie's) $14,157 £7,150

ACS FRANÇOIS (1876–1949) – Working in the fields –
signed - oil on canvas – 83.5 x 67.5cm.
(Hôtel de Ventes Horta) $1,148   £656

ALEX FRASER, R.S.A. – Cobbler outside Ye Olde Shop
– 10 x 8½in.
(Austin & Wyatt) $2,118 £1,100

FRENCH SCHOOL, 18th Century – Portrait of a
gentleman – pastel – oval – 54 x 44cm.
(Sotheby's)   **$4,853**   **£2,789**

FRENCH SCHOOL circa 1810 – A portrait of Napoleon
— oil on canvas – 188.5 x 121cm.
(Sotheby's)   **$43,802**   **£24,200**

FRENCH SCHOOL (late 19th Century) – The first day –
with inscription 'Anker' – oil on canvas – unframed –
76.2 x 62.9cm.
(Christie's)   **$6,618**   **£3,520**

FRENCH SCHOOL, 18th Century – Portrait of a lady –
pastel – oval – 55 x 47cm.
(Sotheby's)   **$7,376**   **£4,239**

FRENCH SCHOOL

FRENCH SCHOOL, 17th Century – Portrait of the
Duchesse de Sully – oil on canvas - 128 x 96cm.
(Sotheby's)   **$5,436   £3,124**

FRENCH SCHOOL, 18th Century – A Sultan and his
favourite – oil on canvas – unframed – 81 x 65cm.
(Christie's)   **$9,256   £4,757**

FRENCH SCHOOL, 19th Century – Pleading with
Napoleon – oil on canvas – 45 x 57cm.
(Finarte Casa d'Aste)   **$6,705   £3,456**

FRENCH SCHOOL (late 19th Century) – The head of
an Arab man – with monogram IHF and dated 95 –
unframed – 64 x 52cm.
(Christie's)   **$4,819   £2,860**

FRENCH SCHOOL – The balloon ascent – bodycolour –
5¼ x 6¾in.
(Christie's)   **$759   £418**

FRENCH SCHOOL

FRENCH SCHOOL (19th Century) – In the park –
53.3 x 35.6cm.
(Christie's) $4,077 £2,420

FRENCH SCHOOL – A lady at her bath (Gabrielle
D'Estrée?) – oval – 67.9 x 49.5cm.
(Christie's) $2,257 £1,210

FRENCH SCHOOL, 17th Century – Portrait of Henri II,
Prince de Condé - oil on canvas – 182 x 123cm.
(Sotheby's) $5,824 £3,347

FRENCH SCHOOL, c. 1800 - Portrait of Napoleon,
small full length, in Coronation robes – 78.1 x 55.2cm.
(Christie's) $1,641 £880

FRIANT

EMILE FRIANT – Bringing the catch ashore – signed
and dated – oil on panel – 29 x 45.5cm.
(Sotheby's)   **$9,845   £5,500**

AXEL FRIDELL (1894–1935) – Gentleman's dinner party
– signed – watercolour, indian ink and gouache –
23 x 49cm.
(AB Stockholms Auktionsverk)   **$3,513   £1,811**

AXEL FRIDELL (1894–1935) – Portrait of the painter
Robert Högfeldt – signed and dated 1914 – oil on canvas –
62 x 46cm.
(AB Stockholms Auktionsverk)   **$711   £372**

AXEL FRIDELL – Self portrait VII 1927–8 – signed –
drypoint engraving on thin laid paper – 19.9 x 14.9cm.
(AB Stockholms Auktionsverk)   **$1,081   £557**

P. FRIED – The courtesan – oil on canvas – signed and
dated – 120 x 80cm.
(Jean-Claude Anaf)   **$4,752   £2,463**

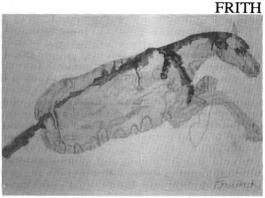

RICHARD-BERNHARDT-LOUIS FRIESE (b. 1854) –
A lion and lioness stalking prey – signed and dated 86 - oil
on canvas – 49.5 x 79.4cm.
(Christie's) $39,270 £23,100

DAME ELISABETH FRINK, R.A. (b.1930) – Reclining
horse – with woven signature – signed and numbered on
reverse – wool tapestry – 173 x 251.5cm.
(Christie's) $6,980 £4,180

ANDREAS FRIIS (late 19th Century) – Children on the
beach, Skagen – signed and inscribed – 30 x 40cm.
(Christie's) $1,075 £638

INNES FRIPP – Girl coaxing a pony – signed –
watercolour – 26 x 36cm.
(Allen & Harris) $1,600 £860

DAME ELISABETH FRINK, R.A. (b. 1930) –
Illustration for Aesop's Fables – signed and dated 68 –
watercolour and pencil – 54.5 x 74.5cm.
(Christie's) $2,561 £1,320

WILLIAM POWELL FRITH, R.A. (1819–1909) – A
sketch for 'Many Happy Returns of the Day' – oil on board
– 40.3 x 75.5cm.
(Christie's) $26,136 £13,200

FROST

ARTHUR BURDETT FROST (1851–1928) – 'Den He
Shuck a Gourd-vine Flower Over de Pot' and Backstage:
Two works – the second, signed – the first, ink wash
heightened with white on paper – the second, watercolour
heightened with white en grisaille on paper – the first,
36.8 x 33.6cm. – the second, 39 x 36.2cm.
(Christie's) **$7,150 £3,718**

ARTHUR BURDETT FROST (1851–1928) – "Here
comes the man I've been laying for." – signed – pen and
black ink and pencil on board – 35.6 x 37.5cm.
(Christie's) **$990 £515**

ARTHUR BURDETT FROST (1851–1928) - The circus
lion on the loose – signed – grey washes, brush and black
ink on board – 37.5 x 55.9cm.
(Christie's) **$4,950 £2,937**

TERRY FROST (b. 1915) – Collage – signed and dated
June '87 – 20½ x 15in.
(David Lay) **$1,000 £500**

LOUIS AGASSIZ FUERTES (1874–1927) – Birds on a
branch – signed – gouache and pencil on board –
36.8 x 29.8cm.
(Christie's) **$8,250 £4,373**

LEONARD JOHN FULLER (b. 1891) – Girl in red kimono reading Velazquez – oil on canvas – framed – 24 x 20in.
(W.H. Lane & Son) $1,728   £900

GAERTNER – Bavarian peasant – signed – oil on canvas – 10 x 8in.
(Du Mouchelles) $350   £188

Follower of THOMAS GAINSBOROUGH – Figures and horses outside a woodland cottage – 45.7 x 63.5cm.
(Christie's) $1,405   £770

PIETRO GABRINI (1865–1926) – Going home, Tivoli – signed – watercolour on paper – 97.8 x 62.2cm.
(Christie's) $6,468   £3,300

EUGENE GALIEN-LALOUE (French 1854–1941) – Place du Châtelet – signed – watercolour – 19 x 31cm.
(AB Stockholms Auktionsverk) $6,449   £3,324

GALIEN-LALOUE

EUGENE GALIEN-LALOUE (French 1854–1941) – Figures laying tram tracks by a fair, Paris – pen and ink, watercolour and bodycolour over traces of pencil – 19 x 30.5cm.
(Sotheby's) $11,071   £6,050

EUGENE GALIEN-LALOUE - Les Quais de la Seine et Notre Dame – signed – gouache – 370 x 540mm.
(Sotheby's) $36,814   £18,407

EUGENE GALIEN-LALOUE (1854–1941) – Boulevard de Palais, Paris – signed – black chalk, watercolour and bodycolour on paper – 20.7 x 33.7cm.
(Christie's) $14,661   £7,480

FRANCESCO MIRALLES Y GALUP – The tambourine girl – signed – oil on panel – 27 x 15.5cm.
(Sotheby's) $5,907   £3,300

G.* GALLI (Italian, 19th/20th century) – Reflections – signed – oil on canvas – 34.9 x 25.4cm.
(Bonhams) $2,022   £1,000

ENRICO GAMBA – The young spectators – signed – watercolour – 22½ x 17in.
(Christie's) $2,667   £1,430

Follower of UBALDO GANDOLFI – A young woman, bust length, holding a mask – in a painted oval – 73.7 x 59.7cm.
(Christie's) **$990 £495**

ENRICO GAMBA – On the terrace – signed and indistinctly inscribed – pencil and watercolour heightened with white – unframed – 15¼ x 9½in.
(Christie's) **$3,077 £1,650**

GAETANO GANDOLFI (1734–1802) – Orpheus and Eurydice – oil on canvas – 42 x 28cm.
(Sotheby's) **$163,020 £85,800**

EMIL GANSO (1895–1941) – Female nudes: Two drawings – the first signed – the first brush and brown ink on paper – the second pencil and brown chalk on paper – both unframed – 47.6 x 36.8cm. - 50.8 x 40cm. – two, one illustrated.
(Christie's) **$1,760 £933**

GARDANNE

ELIZA D. GARDINER (1871–1955) – My pony – colour woodblock – signed – 8 x 7½in. with margins
(Bruce D. Collins)   **$1,100   £595**

STANLEY HORACE GARDINER (b. 1887) – A boy with his model yacht – signed – oil on panel – 14½ x 18in.
(David Lay)   **$798   £420**

AUGUSTE GARDANNE (French 19th Century) – French Foreign Legion drummer – signed – oil on canvas – 13½ x 9½in.
(Du Mouchelles)   **$750   £402**

DANIEL GARDNER (1750–1805) – The Duchess of Devonshire, Lady Melbourne and Mrs Dawson Damer as the three witches from Macbeth – watercolour and bodycolour heightened with red chalk – 38 x 32in.
(Christie's)   **$13,937   £7,700**

Follower of JAN ANTON GAREMYN – The rest on the Flight into Egypt – 62.9 x 54.6cm.
(Christie's)   **$2,614   £1,320**

PROFESSOR THEO GARVE (German, 1902–87) – View of the English church in Frankfurt am Main – signed – oil on canvas – 74 x 59cm.
(Auktionshaus Arnold) $3,906 £2,353

F. GASPAR (1889–1959) - The socialist dream – signed and dated – oil on canvas – 100 x 74cm.
(Hôtel de Ventes Horta) $2,007 £1,147

XAVIER DELLA GATTA – La Tarantella – signed and dated 1818 – pencil and watercolour – 7½ x 10in.
(Christie's) $2,462 £1,320

Follower of HENRI GASCARS – Portrait of a lady, said to be the Duchess of Burgundy, as Minerva, seated small full-length on a draped terrace – 122 x 88.5cm.
(Christie's) $6,098 £3,080

ANNIBALE GATTI (Italian, 1828–1909) - Galileo receiving John Milton – signed – oil on canvas – 99 x 85.7cm.
(Bonhams) $3,033 £1,500

GAUDEFROY

ALPHONSE GAUDEFROY (1845–1936) – In the sculptor Dalou's atelier – signed and dated 89 – oil on canvas – 61 x 50cm.
(Christie's) $21,505 £12,650

PAUL GAUGUIN (1848–1903) – Nave nave fenua 1894 – original woodcut on ivory japan paper – one of edition of 100 – 35.2 x 20.3cm.
(Lempertz) $5,389 £2,778

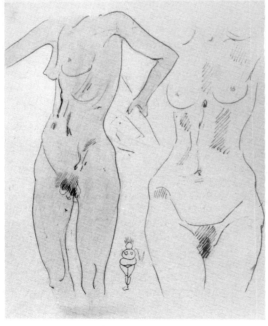

HENRI GAUDIER-BRZESKA (1891–1915) – Two nude female torsos – pen, black ink, grey wash and crayon on grey paper – 30 x 24.5cm.
(Christie's) $1,600 £825

Circle of GIOVANNI BATTISTA GAULLI called Il Baciccio (1639–1709) - Portrait of a cardinal, half length – oil on canvas – 73.5 x 60.5cm.
(Phillips) $4,224 £2,200

PAUL GAVARNI (French, 1804–1866) – The gardener – inscribed, stamped and numbered 52 – pen and brown ink, watercolour and gouache and pencil on paper – 28.3 x 21cm.
(Christie's) $3,080   £1,602

AUGUST GAY (1890–1949) – Street scene – signed – oil on board – 30.5 x 35cm.
(Butterfield & Butterfield) $9,900   £4,853

ALEXANDER GAZONAS (American, 20th Century) – Yachting – signed – watercolour on paper – 14³/₄ x 21¹/₂in.
(Skinner Inc.) $500   £268

PAUL GAVARNI (French, 1804–1866) – Going to war to kill the enemy – signed – watercolour, gouache and pen and grey ink on light tan paper – 33.3 x 20.7cm.
(Christie's) $4,180   £2,174

MABEL GEAR (b. 1900) – A West Highland terrier and two Scotties – signed – watercolour and bodycolour heightened with white – 30.4 x 45.7cm.
(Christie's) $2,090   £1,100

GEER-BERGENSTRAHLE

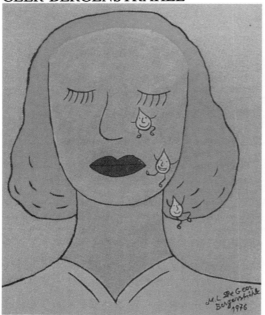

MARIE-LOUISE EKMAN DE GEER-BERGENSTRAHLE (b. 1944) – Weeping lady – signed and dated 1976 – watercolour on silk – 23 x 17cm.
(AB Stockholms Auktionsverk)   **$5,508**   **£2,884**

GEORGE GELDORP (Flemish 1553–1618) – Attributed to – Portrait of a young man with lace collar – signed with monogram – oil on canvas – 77 x 63cm.
(AB Stockholms Auktionsverk)   **$4,836**   **£2,493**

JULES VICTOR GENISSON (1805–1860) – A view in a Gothic church, looking East, with a service taking place – signed and dated 1851 – 74.5 x 94cm.
(Christie's)   **$3,353**   **£1,676**

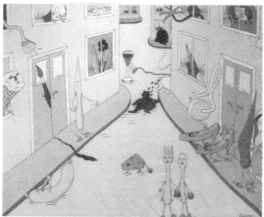

MARIE-LOUISE EKMAN DE GEER-BERGENSTRAHLE (b. 1944) – City II – signed and dated 1976 – watercolour on silk – 61 x 74cm.
(AB Stockholms Auktionsverk)   **$4,798**   **£2,512**

W.B. GELDER – On the Yorkshire coast, probably Runswick Bay – signed – 81 x 99cm.
(Phillips)   **$2,500**   **£1,250**

B. GEORGE (Attributed to Jean Louis Georges 1860–90) – Still life study of lemons and grapes beside green bottle on table top – signed and dated 1882 – inscribed verso 'Jean Louis Georges' – oil on canvas – 13½ x 11½in.
(Hobbs & Chambers)   **$3,938**   **£2,200**

GERMAN SCHOOL

SIR ERNEST GEORGE, R.A. (1839–1922) –
Halberstadt – signed and inscribed – pencil and
watercolour – 13³/4 x 9³/4in.
(Christie's) **$955 £495**

GERMAN SCHOOL – Good looking lad – bears
signature *Steinhardt 1896* – oil on canvas – 66 x 53cm.
(Hôtel de Ventes Horta) **$2,052 £1,066**

GERMAN SCHOOL 19th Century – Two putti in a
garden – oil on canvas – 109 x 160cm.
(Sotheby's) **$8,860 £4,950**

THEODORE GERARD (1829–1895) – Keeping lookout
– signed and dated 60 – oil on panel – unframed –
56 x 49.5cm.
(Christie's) **$9,702 £4,950**

GERMAN SCHOOL (late 19th century) – The
Personification of Music – oil on canvas en grisaille –
117 x 173cm.
(Christie's) **$10,780 £5,500**

GERMAN SCHOOL

GERMAN SCHOOL, 18th century – Lady with
tambourine – oil laid down on canvas – 50 x 41cm.
(Auktionshaus Arnold)   **$1,092   £584**

JEAN LEON GEROME (1824–1904) – The Iliad; and
The Odyssey – both with inscription 'Gérôme' – oil on
canvas – 98.5 x 78cm. – a pair
(Christie's)   **$65,010   £33,000**

JEAN-LEON GEROME (1824–1904) – Portrait of a girl
in a red coat – oil on panel – 16.5 x 10.5cm.
(Sotheby's)   **$5,622   £3,347**

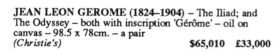

JEAN LEON GEROME (1824–1904) – Napoleon at
Cairo – oil on canvas – 32 x 41cm.
(Christie's) $28,985 £17,050

JEAN LEON GEROME (1824–1904) – Thirst – signed
and inscribed – oil on canvas – 27.5 x 46.5cm.
(Christie's) $46,750 £27,500

LEO GESTEL (1881–1941) – Gitana – signed – oil on
canvas – 120 x 104cm.
(Christie's) $137,784 £71,875

MARK GERTLER (1891–1939) – Portrait of a young
girl - signed and dated 31 - oil on canvas – 41 x 31cm.
(Christie's) $3,031 £1,815

GIOVANNI GIACOMETTI (1868–1934) – Kneeling
male nude – woodcut – 19.5 x 13.3cm.
(Galerie Koller Zürich) $4,747 £2,479

GIACOMETTI

Y. GIANNI – Fisherfolk on the beach, Vesuvius smoking beyond – signed – bodycolour – 7 x 16in.
(Christie's) $799   £440

GIOVANNI GIARDIELLO (late 19th century) – On the Neapolitan coast – signed – oil on canvas – 28.5 x 45.7cm.
(Christie's) $6,037   £3,080

GIOVANNI GIACOMETTI (1868–1934) – Giovane Madre – signed with initials and dated 1910 – oil on canvas – 65.4 x 55.9cm.
(Christie's)   **$151,690**   **£77,000**

GIOVANNI GIACOMETTI (1868–1934) – The evening toilet II – signed – indian ink on pencil – 19.5 x 18.5cm.
(Galerie Koller Zürich)   **$15,825**   **£8,264**

GIROLAMO GIANNI (b. 1837) – St. Paul's Bay, Malta – signed and dated 1872 – oil on canvas – 38 x 73.6cm.
(Christie's)   **$24,794**   **£12,650**

GIUSEPPE GIARDIELLO (late 19th century) – A street scene, Naples – signed – oil on canvas – 40 x 25cm.
(Christie's)   **$6,037**   **£3,080**

EMIL GIES (German, 19/20th century) – Portrait of a child – signed – pastel – 50 x 40cm.
(Auktionshaus Arnold) $608 £325

HARRY PHELAN GIBB (1870–1948) – Resting – oil on board – signed and dated 1914 – 20 x 15in.
(David Lay) $2,200 £1,100

CHARLES HENRY GIFFORD (American, 1839–1904) – Striped Bass on the Shores of Cuttyhunk Island, Fishing Stand Used by the Cuttyhunk Club (1865–1918) Beyond – signed and dated May 1870 – oil on canvas – 35 x 60in.
(Skinner) $25,000 £12,887

CHARLES DANA GIBSON – Conversation on a railway track – pen and ink on card – signed – unframed – 31 x 34cm.
(Bonhams) $400 £200

CHARLES DANA GIBSON (1867–1944) – Dinner party – signed – pen and brush and black ink and pencil on board – 41.8 x 70.4cm.
(Christie's) $1,650 £875

JOHN GIFFORD (19th Century) – A Gordon setter and an English setter with a game basket; and A Gordon and an English setter on the moor – both signed – oil on canvas – a pair (one illustrated) – 29.2 x 39.2cm.
(Christie's) $2,090 £1,100

GIGANTE

GIACINTO GIGANTE (Italian 1806–76) – Italian palacio with figures – signed and dated 1840 – oil on paper laid down on canvas – 43 x 33cm.
(AB Stockholms Auktionsverk)   **$6,449   £3,324**

JOAN GILCHREST – The harbour – initialled – oil on board – 14½ x 23½in.
(David Lay)   **$513   £270**

JOAN GILCHREST – Green fishing boat – oil on board – monogrammed – 15 x 20in.
(David Lay)   **$1,052   £526**

SIR JOHN GILBERT, R.A. – The Standard bearer – signed with monogram and dated 1867 – pen and ink, watercolour and gouache – 17½ x 13½in.
(Tennants)   **$500   £250**

SIR WILLIAM GEORGE GILLIES (1898–1973) – Kippford – signed and dated 1948 – pen and black ink and watercolour – 50.8 x 70.5cm.
(Christie's)   **$17,370   £9,000**

VICTOR GILSOUL (1867–1939) – Canal in Bruges
1903 – signed and dated 1903 – oil on canvas –
80 x 100cm.
(Lempertz) **$16,166 £8,333**

WILHELM GIMMI (Swiss, 1886–1965) – Woman semi
clad with dressing gown – signed and dated 1924 – oil on
canvas – 46 x 55cm.
(germann Auktionshaus) **$23,528 £12,097**

WILHELM GIMMI (Swiss, 1886–1965) – Faun and
Nymph – signed – oil on board – 16.5 x 21.2cm.
(germann Auktionshaus) **$2,987 £1,757**

ERNEST GUSTAVE GIRADOT (Exh. 1880–1904) –
Sisters – signed and dated 1871 – oil on canvas –
22 x 27in. – oval
(David Lay) **$418 £220**

CHARLES GIRON (1850–1914) – Diana and Actaeon –
signed and dated 1879 – oil on canvas – 70.2 x 114.3cm.
(Christie's) **$11,374 £6,050**

ANDRE GISSON (b. 1910) – L'Arc de Triomphe –
signed – oil on canvas – 61 x 91.5cm.
(Pinney's) **$1,871 £1,117**

NINO GIUFFRIDA – Young ballet dancers – signed –
45.6 x 56cm.
(Christie's) **$880 £440**

233

GIUSTI

GIUGLIELMO GIUSTI (Italian, 1824-c. 1916) –
Naples from Posilipos – signed, also inscribed verso –
gouache – 33 x 43.5cm.
(Phillips) **$1,831 £956**

WILLIAM JAMES GLACKENS (1870–1938) – With
the regulars at Port Tampa, Florida, U.S. Cavalry troops
taking their horses for a dash into the Gulf – signed – brush
and black ink heightened with white and pencil on grey-
green paper – 37.5 x 53.5cm.
(Christie's) **$7,700 £4,569**

WILLIAM JAMES GLACKENS (1870–1938) - A Tune
in Court – signed – charcoal, chinese white, pen and brush
and black ink en grisaille on paper – 38.7 x 34.9cm.
(Christie's) **$3,080 £1,602**

WILFRED GABRIEL DE GLEHN (1870–1951) – The
Picnic – Girls on the cliff, Gwendreath, Cornwall – oil on
canvas – bears studio stamp to stretcher – 25 x 30in.
(W.H. Lane & Son) **$17,280 £9,000**

WILLIAM JAMES GLACKENS (1870–1938) –
"Winifred Caton laughed in the face of Cary." – signed -
brush and black ink heightened with white over black
chalk on board – 33.7 x 27.9cm.
(Christie's) **$2,860 £1,697**

ALFRED AUGUSTUS GLENDENING, JUN.
(1861–1907) – From the old favourite tree – signed with
monogram and dated 1886 – oil on canvas –
30.5 x 25.4cm.
(Christie's) **$5,577 £3,300**

JOHN GLOVER (1767–1849) – View of a lake, probably Coniston Water – oil on canvas – 35 x 51½in.
(Russell, Baldwin & Bright) $28,875   £15,000

DOMENICO GNOLI (1933–1970) – Fleet – signed and dated 54 – oil on canvas – 54.4 x 81.5cm.
(Christie's) $71,898   £41,800

PIERRE GOBERT (1662–1744) – Portrait of Louise-Diane d'Orléans, Princess of Conti – oil on canvas – 137 x 100.5cm.
(Sotheby's) $42,705   £24,543

WARWICK GOBLE (circa 1880–circa 1940) – An illustration to Charles Kingley's The Water-Babies: 'Pandora and her Box' – signed – pen and black ink and watercolour heightened with white – 13¼ x 9⅛in.
(Christie's) $3,684   £1,870

ADRIEN GODIEN – The foyer of the Opera – oil on canvas – signed and dated 1900 – 93 x 114cm.
(Jean-Claude Anaf) $7,415   £3,842

JOHN WILLIAM GODWARD – "Absence makes the heart grow fonder" – signed and dated 1912 – 51½ x 31½in.
(Tennants) $160,000   £80,000

GOGH

VINCENT VAN GOGH – Tête de Paysanne – black
chalk, pen and ink and wash – 13 x 10cm.
(Sotheby's)   **$317,900   £187,000**

VINCENT VAN GOGH (1853–1890) – Sien and child
under an umbrella – signed – pencil heightened with white
on paper – 45 x 25.5cm.
(Christie's)   **$275,569   £143,750**

VINCENT VAN GOGH (1853–1890) – Jacob Meyer's
daughter – after Hans Holbein – with signature – pencil on
paper – 42.5 x 30.5cm.
(Christie's)   **$44,779   £23,359**

FRED F. GOLDBERG (20th century) – Cable cars
along Market Street – signed – oil on canvas – 76 x 102cm.
(Butterfield & Butterfield)   **$2,090   £1,024**

HENDRICK GOLTZIUS (1558–1617)– Vulcan in his forge – oil on lozenge-shaped canvas made up to a rectangle – 85 x 83cm.
(Sotheby's)   **$112,860**   **£59,400**

ROGELIO GONZALEZ – World Fair Boulevard, Seville – signed – oil on canvas – 70.2 x 101cm.
(Ritchie's)   **$460**   **£238**

FREDERICK GOODALL (English, 1822–1904) – An Arab warrior – signed with monogram – oil on canvas – 55.8 x 34cm.
(Bonhams)   **$1,618**   **£800**

FREDERICK GOODALL, R.A. (1822–1904) – An Arab beauty – signed with monogram and dated 1871 – 53.3 x 38.2cm.
(Christie's)   **$2,208**   **£1,210**

BERTRAM GOODMAN (1904–) – Fishermen going home – signed and dated 41 – gouache and pencil on brown paper – 59.7 x 52.1cm.
(Christie's)   **$1,320**   **£700**

GOODWIN

ALBERT GOODWIN (1845–1932) – Canterbury – signed and inscribed – pen and ink and watercolour with scratching out – 24.5 x 36cm.
(Phillips)   **$3,636 £1,800**

KONSTANTY GORSKI (late 19th Century) – Resting between shows – signed and dated 88 – on board – 22.8 x 38.7cm.
(Christie's)   **$3,336 £1,980**

ROBIN GOODWIN – The red stole – signed and dated 1949 on reverse – 15½ x 17¾in.
(Tennants)   **$2,400 £1,200**

GEORGE TURLAND GOOSEY – St. Ives Harbour – signed – oil on board – 8 x 10in.
(David Lay)   **$798 £420**

ROBERT JAMES GORDON (English, fl. 1871–1893) – La Liseuse – oil on canvas – signed – 91.4 x 71.8cm.
(Bonhams)   **$6,143 £3,500**

GEORGE TURLAND GOOSEY – Low tide, St. Ives – signed – oil on board – 8 x 10in.
(David Lay)   **$931 £490**

THOMAS COOPER GOTCH, R.W.A. (1854–1931) - The goose girl – signed – oil on panel – 20 x 27cm.
(Phillips)   **$15,299 £9,200**

JEAN GOUWELOOS (Belgian 1865–1934) – On the beach – signed – oil on canvas – 59 x 80cm.
(Sotheby's) $32,208   £17,600

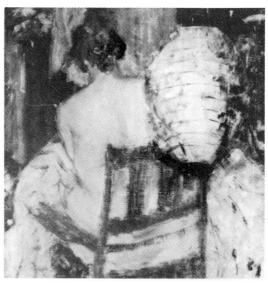

THOMAS COOPER GOTCH, R.W.A. (1854–1931) –
The message - signed – oil on canvas – tondo – 84cm. diameter
(Phillips) $249,450   £150,000

JOHN R. GRABACH (American, 1880–1981) –
Japanese Lantern – signed – oil on canvas – 19 x 18in.
(Skinner) $3,700   £1,907

COMTE HENDRIK GOUDT (1585–1630) – A man
wrapped in a cloak, holding a staff, facing right – pen and
brown ink – 196 x 115mm.
(Christie's) $3,306   £1,699

H. GRADE (late 19th Century) – Playing with Time –
signed – oil on panel – 30.5 x 25.2cm.
(Christie's) $627   £330

GRAEME

COLIN GRAEME (19th Century) – 'Don Puggles', a pug on a bear skin rug – signed, inscribed and dated 86 – oil on canvas – 25.3 x 30.4cm.
(Christie's) **$3,971 £2,090**

LUIS GRANER (1863-1929) - Party – oil on canvas – signed – 64 x 80cm.
(Duran) **$4,294 £2,225**

ANTON GRAFF (German 1736–1813) – Attributed to – Portrait of the Ambassador Bengt Sparre – oil on canvas – oval – 63 x 53cm.
(AB Stockholms Auktionsverk) **$3,940 £2,031**

DUNCAN GRANT (1885-1978) – Boy asleep on a railway carriage – oil on board – 25 x 35cm.
(Christie's) **$3,414 £1,760**

PETER GRAHAM, R.A. (1836–1921) – A rising tide – signed and dated 1899 – oil on canvas – 138.5 x 184.8cm.
(Christie's) **$7,623 £3,850**

DUNCAN GRANT – Still life of jugs and apples – signed – oil on board – 12½ x 15in.
(Riddetts) **$1,183 £650**

240

DUNCAN GRANT (1885–1978) – Psyche and Amor –
watercolour and gouache over ballpoint – 24 x 32cm.
(Phillips) $3,991 £2,400

JOSEF GRASSI, (Attributed to) – Portrait of Duchess
Maria Christine Lichnowsky (1770–1841), half length,
wearing pearls and a white headress – signed Grassy – oval
– unframed – 79.3 x 60.7cm.
(Christie's) $8,206 £4,400

DUNCAN GRANT – Reclining male nude – signed with
initials – watercolour, gouache and pencil – 58.5 x 43cm.
(Christie's) $1,210 £605

GORDON GRANT (1875–1962) – Harbour scenes with
boats: Two watercolours – both signed – both watercolour
and pencil on paper – 40 x 58.4cm.: one illustrated.
(Christie's) $3,190 £1,691

GRAU-SALA

EMILE GRAU-SALA – At the races – oil on panel –
signed and dated on reverse – 46 x 38cm.
(Jean Claude Anaf) $36,722 £21,105

HENRY PERCY GRAY (1869–1952) – Barn on a
hillside – signed and dated 1907 – watercolour on paper –
24 x 33cm.
(Butterfield & Butterfield) $6,600 £3,235

ROBERT GREENHAM, R.A. (1906–1975) – Parisian
girl – signed with initials and dated – oil on board –
19 x 14cm.
(Christie's) $7,161 £3,850

ROBERT GREENHAM (1906–1975) – Jesse Matthews
– signed and dated 34 – oil on board – 25.5 x 20cm.
(Christie's) $1,920 £990

ROBERT GREENHAM, R.A. (1906–1975) – Flowers
and apples, No. 2 – signed and dated – oil on canvas –
46 x 35.5cm.
(Christie's) $3,274 £1,760

ORLANDO GREENWOOD – Self portrait in profile – signed – unframed – 34.2 x 26.6cm.
(Christie's)   **$318**   **£165**

ROBERT GREENHAM, R.A. (1906–1975) - The Broads – signed – oil on board – 25.5 x 34.5cm.
(Christie's)   **$4,776**   **£2,860**

ORLANDO GREENWOOD – Piano solo – inscribed on reverse – 74.3 x 61.5cm.
(Christie's)   **$6,369**   **£3,300**

ROBERT GREENHAM, R.A. (1906–1975) – The Compleat Angler, Marlow – signed with initials and dated 66 – oil on canvas – 42 x 52cm.
(Christie's)   **$9,185**   **£5,500**

ORLANDO GREENWOOD (1892–1989) – Boy on a windowsill (a study for Classical Art Appreciation) – unstretched and unframed – 43.1 x 52cm.
(Christie's)   **$1,274**   **£660**

GREENWOOD

ORLANDO GREENWOOD – The little provincial –
signed and dated 1924 – 39.4 x 30.5cm.
(Christie's)   **$1,698   £880**

ORLANDO GREENWOOD – A negro couple –
45.7 x 38.1cm.
(Christie's)   **$1,486   £770**

ORLANDO GREENWOOD – Pears – signed –
45.6 x 50.7cm.
(Christie's)   **$8,067   £4,180**

WYTY GREER (fl. 1886) – A young girl in the vegetable
garden – signed and dated 1886 – unframed –
66.1 x 48.8cm.
(Christie's)   **$1,297   £770**

MARCO DE GREGORIO (1829–1876) – An Arab boy
and a negro boy smoking hookahs – signed – oil on canvas
– 16.5 x 29cm.
(Christie's)   **$10,780   £5,500**

Manner of JEAN-BAPTISTE GREUZE – The broken
pitcher – oval – 63.5 x 53.3cm.
(Christie's)   **$2,147**   **£1,078**

Follower of JEAN BAPTISTE GREUZE – Portrait of a
young girl – oil on canvas – 56 x 46.5cm.
(Sotheby's)   **$12,122**   **£6,380**

Studio of JEAN BAPTISTE GREUZE (1725–1805) – A
young girl with a basket of apples – oil on panel –
40 x 31.5cm.
(Phillips)   **$21,480**   **£12,000**

Follower of JEAN BAPTISTE GREUZE – Study of two
young girls – pastel – a delineated oval – 405 x 325mm.
(Phillips)   **$3,451**   **£1,800**

GRIGOR'EV

BORIS DMITRIEVICH GRIGOR'EV (1886–1939) –
Portrait of a woman – signed and dated 24 – pencil on
paper – 37.5 x 25.7cm.
(Christie's) $2,574 £1,320

BORIS DMITRIEVICH GRIGOR'EV (1886–1939) –
At the cabaret – signed – pencil on paper – 25.5 x 26.8cm.
(Christie's) $3,003 £1,540

ABEL GRIMMER (Active 1592–before 1619) – The
interior of the Cathedral at Antwerp – signed and dated –
oil on panel – 41 x 57.3cm.
(Sotheby's) $229,900 £121,000

**After JEAN ALEXIS GRIMOUX (French, c.
1680–1733/40)** – Two portraits: A Boy Pilgrim and A Girl
pilgrim (Mme. Dangeville) – unsigned – both identified on
presentation plaques – oil on canvas – 32 x 25in.
(Skinner) $1,500 £773

ATKINSON GRIMSHAW (1836–1893) – In the golden
gloaming – signed and dated 1883+ – oil on canvas –
50.8 x 76.2cm.
(Christie's) $126,324 £63,800

GUNTA LIEPINA GRIVA (b. 1942) – The white feather – signed with monogram – oil on canvas – 60 x 50cm. *(Jean-Claude Anaf)* **$1,180 £616**

GEORGES GROEGAERT – The musical hour – signed – oil on panel – 45 x 38cm. *(Hôtel de Ventes Horta)* **$13,770 £7,869**

WILLIAM H.C. GROOME – The best of friends must part – signed – oil on canvas – 76 x 102cm. *(Sotheby's)* **$18,317 £10120**

GROOT

A. DE GROOT (20th Century) – A Dutch canal town in winter – signed – on panel – 57.2 x 88.9cm.
(Christie's) $4,819 £2,860

JOHANN FRIEDRICH GROOTH called Iwan Fjodorwitsch (German/Russian 1717–1801) – Russian greyhound – signed and dated 1794 – oil on canvas – 70 x 90cm.
(AB Stockholms Auktionsverk) $2,598 £1,339

JAN HENDRIK VAN GROOTVELD (1808–1855) – A maid serving a glass of wine to a sportsman in an inn by candlelight – signed and dated 1834 – oil on panel – 29 x 34cm.
(Christie's) $3,353 £1,676

WILLIAM GROPPER (1897–1977) – Study for "The Student" – signed – pastel on cream paper laid down on board – 51.4 x 35.6cm.
(Christie's) $1,650 £875

GEORGE GROSZ (1893–1959) – People in the coffee house – signed and dated 1918 – watercolour and black ink on paper – 57.1 x 43.8cm.
(Christie's) $368,390 £187,000

GRUNEWALD

HEINRICH FERDINAND GRUNEWALD (German 1802–49) – Pan teaching Bacchus to play the flute – signed – oil on canvas – 38 x 49cm.
(AB Stockholms Auktionsverk) $3,940   £2,031

GEORGE GROSZ (1892–1959) – Berlin street scene – stamped George Grosz Berlin 1930 – black ink, watercolour and thinned oil on paper – 59.7 x 45.7cm.
(Christie's) $56,342   £28,600

ISAAC GRUNEWALD (1889–1946) – Amaryllis – signed – oil on panel – 46 x 38cm.
(AB Stockholms Auktionsverk) $6,574   £3,442

MARY GROVES (fl. 1884–1904) – Revelation – signed – 101.6 x 66.1cm.
(Christie's) $4,417   £2,420

ISAAC GRUNEWALD (1889–1946) – Locks, view of Stockholm with boats – signed – oil on canvas – 54 x 46cm.
(AB Stockholms Auktionsverk) $31,093   £16,279

EMILE ALBERT GRUPPE – A harbour scene, with
moored vessels, in Venezuela – signed – oil on canvas –
24⅝ x 29⅝in.
(Geering & Colyer)   **$2,288   £1,250**

EMILE ALBERT GRUPPE (American, 1896–1978) –
Smith Cove, Gloucester – signed "Emile A. Gruppe" – oil
on canvas – 18 x 20in.
(Skinner Inc.)   **$2,100   £1,126**

EMILE ALBERT GRUPPE (American, 1896–1978) -
Gill Netters – signed – oil on canvas – 25 x 25in.
(Skinner Inc.)   **$4,500   £2,413**

G.S. – Young redhead – signed with monogram – oil on
canvas – 80 x 70cm.
(Hôtel de Ventes Horta)   **$12,381   £6,129**

GUERINO GUARDABASSI – In the campagna; and On
the steps – both signed and inscribed – pencil and
watercolour – a pair – 20⅞ x 15in.: one illustrated.
(Christie's)   **$2,462   £1,320**

GIOVANNI FRANCESCO GUERCINO (Italian 1591–1666) – Manner of – The repentant Magdalen – oil on canvas – 178 x 167cm.
(AB Stockholms Auktionsverk)   **$12,897** **£6,648**

Attributed to JULES GUERIN (American, b. 1866) – Sheep in a barn – signed – oil on canvas – 8 x 10in.
(Selkirk's)   **$375** **£184**

M. GUILLAIN – Solitude – signed – oil on canvas – 82 x 130cm.
(Galerie Moderne)   **$2,112** **£1,106**

GEN. GIOVANNI FRANCESCO BARBIERI GUERCINO (1591–1666) – In the manner of – St. Hieronymus reading – oil on copper – 18.5 x 24cm.
(Lempertz)   **$6,953** **£3,973**

ARMAND-MARIE GUERIN (French, 1913–1983) – Two barges – signed – oil on artist's board – 46 x 55cm.
(germann Auktionshaus)   **$925** **£543**

ARMAND GUILLAUMIN (1841–1924) – A portrait of Mr. Martinez – signed – pastel on paper – 43.5 x 35cm.
(Christie's)   **$10,334** **£5,391**

GUINOVART

JOSE GUINOVART (b. 1927) – Che in the guerillas – signed – oil on panel – 44 x 40cm.
(Duran) **$5,054 £2,639**

KARL GUNSCHMANN (German, b. 1895) – Semi nude with fruit – signed with monogram and dated 1935 – oil on board – 135 x 111cm.
(Auktionshaus Arnold) **$7,893 £4,221**

SIR HERBERT JAMES GUNN, R.A. (1893–1964) – Sunbathers – oil on canvas – 35.5 x 46cm.
(Christie's) **$58,784 £35,200**

FRANCISCUS GYSBRECHTS (active c. 1674) – Still life of a covered chalice, a shell and a book in a stone niche with an artist's palette and the reverse of a painting – signed – oil on canvas – 95 x 73cm.
(Phillips) $10,956   £5,500

FELICE GUSSONI (fl. 1885–1908) – Girl with flowers – signed – oil on canvas – 100 x 63cm.
(Finarte Casa d'Aste) $4,478   £2,336

Follower of PIETER GYSELS (1621–1690) – A carriage on a village road by a inn, a windmill beyond – oil on panel – 18.9 x 21.3cm.
(Christie's) $15,246   £7,700

ROBERT GWATHMEY (1903–1988) – Tending the fields – signed – oil on canvas – 41 x 36cm.
(Christie's) $5,280   £2,798

CARL HAAG (1820–1915) – La illah ill allah – signed – inscribed and dated 1875– pencil and watercolour with gum arabic on paper – 46.4 x 89.6cm.
(Christie's) $16,456   £9,680

HAGBORG

AUGUST HAGBORG (1852–1921) – 'Haste', coastal
scene with crew and lifeboat – signed – oil on canvas –
51 x 85cm.
(AB Stockholms Auktionsverk) $40,125   £20,683

KARL HAGEDORN (1889–1969) – Home Defence –
signed and dated 40 – oil on panel – 36.5 x 76cm.
(Christie's) $2,881   £1,485

KARL HAGEDORN (1889–1969) – A wash stand – oil
on canvas-board – 52 x 44.5cm.
(Christie's) $16,533   £9,900

M. HAGEMANS (Belgian, 1852–1917) – Towards the
meadow – signed – watercolour on paper – 46 x 31cm.
(Hôtel de Ventes Horta) $2,839   £1,475

KARL HAGEDORN (1889–1969) – In Training – signed
and dated 40 – oil on panel – 30.5 x 76cm.
(Christie's) $2,881   £1,485

MAURICE HAGEMANS (Belgian 1852–1917) –
Grazing – watercolour on paper – signed
(Hôtel de Ventes Horta) $2,794   £1,440

F. HALL – Half length portrait of a young country boy –
signed – oil – 24 x 17in.
(G.A. Key)   **$107   £55**

GEORGE HENRY HALL (1825–1913) – Still life with
watermelon – signed and dated 1868 – oil on panel –
22.2 x 28cm.
(Christie's)   **$15,400   £8,008**

THOMAS P. HALL – The lesson – signed with
monogram and dated 1856 – oil on canvas – unframed –
33 x 43cm.
(Sotheby's)   **$7,964   £4,400**

SAMUEL BARUCH HALLE (1824–1889) – Mother's
pet – signed and dated 1860 – oil on canvas –
125.4 x 100.4cm.
(Christie's)   **$20,449   £12,100**

A. HALLET (Belgian, 1890–1959) – The Hogebridge at
Malines – signed – oil on canvas – 70 x 80cm.
(Hôtel de Ventes Horta)   **$8,204   £4,262**

ANDRE HALLET (1890–1959) – Main square in
Brussels, 1931 – signed – oil on board – 45.3 x 37.8cm.
(Hôtel de Ventes Horta)   **$10,163   £5,031**

HAMILTON

LETITIA MAY HAMILTON, R.H.A. (1878–1964) –
Errisbeg, Roundstone – signed with initials – oil on canvas
– 51 x 61cm.
(Phillips)   **$3,825 £2,300**

SIGMUND WALTER HAMPEL (Austrian 1868–1949)
– A girl reading – signed and dated – oil on panel –
37 x 48cm.
(Sotheby's)   **$26,169 £14,300**

ADRIAEN HANNEMAN (1601–1671) – Portrait of a
young girl, seated holding a bread roll in her hand – on
canvas – oval – 73 x 59.5cm.
(Phillips)   **$32,220 £18,000**

JOHANN HAMZA (Austrian 1850–1927) – The
christening – signed and inscribed – oil on panel –
45 x 36cm.
(Sotheby's)   **$18,117 £9,900**

JOSEF THEODOR HANSEN (1848–1912) – The
entrance to the Senato, Doge's Palace, Venice – signed and
dated 1881 – oil on panel – 32.4 x 23.8cm.
(Christie's)   **$12,505 £6,380**

FREDERICK DANIEL HARDY (1826–1911) – The first sewing lesson – signed and dated 1889 – oil on panel – 17.8 x 14cm.
(Christie's) $3,718 £2,200

JOSEF THEODORE HANSEN (1848–1912) – Conseil Salen, Stockholm – signed – inscribed and dated - oil on canvas – 36 x 54cm.
(Christie's) $15,334 £9,020

Follower of PIETER HARDIME – Tulips, roses, narcissi and other flowers in a vase on a ledge – 76.2 x 63.5cm.
(Christie's) $11,000 £5,500

HEYWOOD HARDY (1843–1933) – The peacemaker – signed – oil on canvas – 63.8 x 48.2cm.
(Christie's) $29,722 £15,400

HARRIS

EDWIN HARRIS (1855–1906) – The fisherman – oil on canvas – 37 x 29cm.
(Christie's) $3,490 £2,090

WILLIAM E. HARRIS (English, 19th Century) – 'Harvest Time, Dorney, near Windsor – oil on canvas – signed and dated '98 – 50.8 x 76.2cm.
(Bonhams) $7,898 £4,500

EDWIN HARRIS (1855–1906) – Head of a fisherman – oil on panel – signed
(David Lay) $1,900 £950

JOHN CYRIL HARRISON – Yellowhammers, an autumn landscape – signed – watercolour - 9¹/₂ x 6¹/₂in.
(G.A. Key) $2,242   £1,150

J K HARVEY (English, circa 1800) – Interior with woman and washtub – signed – oil on canvas – 51 x 41cm.
(AB Stockholms Auktionsverk) $5,374   £2,770

MARSDEN HARTLEY (1877–1943) – Bird of paradise – signed – oil on canvas – 50.8 x 61cm.
(Christie's) $33,000   £17,160

GERTRUDE HARVEY – Flowers in a bowl – oil on board – signed – 15¹/₂ x 17¹/₂in.
(David Lay) $1,061   £580

JOHN RABONE HARVEY (fl. 1866–1933) – A smooth-haired Fox Terrier on a sofa – signed – oil on canvas – 53.3 x 43.2cm.
(Christie's) $3,553   £1,870

HAROLD HARVEY – Sea pinks – signed and dated 1913 – inscribed on the reverse with title – oil on canvas – 35 x 16cm.
(Phillips)   **$59,868   £36,000**

FREDERICK CHILDE HASSAM (1859-1935)—The mantle piece—signed and dated 1912 on the reverse—oil on panel—19 x 25.5cm.
(Christie's)   **$28,600 £15,158**

ANTOINETTE-CECILE-HORTENSE
HAUDEBOURT née LESCOT (1784–1845) – The two
sisters – trace of signature – oil on canvas – 161 x 192.5cm.
(Sotheby's) $29,284   £16,734

FREDERICK CHILDE HASSAM, (1859–1935) - The
El, New York – signed and dated 1894 – oil on canvas –
45.7 x 35.5cm.
(Christie's) $528,000   £274,560

JO KOSTER-VAN HATTUM (1869–1944) – A view of a
farmyard with a girl in costume, Staphorst – signed and
dated 1912 – oil on canvas – 34.5 x 45.5cm.
(Christie's) $12,401   £6,469

HENRI HAYDEN – Nature morte aux fruits et pichet
bleu – signed and dated 1915 – oil on canvas –
55.5 x 46cm.
(Sotheby's) $56,100   £33,000

HAYGREEN

PHILIP HAYGREEN – Trafalgar Square – signed – oil on panel – 24 x 34cm.
(Christie's)   **$11,940 £7,150**

GEORGE A. HAYS (1854–1945) – Team of oxen – oil on canvas – signed – 35¼ x 61in.
(Bruce D. Collins)   **$4,000 £2,162**

JOSEPH HEICKE – The ambush – signed – glazed watercolour on paper – 40 x 51cm.
(Hôtel de Ventes Horta)   **$1,722 £984**

CORNELIS DE HEEM (1631–1695) – A still life on a ledge covered by a blue cloth, on which rests a roemer, oysters, a lobster, a bunch of white grapes and a silver pepper pot – signed – oil on copper – 36 x 44.5cm.
(Phillips)   **$318,720 £160,000**

JOHANNES HERMANUS VAN DER HEIJDEN (1825–1907) – A view in Amsterdam with a carriage on a canal – signed – oil on panel – 26.5 x 37cm.
(Christie's)   **$4,560 £2,280**

FERDINAND HEILBUTH (1826-1889) – The boating party – signed and dated 85 – oil on panel – 50.8 x 73.6cm. *(Christie's)* **$37,400 £22,000**

JOHANN ADALBERT HEINE (b. 1850) – Merry company – signed and inscribed – oil on panel – 21.9 x 27cm. *(Christie's)* **$6,204 £3,300**

KARL ADAM HEINISCH (1847–1923) – A winter landscape with a shepherdess and sheep by cottages – signed – oil on panel – unframed – 15.2 x 27.3cm. *(Christie's)* **$9,918 £5,060**

JOSEPH HEINZ, Follower of – A woman's bath-house – oil on panel – 55.7 x 78.1cm. *(Christie's)* **$14,386 £7,150**

PAUL CESAR HELLEU (1859–1927) – Portrait of Annette, bust length wearing a white hat – signed and inscribed – pastel on canvas – 64.8 x 52.1cm. *(Christie's)* **$97,240 £57,200**

PAUL-CESAR HELLEU (1859–1927) – The Duchess of Marlborough seated in a chair – signed and inscribed by the sitter – coloured chalks on paper – 49 x 36cm. *(Christie's)* **$10,835 £5,500**

HELLEU

PAUL CESAR HELLEU (1859–1927) – Madame Helleu à Fladbury chez John Singer Sargent – signed – oil on canvas – 54 x 73cm.
(Christie's) **$145,860 £85,800**

BARTHOLOMEUS VAN DER HELST (Dutch 1612–70) – Portrait of a man – signed and dated 1655 – oil on panel – 72 x 57cm.
(AB Stockholms Auktionsverk) **$5,552 £2,862**

BARTHOLOMEUS VAN DER HELST (Dutch 1612–70) – Follower of – Portrait of a man with helmet – oil on canvas – 89 x 72cm.
(AB Stockholms Auktionsverk) **$3,583 £1,847**

**Circle of JAN SANDERS VAN HEMESSEN (c.
1504–1566) after Lorenzo Lotto** – Christ and the woman
taken in adultery – oil on panel – 113 x 135cm.
(Phillips) $5,976   £3,000

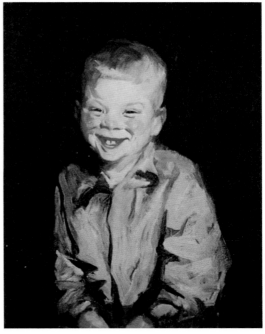

B. BENEDICT HEMY – Holy Island Castle, with sailing
vessel docked – signed – oil on canvas – 11½ x 17½in.
(Hobbs & Chambers) $501   £280

ROBERT HENRI (1865–1929) – Jobie, the laughing boy
– signed – oil on canvas – 61 x 50.5cm.
(Christie's) $55,000   £28,600

FRANTS HENNINGSEN (Danish 1850–1908) – Woman
carrying kindling – signed with monogram and dated 85 –
pastel – 60 x 50cm.
(AB Stockholms Auktionsverk) $3,224   £1,662

ROBERT HENRI (1865-1929) – Little girl in red stripes
– signed – oil on canvas – 61.3 x 50.8cm.
(Christie's) $66,000   £34,320

ROBERT HENRI (1865–1929) – Boy with green cap
(Chico) – signed – oil on canvas – 61 x 51cm.
(Christie's)   **$88,000   £45,760**

AUGUSTE HERBIN (1882–1960) – The harbour – signed
– oil on canvas – 100 x 73cm.
(Galerie Koller Zürich)   **$126,612   £66,116**

ERNST HENSELER (b. 1852) – The Rendez-vous –
signed – oil on board – 49.5 x 71.2cm.
(Christie's)   **$17,248   £8,800**

WILSON HEPPLE (1854–1937) – The Artist's kittens –
signed – oil on canvas – 45.7 x 35.6cm.
(Christie's)   **$3,553   £1,870**

AUGUSTE HERBIN (1882–1960) – Countryside –
signed – oil on panel – 46.5 x 27cm.
(Christie's)   **$42,713   £22,281**

KORNEL HERNADI-HERZEL – Flirtation in the inn –
signed and dated – oil on canvas – 129 x 96.5cm.
(Sotheby's) **$11,814 £6,600**

Follower of JOHN FREDERICK HERRING, JNR. –
Horses, chickens, ducks and a goat in a farmyard – with
signature – oil on board – oval – 43.2 x 50.8cm.
(Christie's) **$1,424 £715**

JOHN FREDERICK HERRING, SEN. (1795–1865) –
Two Lurchers – signed with initials and dated 1851 – oil
on board – 25.3 x 34.3cm.
(Christie's) **$8,360 £4,400**

DANIEL HERNANDEZ – Eugenie and Père Grandet –
signed – pen, black ink and grey wash heightened with
bodycolour and white – 9³/₄ x 7¹/₂in.
(Christie's) **$97 £55**

ALBERT HERTER (b. 1871), American school – Girl in
kimono – signed and dated 74 – oil on canvas –
54.5 x 50cm.
(Sotheby's) **$9,371 £5,578**

HEYER

ARTHUR HEYER (1872–1931) – White Persian kittens with a bee – signed – oil on canvas – 50.8 x 71.2cm.
(Christie's)   **$4,598 £2,420**

A.J. HEYMANS (Belgian, 1839–1921) – The pond – signed – oil on canvas – 81 x 146cm.
(Hôtel de Ventes Horta)   **$9,467 £4,918**

GEORGE ELGAR HICKS (1824–1914) – Portrait of the Duchess of St. Albans, seated half length, with her son – signed and dated 1875 – oil on canvas – 91.5 x 71cm.
(Christie's)   **$32,505 £16,500**

GEORGE ELGAR HICKS (English 1824–1914) – The General Post Office (one minute to six) – signed and dated 1860 – oil on canvas – – 89 x 135cm.
(Sotheby's)   **$418,110 £231,000**

DEREK HILL (b. 1916) – Hunting in Limerick – oil on canvas – 76 x 115cm.
(Christie's)   **$6,980**   **£4,180**

TRISTRAM HILLIER, R.A. (b. 1905) – Hulks on a Portuguese beach – signed and dated 67 - oil on canvas – 51 x 61cm.
(Christie's)   **$14,696**   **£8,800**

TRISTRAM HILLIER, R.A. (1905-1983) – Spanish landscape – signed – oil on panel – 13 x 18cm.
(Phillips)   **$4,324**   **£2,600**

ROGER HILTON (1911–1975) – Untitled, 1970 – signed and dated 70 – oil on canvas – 140 x 153cm.
(Christie's)   **$53,350**   **£27,500**

CLAUDE RAGUET HIRST (1855–1942) – Poems of William Cowper – signed and inscribed – oil on canvas – 20.5 x 25.5cm.
(Christie's)   **$30,800**   **£16,324**

HITCHENS

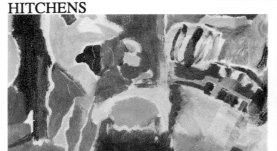

IVON HITCHENS (1893–1979) – Interior, red sunlight – signed – inscribed and dated on a label on the stretcher 1960 – oil on canvas – 56 x 84cm.
(Christie's)   **$44,814   £23,100**

FRANCES HODGKINS (1869–1947) – The bridge – signed and dated 1940 – gouache – 45 x 53.5cm.
(Phillips)   **$16,630   £10,000**

GEORGE HITCHCOCK (1850–1913) – A Normandy farmhouse – oil on canvas – 40.3 x 56cm.
(Christie's)   **$18,700   £9,724**

FERDINAND HODLER (1853–1918) – Die Cempfindung I: Study – signed – gouache, pastel and pencil on paper – 34.9 x 32.4cm.
(Christie's)   **$122,265   £71,500**

OLLE HJORTZBERG (1872–1959) – Still life with yellow rose in a ceramic vase – signed and dated 52 – oil on canvas – 64 x 49cm.
(AB Stockholms Auktionsverk)   **$10,482   £5,488**

ABRAHAM VAN DER HOEF (Dutch, 17th C.) – Cavalry engagement – oil on panel – 48 x 63.5cm.
(Hôtel de Ventes Horta)   **$4,346   £2,240**

VAN DER HOEF – The ambush – faintly signed – oil on panel – 32 x 43cm.
(Hôtel de Ventes Horta) **$1,435 £820**

R.A. HOGER (1876–1928) – Schubert sitting in a park with other figures – signed – oil on canvas – 35½ x 48½in.
(Du Mouchelles) **$1,500 £761**

ROBERT HOGFELDT (1894–1986) – Antique dealing – signed – oil on canvas – 73 x 60cm.
(AB Stockholms Auktionsverk) **$2,754 £1,442**

HEINRICH HOERLE (1895–1936) – Woman – signed with monogram – oil on wood – 70 x 46cm.
(Lempertz) **$44,459 £22,917**

JONAS HOFFMANN (1731–1780) – Hercules freeing Promethus – signed and dated 1770 – oil on canvas – 193 x 127cm.
(Sotheby's) **$29,117 £16,734**

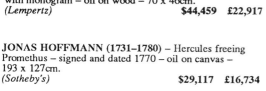

ROBERT HOGFELDT (1894–1986) – Jesus in the Temple – signed – oil on canvas – 60 x 73cm.
(AB Stockholms Auktionsverk) **$2,221 £1,163**

271

HOLBEIN

After HANS HOLBEIN II – Portrait of Nicholas Kratzer
– oil on panel – 81.8 x 63.5cm.
(Christie's) **$5,976 £2,970**

CARL HOLSØE – A lady with a tray – signed – oil on
canvas – 37 x 28cm.
(Sotheby's) **$7,482 £4,180**

HIPPOLYTE-DOMINIQUE HOLFELD – Three
children playing (Possibly known as Family Prayers) –
signed and dated 1852 – oil on canvas – oval –
65.7 x 81.3cm.
(Ritchie's) **$1,470 £762**

JOHN HOLLAND JNR. (English, 1830–1886) – Young
faggot gatherers – signed – oil on canvas – unframed –
35.6 x 53.3cm.
(Bonhams) **$1,517 £750**

CARL HOLSØE (1863–1935) – A woman reading in an
interior – signed – oil on canvas – 57.2 x 50.7cm.
(Christie's) **$26,004 £13,200**

CARL HOLSØE (1863–1935) – A woman reading in an
interior – signed and dated 02 – oil on panel –
31.7 x 41cm.
(Christie's) **$16,544 £8,800**

HOOK

MELCHIOR DE HONDECOETER (1636–1695) – An
assembly of birds in a park setting; an owl holding a scroll
– signed – oil on canvas – 153 x 188cm.
(Sotheby's) $647,900   £341,000

CARL HOLSOE (Danish 1863–1935) – Interior with old
woman and tray – signed – oil on panel – 46 x 56cm.
(AB Stockholms Auktionsverk) $4,836   £2,493

Circle of MELCHIOR DE HONDECOETER
(1636–1695) – Poultry in a farmyard – unframed –
124.3 x 162.6cm.
(Christie's) $8,712   £4,400

WILLIAM HOLYOAKE, R.B.A. (1834–1894) – The
lover's vows – signed – oil on canvas – 101.5 x 122cm.
(Christie's) $25,476   £13,200

BERNARD DE HOOG (1867–1943) – The little family –
signed – oil on canvas – 101.6 x 120.7cm.
(Christie's) $24,816   £13,200

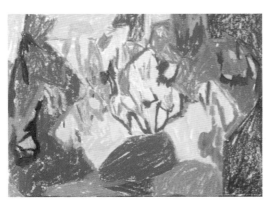

ADOLF HOLZEL (1853–1934) – Metaphorical
composition – pastel on paper – 37 x 70cm.
(Lempertz) $12,125   £6,250

JAMES CLARKE HOOK, R.A. (1817–1907) – The
fisherman's return – signed – oil on canvas –
64.8 x 100.3cm.
(Christie's) $5,663   £2,860

HOREMANS

JAN JOSEPH HOREMANS (Flemish 1682–1759) –
Attributed to – Interior with figures round a sickbed – oil
on canvas – 50 x 57cm.
(AB Stockholms Auktionsverk)   **$6,270   £3,232**

JOHN CALLCOTT HORSLEY, R.A. – The poet's
theme – indistinctly signed – oil on canvas – 136 x 107cm.
(Sotheby's)   **$26,879   £14,850**

GEORGE W. HORLOR (fl. 1849–1891) – The Lords of
the Isles – signed and dated 1881 – oil on canvas –
unframed – 33 x 41.9cm.
(Christie's)   **$9,148   £4,620**

WILLIAM B. HOUGH (Exh. 1857–1894) – Still life of
raspberries – signed – watercolour and bodycolour –
25.5 x 36cm. and companion Strawberries, a pair.
(Phillips)   **$8,234   £4,600**

GEORGE W. HORLOR (English circa 1800) – Calves,
pony and a dog with sheep in a highland landscape –
signed – oil on canvas – 66 x 102cm.
(AB Stockholms Auktionsverk)   **$1,882   £970**

J.J. HOVENER (c. 1900) – On the beach, Ostend –
signed – on canvas laid down on panel – unframed –
59 x 79cm.
(Christie's)   **$4,448   £2,640**

KEN HOWARD, A.R.A. (b. 1932) – Sara in the studio -
signed – oil on canvas – 40.5 x 51cm.
(Christie's)   **$3,122**   **£1,870**

JAN VAN HUCHTENBURG (1647–1733) – A cavalry
skirmish – 57.5 x 74.5cm.
(Christie's)   **$10,454**   **£5,280**

KEN HOWARD, A.R.A. (b. 1932) – Danny and the
Omani coffee pot – signed – oil on canvas – 122 x 102cm.
(Christie's)   **$6,402**   **£3,300**

KARL HUCK (1876–1926) – A hunting falcon in a
mountainous landscape (recto); and a Deer in a wooded
landscape (verso) – signed recto – oil on canvas –
unframed – 213 x 190.5cm.
(Christie's)   **$10,780**   **£5,500**

KEN HOWARD, A.R.A. (b. 1932) – Seated nude in the
studio – signed and dated 86 - oil on canvas – 48 x 58.5cm.
(Christie's)   **$3,674**   **£2,200**

WILLIAM HUGGINS (1820–1884) – A lion in a jungle
landscape – signed and dated 1867 – oil on canvas –
71.1 x 91.5cm.
(Christie's)   **$11,154**   **£6,600**

HUGHES

EDWARD ROBERT HUGHES (1851–1914) – Portrait of Hilda Virtue Tebbs, bust length, looking to the right – signed, inscribed and dated 1897 – red chalk – 24 x 20in.
(Christie's) **$7,218 £3,740**

ARTHUR HUGHES (English 1832–1915) – Good night – signed – oil on canvas – 99 x 64.8cm.
(Sotheby's) **$99,550 £55,000**

Circle of PIERRE-NICOLAS HUILLIOT (1674–1751) – A sculpted urn adorned with flowers, silver-gilt platters and ewers and musical instruments in a stone recess – a trompe-l'oeil overdoor – unframed – 50.4 x 213cm.
(Christie's) **$8,712 £4,400**

FREDERICK WILLIAM HULME (1816–1884) – Bettws-y-Coed, North Wales – signed – oil on canvas – 51 x 71cm.
(Christie's) **$10,454 £5,280**

FRIEDENSREICH HUNDERTWASSER (Austrian, b. 1928) – The city is a woman's coiffure, 1962 – signed and dated – mixed media on paper laid down on canvas– 65 x 50cm.
(germann Auktionshaus) **$106,111 £55,555**

EDGAR HUNT – A rooster and a hen with their chicks – signed and dated '09 – oil on canvas – 20.5 x 25.5cm.
(Sotheby's) $10,751 £5,940

CHARLES HUNT (1803–1877) – The rival suitors – signed and dated 1876 – oil on canvas – 91.5 x 148cm.
(Christie's) **$10,615 £5,500**

CHARLES HUNT JNR. (fl. 1880–1900) – Mishap at the crossroads – signed and dated 1880 – oil on canvas – 102.3 x 151.7cm.
(Christie's) $44,616 £26,400

EDGAR HUNT – Chickens and a goat; Chickens, a pony and a donkey – a pair – both signed and one dated 1915 – oil on canvas – each 28 x 38cm.
(Sotheby's) $33,847 £18,700

CHARLES HUNT, JUN. (d. 1900) – The game of draughts – signed and dated 91 – oil on canvas – 51 x 76cm.
(Christie's) $24,414 £12,650

EDGAR HUNT (1876–1953) – Chickens and goats feeding in a farmyard – signed and dated 1944 – oil on canvas – 28.6 x 38.7cm.
(Christie's) $22,308 £13,200

WALTER HUNT – Calves by a pond – signed and dated 1919 – oil on canvas – 51 x 76cm.
(Sotheby's) $27,874 £15,400

HUNT

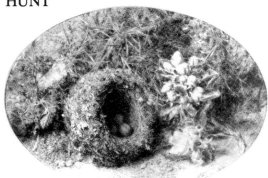

WILLIAM HENRY HUNT (1790–1864) – Apple blossom and a bird's nest on a mossy bank – watercolour heightened with white – oval – 8¹/₂ x 12in.
(Christie's)   **$2,167**   **£1,100**

Attributed to WILLIAM HUNT (American, 1824–1879) – Sorting grain/An interior genre scene – indistinctly signed – oil on canvas – 25³/₄ x 21in.
(Skinner Inc.)   **$300**   **£161**

GEORGE SHERWOOD HUNTER – Newlyn, George V's Coronation Procession on the new road returning from Penzance – inscribed on the stretcher, unframed – 30.4 x 45.7cm.
(Christie's)   **$2,090**   **£1,045**

GEORGE SHERWOOD HUNTER (c1850–1919) – Enjoying life, Volendam, Zuider Zee – signed and inscribed on the reverse – 45.7 x 30.4cm.
(Christie's)   **$4,840**   **£2,420**

GEORGE SHERWOOD HUNTER – H.M.S. Renard and Torpedo-Catcher H.M.S. Ferret off Newlyn pier – signed with initials – inscribed and dated 13 June 1896 – unframed – 20.2 x 26.7cm.
(Christie's)   **$2,090**   **£1,045**

GEORGE SHERWOOD HUNTER (c1850–1919) –
Figures on a beach, Brittany – unframed – 32.4 x 45.7cm.
(Christie's) $8,800 £4,400

LOUIS BOSWORTH HURT (1856–1929) – Through the
glen: The Mantle of Winter (Glencoe, Argyle) – signed –
oil on canvas – 61 x 101.6cm.
(Christie's) $39,204 £19,800

LOUIS BOSWORTH HURT (1856–1929) – A rest by
the way – signed and dated 1892 – oil on canvas –
92.5 x 77cm.
(Christie's) $19,602 £9,900

ROBERT GEMMELL HUTCHISON – 'A feed of
carrots' – gouache – signed – 16.5 x 21.6cm.
(Bonhams) $4,044 £2,400

ROBERT GEMMELL HUTCHISON, R.S.A., R.S.W., R.O.I. (1855–1936) – Reflections – signed – oil on canvas – 63.5 x 76.8cm.
(Christie's)   **$30,880 £16,000**

FILIPPO INDONI (Italian 19th Century) – Courtship in the farmyard – signed and inscribed – watercolour – 100 x 66.5cm.
(Sotheby's)   **$7,045 £3,850**

FILIPI INDONI (Italian 19th Century) – A young peasant couple by the temple of Vesta, Rome – signed – watercolour – 73.5 x 53cm.
(Sotheby's)   **$3,019 £1,650**

JAMES DICKSON INNES (1887–1914) – The Corbières Mountains – signed and indistinctly inscribed on the reverse – oil on panel – 28 x 37.5cm.
(Christie's) $15,015   £7,700

EUGENE ISABEY (French 1803–86) – Streetscene – signed and dated 1859 – oil on canvas – 115 x 81cm.
(AB Stockholms Auktionsverk) $11,644   £6,002

LOUIS-GABRIEL-EUGENE ISABEY (1803–1886) – Portrait of a lady, bust length – stamped – oil on canvas – 72.4 x 61.5cm.
(Christie's) $11,858   £6,050

LOUIS-GABRIEL-EUGENE ISABEY (1803–1866) – Cliffs near Etretat – watercolour heightened with gouache – 247 x 335mm.
(Sotheby's) $13,833   £6,916

LOUIS-GABRIEL-EUGENE ISABEY (1803–1866) – A Normandy cottage and gate – watercolour – 320 x 238mm.
(Sotheby's) $4,574   £2,287

ISABEY

ISAAC ISRAELS (1865–1934) – Women dancing at a café, Amsterdam – signed – 80 x 75cm.
(Christie's)   **$241,400   £120,700**

LOUIS-GABRIEL-EUGENE ISABEY (1803–1866) –
Sketch for a farm in Normandy – watercolour –
255 x 175mm.
(Sotheby's)   **$3,570   £1,785**

KARL ISAKSON (1878–1922) – Still life with flowers in
vase - oil on canvas – 67 x 53cm.
(AB Stockholms Auktionsverk)   **$8,175   £4,280**

ISAAC ISRAELS (1865–1934) – Women in the sewing
studio of Pacquin, Paris – signed – 60 x 48.5cm.
(Christie's)   **$48,280   £24,140**

ISAAC ISRAELS (1865–1934) – A girl, full length, dressed in a red bathing suit at the beach – signed – oil on canvas – 50 x 40cm.
(Christie's)   **$41,340   £21,565**

JOSEF ISRAELS (Dutch 1824–1911) – Making pancakes – signed – watercolour – 33.5 x 18cm.
(Sotheby's)   **$9,058   £4,950**

ISAAC ISRAELS (1865–1934) – A girl in white at the Boulevard – black chalk and pastel on paper – 56 x 38cm.
(Christie's)   **$55,114   £28,750**

ITALIAN SCHOOL, 19th/20th Century – The Evening's Entertainment – signed Augusta Daini – oil on canvas – 21½ x 29in.
(Skinner)   **$2,500   £1,289**

ITALIAN SCHOOL

ITALIAN SCHOOL, 17th century – Angelica & Medoro – oil on canvas – 200 x 270cm.
(Finarte) **$13,762 £7,243**

ITALIAN SCHOOL, 18th century – Portrait of a gentleman – oil on canvas – 84 x 73cm. – one of a pair.
(Finarte) **$6,705 £3,456**

ITALIAN SCHOOL, 17th century – Portrait of a gentleman – oil on canvas – 48 x 37cm.
(Finarte) **$5,182 £2,727**

ITALIAN SCHOOL

ITALIAN SCHOOL 19th/20th Century – A view of Santa Lucia, Naples – titled on the border – gouache – 42.5 x 64.5cm.
(Sotheby's)   **$5,636**   **£3,080**

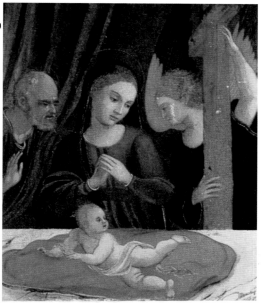

ITALIAN SCHOOL – The Holy Family with an Angel presenting the Cross – oil on panel – 52.1 x 44.4cm.
(Christie's)   **$3,267**   **£1,650**

ITALIAN SCHOOL, 17th Century – Vase of flowers – oil on canvas – 64 x 50cm.
(Sotheby's)   **$11,646**   **£6,693**

ITALIAN SCHOOL, late 18th Century – The Madonna and Child – 50.2 x 40.3cm.
(Christie's)   **$1,744**   **£935**

JACK

RICHARD JACK, R.A. (1866–1952) – Beach huts –
signed and dated 96 – oil on panel – 20 x 29cm.
(Christie's) $2,388 £1,430

FREDERICK WILLIAM JACKSON (1859–1918) – A
Bazaar in Tangier – signed – pencil, watercolour and
bodycolour – 10½ x 14½in.
(Christie's) $1,517 £770

ANTONIO JACOBSEN (1850–1921) – Storm King,
1894 – signed and dated 1894 – oil on canvas –
56 x 91.5cm.
(Christie's) $14,300 £7,436

**ANTONIO NICOLO GASPARO JACOBSEN
(1850–1921)** – The Grand Banks fishing schooner
Albertina – signed and dated 1906 – 56 x 91.5cm.
(Christie's) $37,774 £18,700

ROBERT JACOBSEN (Danish, b. 1912) – Composition
– signed – watercolour and collage – 64 x 98cm.
(AB Stockholms Auktionsverk) $2,932 £1,535

JULES-LEON-EDOUARD JACQUET (fl. 1879) –
Femme au Chapeau noir – signed – oil on panel –
45.8 x 36.8cm.
(Christie's) $2,482 £1,320

HELGA JAKSONE (b. 1959) – The evening – oil on
panel – 100 x 120cm.
(Jean-Claude Anaf) $1,101 £575

DAVID JAMES (fl. 1881–1898) – An Atlantic roller –
signed and dated 95 – oil on canvas – 63.5 x 127cm.
(Christie's)   **$26,026   £15,400**

WILLIAM JAMES (Active 1761–1771) - The Bucintoro
returning to the Molo on Ascension Day, Venice – oil on
canvas – 75.5 x 128cm.
(Phillips)   **$55,776   £28,000**

JOSE MARIA JARDINES (b. 1862) – A drover and
cattle in a landscape – signed – 66 x 81.4cm.
(Christie's)   **$4,819   £2,860**

Attributed to ETIENNE JEAURAT (1699–1789) –
Venus lighting Cupid's Torch; and the Triumph of Venus –
one signed (?) 'JEAURAT. PINX' – 62.2 x 129.5 and
61.9 x 123.8cm. – a set of two
(Christie's)   **$32,670   £16,500**

ALBERT JANESCH (1889) – Flowers – oil on panel –
signed and dated 1923 – 87 x 72.5cm.
(Duran)   **$8,083   £4,188**

CH. JENOT (19th Century) – Elegant company playing
chess – signed – 64.8 x 95.3cm.
(Christie's)   **$10,750   £6,380**

JENSEN

JOHAN LAURENTS JENSEN (Danish 1800–56) – Still life with oranges, flowers and nuts – signed – oil on panel – 51 x 38cm.
(AB Stockholms Auktionsverk) **$13,972 £7,202**

JOHAN LAURENTS JENSEN (Danish 1800–56) – Still life with flowers – signed – oil on panel – 33 x 26cm.
(AB Stockholms Auktionsverk) **$11,107 £5,725**

CARLO CHRISTOFFE HORNUNG JENSEN (1882-1960) – The Water Garden – signed and dated 'C. Hornung Jensen 1939' – oil on canvas – 28 x 32½in.
(Christie's) **$7,612 £4,400**

MISS AMBROSINI JEROME (fl. 1840–1871) – Fleur de Marie at the Farm of Bouqueval – signed and dated 1844 – oil on canvas – 76 x 63cm.
(Christie's) **$4,246 £2,200**

LUIS JIMENEZ Y ARANDA (1845–1928) – Meeting Grandmother – signed and inscribed – oil on canvas – 76.2 x 117.5cm.
(Christie's) **$54,175 £27,500**

LUIS JIMENEZ Y ARANDA (Spanish 1845–1928) – Potato picking at Pontoise – signed and dated Pontoise 1895 – oil on canvas – 87 x 123cm.
(Sotheby's)
$89,595   £49,500

LENNART JIRLOW (b. 1936) – French café – interior – signed – oil on canvas – 50 x 60cm.
(AB Stockholms Auktionsverk) $24,874   £13,023

LENNART JIRLOW – Landscape artists, poster, 1976 – colour lithograph – 154 x 109cm.
(AB Stockholms Auktionsverk) $1,297   £669

ERLING JOHANSSON (b. 1934) – Model with birds – signed and dated 69 – oil on canvas – 66 x 120cm.
(AB Stockholms Auktionsverk) $1,866   £977

JOHN

AUGUSTUS JOHN (1876–1961) – Self-portrait – signed
– oil on panel – 15.9 x 18.4cm.
(Christie's) **$6,980 £4,180**

AUGUSTUS JOHN, O.M., R.A. (1878–1961) - A young
girl standing (Study) – signed twice – thinned oil over
pencil on panel – 49.5 x 27.5cm.
(Phillips) **$12,472 £7,500**

AUGUSTUS JOHN, O.M., R.A. (1878–1961) – Romilly
John – oil on panel – 40 x 30.5cm.
(Christie's) **$20,377 £10,450**

AUGUSTUS JOHN (1876–1961) – Portrait of Brigit
Macnamara – signed – oil on canvas – 41 x 34cm.
(Christie's) **$7,715 £4,620**

Circle of ANTONIO JOLI (1700–1777) – Christ healing the soldier – 75.6 x 62cm.
(Christie's) **$9,148 £4,620**

AUGUSTUS JOHN (1876–1961) – The Little Railway, Martigues - signed - oil on canvas – 54 x 73cm.
(Christie's) **$17,451 £10,450**

CLARENCE JOHNSON (1894–1981) – Pennsylvania hillsides – signed – oil on canvas – 50 x 61cm.
(Christie's) **$22,000 £11,440**

ANTONIO JOLI (circa 1700–1777) – A Capriccio, including a scene with the French Ambassador approaching the King of Siam's Palace in a state barge – oil on canvas – 113 x 147.2cm.
(Sotheby's) **$501,600 £264,000**

EINAR JOLIN (1890–1976) – Picture of Stockholm from Skinnarvikspark – winter scene in evening light – signed and dated 1937 – oil on canvas – 83 x 116cm.
(AB Stockholms Auktionsverk) **$26,650 £13,953**

ALEXANDER JOHNSTON (1815–1891) – The flirt – signed – oil on canvas – 92.1 x 70.5cm.
(Christie's) **$10,454 £5,280**

JOLIN

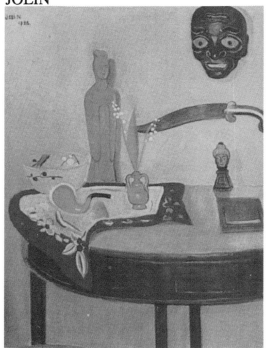

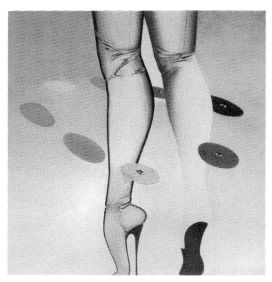

ALLEN JONES, R.A. (b. 1937) – Gallery gasper – signed and inscribed on the stretcher – oil on canvas – 92 x 92cm.
(Christie's) $49,082 £25,300

EINAR JOLIN (1890–1976) – Still life with Chinese objects on mahogany table – signed and dated 1928 – oil on canvas – 65 x 54cm.
(AB Stockholms Auktionsverk) **$2,842 £1,488**

JOE JONES (1909–1963) – Threshing – signed and dated 1935 – oil on masonite – 93.5 x 124cm.
(Christie's) **$6,600 £3,498**

EINAR JOLIN (1890–1976) – View from my window, town with bridge – signed and dated 1921 – oil on canvas – 49 x 39cm.
(AB Stockholms Auktionsverk) **$3,553 £1,860**

SVEN JONSON (1902–81) – "Nocturne" – signed – oil on canvas – 38 x 46cm.
(AB Stockholms Auktionsverk) **$7,107 £3,721**

After JACOB JORDEANS – The washing and anointing of the body of Christ – unframed – 117 x 155cm.
(Christie's)   **$2,667**   **£1,430**

JESSIE JOY – Richmond upon Swale, North Yorkshire – signed and dated 1876 – watercolour – 51 x 74cm.
(Phillips)   **$1,560**   **£780**

CHARLES JACOB JUNG (1880–1940) – Winter morning – oil on canvas – 79 x 101cm.
(Christie's)   **$8,800**   **£4,576**

ERNST JOSEPHSON (1851–1906) – Queen with flower – signed – indian ink – 17.5 x 8cm.
(AB Stockholms Auktionsverk)   **$1,441**   **£743**

E. JOUAS – Birthday present – signed – oil on canvas – 46 x 65cm.
(Hôtel de Ventes Horta)   **$2,009**   **£1,148**

AIJA JURJANE – Games – signed and dated 90 – oil on canvas – 60 x 80cm.
(Jean-Claude Anaf)   **$393**   **£205**

JURJANS

JURIS JURJANS (b. 1944) – Bird – signed with
monogram – oil on canvas – 65 x 70cm.
(Jean-Claude Anaf) $314 £164

HENRY JUTSUM - Cattle by stream with figures and
dogs – signed and dated 1845 – watercolour –
10$\frac{1}{2}$ x 17$\frac{1}{4}$in.
(Hobbs & Chambers) $1,790 £1,000

CARL JUTZ (1838–1916) – The poultry yard – signed –
oil on wood – 26 x 34cm.
(Lempertz) $22,020 £12,583

FREDERIK HENDRIK KAEMMERER (Dutch
1839–1902) – Interior with woman writing a letter – signed
– oil on canvas – 40 x 25cm.
(AB Stockholms Auktionsverk) $11,465 £5,910

OLLE KAKS (b. 1941) – "Emblem II" – signed and dated
74 – oil on canvas – 92 x 73cm.
(AB Stockholms Auktionsverk) $5,153 £2,698

KAT

ABRAHAM VAN KALRAET – Still life with peaches, gooseberries and cherries – oil on panel – signed with monogram – 43.5 x 57.5cm.
(Sotheby's)   **$18,441 £10,598**

C. GORAN KARLSSON (b. 1944) – Geometric composition – signed and dated 87 – tempera – 77 x 58cm.
(AB Stockholms Auktionsverk)   **$3,197 £1,674**

KASPARUS KARSEN (1810–1896) – A view in a Dutch town with children watching a traveller – signed – 41 x 65cm.
(Christie's)   **$60,350 £30,175**

MAX KAMPF (Swiss, b. 1912) – Three figures – signed and dated 1963 – oil and tempera on paper – 99 x 108cm.
(germann Auktionshaus)   **$3,921 £2,016**

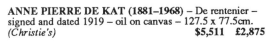

MAURICIO FLORES KAPEROTXIPI (b. 1901) – A glass of wine – signed – oil on canvas – 61 x 50cm.
(Duran)   **$5,065 £2,639**

ANNE PIERRE DE KAT (1881–1968) – De rentenier – signed and dated 1919 – oil on canvas – 127.5 x 77.5cm.
(Christie's)   **$5,511 £2,875**

KAVLI

ARNE KAVLI – An elegant woman seated at a table – signed and dated – oil on canvas – 65 x 77cm.
(Sotheby's) $14,767   £8,250

FELIX KELLY (b. 1916) – St Martin-in-the-Fields from Trafalgar Square – signed and dated 51 – oil on board – 51 x 38cm.
(Christie's) $6,402   £3,300

SIR GERALD KELLY – Ma Seyn Sin – oil on canvas – 72.5 x 47cm.
(Bonhams) $2,200   £1,100

ROBERT KEMM (19th Century) – Fair in Granada – oil on canvas – signed – 92 x 140cm.
(Duran) $15,156   £7,853

JEKA KEMP (1876–1967) – The Black Poodle – signed – watercolour and bodycolour – 38 x 38cm.
(Christie's) $4,408   £2,640

LUCY KEMP-WELCH (1869–1958) A handsome pair –
signed with initials and dated 1915 – watercolour and
gouache heightened with white over traces of pencil –
36.5 x 26cm.
(Phillips)   **$11,641   £7,000**

LUCY KEMP-WELCH (1869–1958) A bad place to leap
– signed – pen and ink and coloured washes heightened
with white over traces of pencil – 30 x 18.5cm.
(Phillips)   **$4,989   £3,000**

LUCY KEMP-WELCH (1869–1958) My Mother and I –
signed and dated 1915 – oil and watercolour on grey paper
– 40 x 28cm.
(Phillips)   **$29,102   £17,500**

LUCY KEMP-WELCH (1869–1958) – Fire! – signed
with initials – oil on canvas – 43 x 33cm.
(Phillips)   **$29,934   £18,000**

KEMP-WELCH

ROCKWELL KENT (1882–1971) – Woodsman from "This is My Own" – signed – pen and brush and black ink on paper – 11.4x 16.5cm.
(Christie's)   **$935**   **£496**

LUCY KEMP-WELCH (1869–1958) Down! –signed with initials and dated 1915 – watercolour and gouache heightened with white over races of pencil – 29.5 x 20cm.
(Phillips)   **$13,304**   **£8,000**

CECIL KENNEDY (b. 1905) – Summer flowers in a basket – signed – oil on canvas – 62 x 75.5cm.
(Christie's)   **$12,441**   **£6,380**

FERNAND KHNOPFF (Belgian 1858–1921) – Portrait de femme – oil on canvas laid down on board – 14 x 11.5cm.
(Sotheby's)   **$49,775**   **£27,500**

JOHN T. EARDLEY KENNEY – Heading for the post – signed and dated '58 – 61 x 82.5cm.
(Christie's)   **$1,153**   **£605**

NORA KIDDER – Yellow roses – oil on board – initialled – 12 x 16in.
(David Lay)   **$347**   **£190**

GEORGE GOODWIN KILBURNE (1839–1924) – The letter – signed – oil on canvas – 71.1 x 91.4cm.
(Christie's) **$9,295** **£5,500**

R. KIMPE (1855–1970) – Hôtel Noir – oil on canvas – signed – 105 x 86cm.
(Hôtel de Ventes Horta) **$6,208** **£3,200**

GEORGE GOODWIN KILBURNE – Listening to a story – watercolour – signed – 21 x 28.2cm.
(Bonhams) **$4,718** **£2,800**

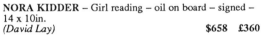

NORA KIDDER – Girl reading – oil on board – signed – 14 x 10in.
(David Lay) **$658** **£360**

KIMPE

OREST ADAMOVICH KIPRENSKII (1782–1836) –
Portrait of Prince Evgenii Grigor'evich Gagarin as a child –
inscribed, initialled and dated 1812 – oil on canvas –
55.8 x 49.2cm.
(Christie's) $42,900 £22,000

R. KIMPE (1855–1970) – The mermaid – oil on canvas –
signed – 130 x 105cm.
(Hôtel de Ventes Horta) $7,450 £3,840

HAYNES KING (1831–1904) – The morning paper –
signed and dated 1878 – oil on canvas – 61 x 51cm.
(Christie's) $11,154 £6,600

ERNST LUDWIG KIRCHNER (1880–1938) – Seated
female nude – with Nachlass stamp on the reverse – pastel
and charcoal on paper - 90.2 x 69.2cm.
(Christie's) $346,720 £176,000

ERNST LUDWIG KIRCHNER (1880–1938) – Seated female nude – signed and dated 07 – watercolour on pencil drawing on paper – 43.1 x 33.4cm.
(Lempertz)   **$161,666   £83,333**

MOISE KISLING (1891–1953) – The waitress – signed – oil on canvas – 35.5 x 27.5cm.
(Christie's)   **$108,350   £55,000**

MOISE KISLING – Landscape in the Midi – oil on canvas – signed – 60 x 73cm.
(Jean-Claude Anaf)   **$85,567   £44,335**

301

KISLING

MOISE KISLING – Les deux amies – signed – oil on canvas – 73 x 60cm.
(Sotheby's) $224,400 £132,000

ESTHER KJERNER (1873–1952) – Still life with yellow roses in a blue jug – signed and dated 50 – oil on panel – 41 x 43cm.
(AB Stockholms Auktionsverk) $8,061 £4,155

JOSEPH KLAUS (late 19th Century) – A basket of Roses – signed – oil on canvas – 55.9 x 70.5cm.
(Christie's) $6,204 £3,300

MOISE KISLING (1891–1953) – Le Vase de Narcisses – signed – oil on canvas – 41 x 33cm.
(Christie's) $150,480 £88,000

PAUL KLEE (1879–1940) – Mystical landscape – signed and dated 1917 – watercolour and gouache on paper – 16 x 24.5cm.
(Lempertz) $404,166 £208,333

GUSTAV KLIMT (1862–1918) – Mother and daughter (recto) – stamped – pencil on paper – 56.5 x 37.2cm.
(Christie's) $34,672   £17,600

GUSTAV KLIMT (1862–1918) – Sitzende Halbakt – bears Nachlass stamp – pencil and coloured chalk on paper – 55 x 36.5cm.
(Christie's) $112,860   £66,000

JOHANNES CHRISTIAAN KAREL KLINKENBERG (1852–1924) – A view of the Gelderse Kade, Amsterdam, towards the Schreierstoren – signed – 39 x 47.5cm.
(Christie's) $46,939   £23,470

F.V. KNAPP (1838–1869) – Pair of still lifes with flowers – oil on panel – one signed – 42 x 30cm.
(Duran) $6,062   £3,141

DAME LAURA KNIGHT, R.A. – A strawberry roan in a
landscape – signed – watercolour – 54.5 x 76.2cm.
(Christie's) $6,270   £3,300

DAME LAURA KNIGHT, R.A. (1877–1970) – A
Chinese juggler – signed with initials and dated 1933 –
watercolour, bodycolour, black crayon and charcoal –
35.5 x 26.5cm.
(Christie's) $6,429   £3,850

DAME LAURA KNIGHT, R.A. (1877–1970) – The
Nursery – signed – oil on canvas – 29 x 34cm.
(Christie's) $20,207   £12,100

DAME LAURA KNIGHT, R.A. (1877–1970) – Taking a
call – signed and dated 1922 – oil on canvas – 60 x 51cm.
(Christie's) $15,249   £7,920

HAROLD KNIGHT, R.A. (1874–1961) – Afternoon tea –
signed – oil on canvas – 193 x 152cm.
(Christie's) $154,440   £79,200

WILLIAM HENRY KNIGHT – Peace versus War – a quarrelsome neighbour – signed and dated 1862 – 45 x 54.5cm.
(Anderson & Garland) **$18,165 £10,500**

JAN HERMANUS KOEKKOEK (1778–1851) – A coastal landscape on the Zuider Zee with figures repairing a boat – signed – oil on canvas – 37 x 59cm.
(Christie's) **$52,008 £26,400**

WILLEM KOEKKOEK (1839–1895) – Winter: A view in a town with several figures in a snowy street, a peasant pushing a sledge along a frozen canal – signed – 44 x 60cm.
(Christie's) **$97,230 £48,615**

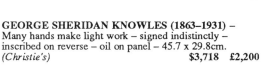

GEORGE SHERIDAN KNOWLES (1863–1931) – Many hands make light work – signed indistinctly – inscribed on reverse – oil on panel – 45.7 x 29.8cm.
(Christie's) **$3,718 £2,200**

GEORGE SHERIDAN KNOWLES – The red red rose – signed – 45.7 x 30.5cm.
(Christie's) **$4,382 £2,200**

WILLEM KOEKKOEK (1839–1895) – A view in a town with women conversing and a horse-drawn cart passing by – signed – 41 x 53cm.
(Christie's) **$33,528 £16,764**

KOEKKOEK

WILLEM KOEKKOEK (1839–1895) – Numerous
figures on a quay in a town with a moored hay-barge –
signed and dated 61 – 66 x 92cm.
(Christie's)   **$28,163**   **£14,082**

WILLEM KOEKKOEK (1839–1895) – A Dutch street
scene – signed – oil on canvas – 50.8 x 38.1cm.
(Christie's)   **$12,408**   **£6,600**

ALEXANDER KOESTER (1864–1932) – Small talk –
signed – oil on canvas laid down on wood – 45.5 x 76cm.
(Lempertz)   **$69,536**   **£39,735**

OSKAR KOKOSCHKA (1886–1980) – Portrait of Dr.
Rudolf Blümner – signed with initials – oil on canvas –
80 x 57.1cm.
(Christie's)   **$1,950,300**   **£990,000**

OSKAR KOKOSCHKA – Bildnis Eines Mädchen –
signed – watercolour – 68 x 51cm.
(Sotheby's)   **$37,400**   **£22,000**

SERGEI KOLESNIKOV (Russian 1889–1947) – Still life with melon – signed and dated 1936 – oil on canvas – 121 x 166cm.
(AB Stockholms Auktionsverk)   **$13,793   £7,110**

OSKAR KOKOSCHKA (1886–1980) – Portrait of a young girl – watercolour – signed – 64.3 x 46.5cm.
(Lempertz)   **$41,764   £21,528**

KARL IVANOVICH KOLLMANN (1788–1846) – Seven scenes illustrating Russian life and types – one signed and dated lower left 1820 – pencil and watercolour on paper – 16.5 x 21cm. – one illustrated
(Christie's)   **$5,577   £2,860**

HEINRICH CHRISTOPH KOLBE (German, 1771–1836) – Portrait of the brother and sister Robert and Alwine Uellenberg, half length – signed – oil on canvas – 70 x 60cm.
(Kunsthaus am Museum)   **$6,724   £3,466**

PETR PETROVICH KONCHALOVSKI (1876–1956) – Still life with a teapot and a lemon – signed with initials and dated 1929 – oil on canvas – 17 x 23.1cm.
(Christie's)   **$6,435   £3,300**

KONOW

JURGEN VON KONOW (1915–59) – The theatre, Stockholm – signed and dated 1947–48 – oil on panel – 80 x 100cm.
(AB Stockholms Auktionsverk) **$2,664 £1,395**

CORNELIS KOPPENOL – Paddling at low tide – oil on panel – signed – 70 x 100.5cm.
(Bonhams) **$6,000 £3,000**

KONSTANTIN ALEKSEEVICH KOROVIN (1861–1939) – Evening serenade – signed, dated and inscribed in 1915 – oil on canvas – 88.4 x 66.5cm.
(Christie's) **$21,450 £11,000**

LEOPOLD KOWALSKY (Polish b. 1856) – Springtime – signed – oil on canvas – 195 x 300cm.
(Sotheby's) **$28,785 £15,730**

DAVID VON KRAFFT (1665–1724) – Follower of – Portrait of Karl XII – half length
(AB Stockholms Auktionsverk) **$2,687 £1,385**

DAVID VON KRAFFT (1665–1724) – Attributed to – Portrait of Queen Hedvig Eleonora – oil on canvas – 140 x 120cm.
(AB Stockholms Auktionsverk) **$7,164 £3,693**

PER KRAFFT (1777–1863) – Portrait of Magistrate
Anders Reimers – half length – signed and dated 1807 – oil
on canvas – 72 x 62cm.
(AB Stockholms Auktionsverk)   **$1,523   £785**

JACOB KRAMER (1892–1962) – Portrait of a lady –
signed lower left Kramer – oil on canvas – 75 x 63cm.
(Christie's)   **$7,161   £3,850**

IVAN NIKOLAEVICH KRAMSKOI (1837–1887) –
Portrait of a Russian General seated on a bench – signed
and inscribed – oil on canvas – 77.5 x 57cm.
(Christie's)   **$21,450   £11,000**

CORNELIUS KRIEGHOFF (1812–1872) – Sleigh ride
– signed and dated 1856 – oil on canvas – 33.2 x 46cm.
(Christie's)   **$33,000   £17,160**

ABRAHAM LEON KROLL (1884–1974) – Naomi -
signed – oil on canvas – 61 x 51cm.
(Christie's)   **$11,000   £5,830**

ABRAHAM LEON KROLL (1884–1974) – Niles Beach
– signed and dated 1913 – oil on canvas – 66 x 81.5cm.
(Christie's)   **$46,200   £24,024**

KROLL

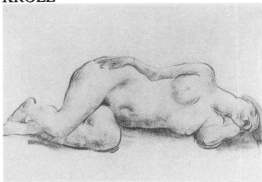

LEON KROLL (1884–1974) – Nude sleeping – signed - charcoal on paper – 35.6 x 53.3cm.
(Christie's) **$880 £466**

CARL GOTTHELF KUCHLER (German, 1807–1843) – Hylas with three naiads – signed and dated 1836 – oil on paper laid down on canvas – 29.5 x 22.5cm.
(Kunsthaus am Museum) **$5,380 £2,773**

JOHAN KROUTHEN (1858–1932) – Coastal landscape with red cottage – signed – oil on canvas – 50 x 75cm.
(AB Stockholms Auktionsverk) **$11,644 £6,002**

JOHAN KROUTHEN (1858–1932) – Bathing beach in summer with figures, boats and beach huts, Falsterbo – signed and dated 1916 – oil on canvas – 100 x 150cm.
(AB Stockholms Auktionsverk) **$46,574 £24,007**

CARL HERMANN KUECHLER (1866–1903) – At the races – signed – oil on board – 30 x 24cm.
(Christie's) **$6,618 £3,520**

HANS FRIEDRICH JOH KUGLER (1840–1873) – The heirs – signed - oil on canvas – 98 x 140cm.
(Hôtel de Ventes Horta)   **$6,597**   **£3,770**

YASUO KUNIYOSHI (1893–1953) – I was just married – signed – oil on canvas – 46 x 34.2cm.
(Christie's)   **$286,000**   **£148,720**

WILHELM KUHNERT (1865–1926) – Tigers stalking their prey – signed – oil on canvas – 94.3 x 149.5cm.
(Christie's)   **$91,014**   **£46,200**

CHARLES EUPHRASIE KUWASSEG (French 1833–1904) – A view of Lucerne – signed – oil on canvas – 30.5 x 50.5cm.
(Sotheby's)   **$12,480**   **£6,820**

LAFRENSEN

CELSO LAGAR (1891–1966) – The Ile de St Louis in
the River Seine – oil on canvas – signed – 56 x 69cm.
(Duran) $32,841 £17,016

Attributed to NIKLAS LAFRENSEN II (1737–1807) –
A studio with an artist and his model – oil on copper –
21.7 x 18cm.
(Christie's) $3,267 £1,650

LOUIS-JEAN-FRANÇOIS LAGRENEE (1725–1805) –
Aurora rising – oil on canvas – 121 x 170.5cm.
(Sotheby's) $46,587 £26,774

JEAN-JACQUES LAGRENEE (1739–1821) –
Telemachus and Mentor on the Isle of Calypso – signed
and dated 1777 – brush and brown wash on black stone –
415 x 550mm.
(Sotheby's) $7,809 £3,904

CELSO LAGAR (1891–1966) - The three clowns –
watercolour – signed – 32.5 x 25cm.
(Duran) $2,779 £1,440

312

Follower of JEAN-JACQUES LAGRENEE called LE JEUNE – Spring, Summer, and Autumn – (one illustrated) a set of three – all oil on canvas – each 120 x 92.5cm. *(Sotheby's)* **$45,980 £24,200**

MARIANO BARBASAN LAGUERUELA (1864–1924) – Celebrating St Josephs Day – watercolour and ink on stamped paper – dated 1910 – 27 x 20cm. *(Duran)* **$1,595 £833**

HENRI-ADOLPHE LAISSEMENT (d. 1921) – Reconcilable differences – signed – oil on canvas – 89 x 117cm.
(Christie's) **$13,090 £7,700**

CAMILLE LAMBERT – Self portrait – signed – canvas laid down on board – 48.5 x 36cm.
(Christie's)   **$1,672   £880**

HENRY LAMB, R.A. (1883–1960) – Portrait of a lady, full length, in a blue dress – signed and dated 1908 – oil on canvas – 199 x 99cm.
(Christie's)   **$34,903   £20,900**

HENRY LAMB, R.A. – Portrait of a young girl – signed and dated 1909 – pencil – 29.8 x 22.2cm.
(Christie's)   **$2,090   £1,045**

EGISTO LANCEROTTO (Italian 1848–1916) – A toast to the bride – signed and inscribed – oil on canvas – 117 x 83.5cm.
(Sotheby's)   **$20,130   £11,000**

NICOLAS LANCRET (1690–1743) – The marmoset shower – oil on canvas – 75 x 62cm.
(Christie's)   **$74,926   £38,510**

NICHOLAS LANCRET, Follower of – Children playing with a loopstoel on a terrace – 85.1 x 85.1cm.
(Christie's)   **$2,213   £1,100**

ANDREA LANDINI (b. 1847) – L'Impatient – signed – oil on canvas – 46.1 x 38.1cm.
(Christie's)   **$14,062   £7,480**

Follower of SIR EDWIN LANDSEER, R.A. – A Distinguished Member of the Humane Society – oil on canvas – 71.1 x 91.5cm.
(Christie's)   **$836   £440**

CURT A. LANDWEHR (German, 1920–88) – Interior with men playing dice – signed – oil on canvas – 79 x 69cm.
(Auktionshaus Arnold)   **$1,214   £649**

Attributed to GIOVANNI BATTISTA LANGETTI – The Penitent Saint Jerome – unframed – 85.1 x 100.3cm.
(Christie's)   **$6,600   £3,300**

LANGEVELD

FRANS LANGEVELD (1877–1939) – Prinseneiland,
Amsterdam – signed, and inscribed and dated September
1937 – 36 x 53.5cm.
(Christie's) $5,364 £2,682

FRANS LANGEVELD (Dutch, 1877–1939) – Woman
milking cow – signed – oil on canvas – 20 x 16in.
(Du Mouchelles) $1,500 £761

WALTER LANGLEY (1852–1922) – On the quay –
signed – oil on canvas-board – 37 x 32cm.
(Christie's) $16,533 £9,900

WALTER LANGLEY (1852–1922) – Young
fisherwoman – watercolour – signed – 5³/₄ x 4¹/₂in.
(David Lay) **$1,640 £820**

WALTER LANGLEY (1852–1922) – Distant thoughts –
signed and dated 87 – watercolour and bodycolour –
46.5cm x 60.5cm.
(Christie's) **$7,936 £4,070**

WALTER LANGLEY (1852–1922) – Rubbing tobacco –
signed and dated 1881 – watercolour – 14 x 10in.
(David Lay) **$4,370 £2,300**

VICTORIANO CODINA Y LANGLIN – A female nude by a pool – signed and dated – oil on canvas – 19 x 14.5cm.
(Sotheby's) **$7,876 £4,400**

MARK W. LANGLOIS (English, 19th century) – 'Pancake Day' – signed – oil on canvas – 53.3 x 43.2cm. – and companion piece, a pair.
(Bonhams) **$3,437 £1,700**

P*** LAPRIA (Italian 20th Century) – Naples from the Carmine – signed and titled – gouache – 41.5 x 61cm.
(Sotheby's) **$8,052 £4,400**

MARK W. LANGLOIS (circa 1900) – A day off – signed – oil on canvas – 53.3 x 43.2cm.
(Christie's) **$1,445 £79?**

NICOLAS DE LARGILLIERE (1656–1746) – Portrait of a lady – oil on canvas – oval – in a carved wood frame – 80 x 63.5cm.
(Sotheby's) **$29,260 £15,400**

NICOLAS DE LARGILLIERRE (1656–1746) – Portrait of Philippe de Bourbon, Duc de Chartres, future Duc d'Orléans then Régent of France (1674–1723) - oil on canvas – 101 x 80.5cm.
(Sotheby's)   **$38,823**   **£22,312**

BARTA LASZLO (Hungarian, b. 1927) – An artist with his canvases – signed – oil on board – 15$^{1}/_{2}$ x 12in.
(Du Mouchelles)   **$600**   **£322**

CARL LARSSON (1852–1919) – Empire, 1891 – signed with initials – etching on laid paper – 19.5 x 31.7cm.
(AB Stockholms Auktionsverk)   **$1,171**   **£604**

P. DE LASZLO (late 19th Century) – An Arab beauty – signed and dated 1891 – 76.2 x 50.8cm.
(Christie's)   **$4,819**   **£2,860**

LATTARD

PHILLIP LATTARD (American, 19th/20th Century) –
Young Woman by a Lily Pond – signed and dated 02 – oil
on canvas – 18 x 22in.
(Skinner) $2,000 £1,031

MARIE LAURENCIN – L'infante Marie – signed and
dated 1935 – oil on canvas – 41 x 33cm.
(Sotheby's) $345,950 £203,500

GASPARD DE LATOIX (active late 19th century) –
Waiting for the beef issue – signed – watercolour on paper
– 36.2 x 26.3cm.
(Christie's) $6,050 £3,206

MARIE LAURENCIN – Trois filles – signed – oil on
canvas – 63 x 50cm.
(Sotheby's) $467,500 £275,000

MARIE LAURENCIN (1885–1956) – Two sisters with cello – signed and dated 1913 – oil on canvas – 115.9 x 89cm.
(Christie's) **$823,460 £418,000**

MARIE LAURENCIN – Bouquet de fleurs – signed – oil on canvas – 61 x 38cm.
(Sotheby's) **$112,200 £66,000**

MARIE LAURENCIN (1885–1956) – Femme decolletée au Collier de Perles – signed – oil on canvas – 55 x 46cm.
(Christie's) **$413,820 £242,000**

ALEXANDER LAUREUS (Finnish 1783–1823) – Woman sewing in her nightgown – signed and dated 1816 – oil on canvas – 34 x 27cm.
(AB Stockholms Auktionsverk) **$17,018 £8,772**

321

LAUWERS

JOHN H LAVER – Farm scene with two row boats laden with hay – signed and dated 1937 – oil on canvas – 71 x 90cm.
(Allen & Harris) $1,116 £600

JACOBUS JOHANNES LAUWERS – The courtyard of an inn – signed – on panel – 36.8 x 31cm.
(Christie's) **$3,080 £1,540**

AUGUST LAUX (1847–1921) – Raspberries and sweet pea – signed – oil on canvas – 30.5 x 41cm.
(Christie's) **$7,700 £4,081**

CYRIL LAVENSTEIN – The harbour at Mevagissey, Cornwall – signed and dated '40 – pencil and watercolour – 11½ x 13¾in.
(Tennants) $840 £420

GEORGES-AUGUSTE-ELIE LAVERGNE (1863–1942) – David with the head of Goliath – signed and dated 1894 – oil on canvas – 228 x 121.3cm.
(Christie's) **$14,085 £7,150**

SIR THOMAS LAWRENCE, P.R.A. (1769–1830) –
Portrait of a lady, bust length, in profile to the left, in a
white dress, with powdered hair - signed – inscribed and
dated 1784 – pastel – oval – 11³/₄ x 9³/₄in.
(Christie's) $2,190   £1,210

SIR JOHN LAVERY, R.A. (1856–1941) – Girl in a
bonnet – signed and dated - oil on canvas – unframed –
81.5 x 48cm.
(Christie's) $6,138   £3,300

DOUGLAS LAWLEY (1906–1971) – Black horse with
the red blanket, Place d'Armes, Quebec – signed – oil on
board – 22.8 x 30.5cm.
(Pinney's) $1,275   £761

Follower of SIR THOMAS LAWRENCE, P.R.A. –
Portrait of a lady, seated half length, in a black dress and a
white lace bonnet, holding a sketch book and pen –
91.4 x 76.2cm.
(Christie's) $2,208   £1,210

LAWSON

ERNEST LAWSON (1873-1939) – The Flatiron Building
– signed – oil on academy board – 53 x 38.8cm.
(Christie's)   **$374,000   £194,480**

JOSE OTERO LAXEIRO (b. 1908) – Nude – mixed
media – signed – 21.5 x 23cm.
(Duran)   **$3,789   £1,963**

E*** LAYNAUD – Figures on a beach – signed – oil on
panel – 10 x 11½in.
(Tennants)   **$3,200   £1,600**

Folower of GREGORIO LAZZARINI – The Good
samaritan – oil on canvas – 189 x 148cm.
(Phillips)   **$19,872   £10,350**

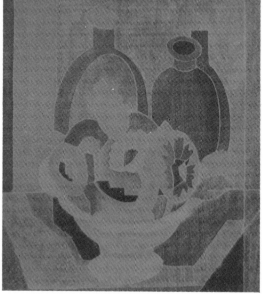

BLANCHE LAZZELL (1878–1956) – Marigolds, 1930 –
colour woodblock print – signed – 14 x 12in. with margins
(Bruce D. Collins)   **$4,675   £2,527**

BENJAMIN WILLIAMS LEADER, R.A. (1831–1923)
– Fishing by the mill – signed and dated 1867 – oil on
board – 35.5 x 30.5cm.
(Christie's)   **$6,098**   **£3,080**

HENRI LEBASQUE (1865–1937) – Fillette à la Fenêtre
– signed – oil on canvas – 55.4 x 46.3cm.
(Christie's)   **$188,100**   **£110,000**

**EDWARD CHALMERS LEAVITT (American,
1842–1904)** – Still Life with Grapes – signed and dated
1870 – oil on canvas – 30¹/₂ x 25in.
(Skinner)   **$3,100**   **£1,598**

HENRI LEBASQUE (1865–1937) – Odalisque – signed –
oil on canvas – 72.5 x 99cm.
(Christie's)   **$303,380**   **£154,000**

HENRI LEBASQUE (1865–1937) – Le Parc Monceau –
signed – oil on canvas – 40.6 x 30.4cm.
(Christie's)   **$60,676**   **£30,800**

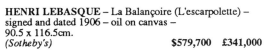

HENRI LEBASQUE – La Balançoire (L'escarpolette) –
signed and dated 1906 – oil on canvas –
90.5 x 116.5cm.
(Sotheby's)   **$579,700**   **£341,000**

HENRI LEBASQUE (1865–1937) – Reclining nude – oil
on canvas – 33.3 x 41.3cm.
(Christie's)   **$60,676**   **£30,800**

HENRI LEBASQUE – La promenade – signed – oil on
canvas – 60 x 50cm.
(Sotheby's)   **$187,000**   **£110,000**

HENRI LEBASQUE – Nu au coussin espagnol – signed –
oil on canvas – 81.5 x 117cm.
(Sotheby's)   **$486,200**   **£286,000**

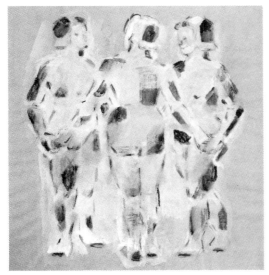

WILLIAM LEE (1810–1865) – Mother Love –
watercolour - signed and dated 1858 – 20¹/₂ x 23¹/₂in.
(GA Canterbury Auction Galleries) **$4,053 £2,100**

BART VAN DER LECK (1876–1958) – Three Graces –
pencil and watercolour on paper – 52 x 47cm.
(Christie's) **$20,666 £10,781**

WILLIAM LEE-HANKEY – Street market – oil on
canvas – signed – 51 x 61cm.
(Bonhams) **$14,000 £7,000**

PAUL LEDUC (Belgian School, 19th Century) – Old
lane at Menton – signed – oil on canvas – 60 x 45cm.
(Galerie Moderne) **$9,837 £5,137**

**CORNELIS VAN LEEMPUTTEN (Belgian,
1841–1902)** – Farm Scene with Sheep and Chickens –
signed – oil on canvas – 22¹/₄ x 30in.
(Skinner) **$850 £438**

LEEMPUTTEN

**ALEXID DE LEEUW and CORNELIS VAN
LEEMPUTTEN** – A shepherd with his flock in a winter
landscape – signed by both artists – 38¹/₂ x 30in.
(Tennants)   **$4,800   £2,400**

**ROBERT-JACQUES-FRANÇOIS LEFEVRE
(1755–1830), Studio of** – Portrait of First Consul
Bonaparte – oil on canvas – oval – 59 x 48cm.
(Sotheby's)   **$4,881   £2,789**

ADOLPHE LEFEVRE (1934–1868) – Faust and
Margarethe leaving the church – signed – dated on reverse
– on panel – 21.5 x 16.5cm.
(Christie's)   **$2,409   £1,430**

FERNAND LEGER – Two women – pen and ink over
pencil – 33.5 x 26cm.
(Sotheby's)   **$44,880   £26,400**

FERNAND LEGER (1881–1955) – Composition with parrot – signed with initials and dated 51 – oil and gouache on paper laid down on canvas – 40 x 60.3cm.
(Christie's)   **$303,380**   **£154,000**

FERNAND LEGER – Le papillon – signed and dated '36 – oil on canvas – 46.2 x 56.2cm.
(Sotheby's)   **$112,200**   **£66,000**

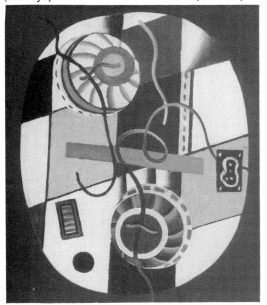

FERNAND LEGER (1881–1955) – Nature morte aux Los anges – signed and dated – oil on canvas – 65.2 x 54cm.
(Christie's)   **$587,400**   **£330,000**

WILHELM LEHMBRUCK (1881–1918) – Lot and his daughter – oil on canvas – 81 x 65.4cm.
(Christie's)   **$314,215**   **£159,500**

CHARLES LEICKERT (1816-1907) – Summer: A view in a town with villagers on a quay – Winter: A view in a town with several figures in a snowy street – both signed – one dated 90, the other dated 79 (?) – oil on panel – 36 x 27cm. – one illustrated
(Christie's)   **$25,481**   **£12,740**

LEIGHTON

FREDERIC, LORD LEIGHTON (English 1830–96)
–The maid with the golden hair – oil on canvas –
83.2 x 61.6cm.
(Sotheby's) $378,290   £209,000

FREDERIC, LORD LEIGHTON, P.R.A., R.W.S.
(English 1830–96) – Dante in exile – oil on canvas –
152.5 x 254cm.
(Sotheby's) $2,009,100 £1,110,000

EDMUND BLAIR LEIGHTON (1853–1922) – The love
letter – signed with initials – oil on panel – 20.3 x 12.7cm.
(Christie's) $10,454   £5,280

FREDERIC, LORD LEIGHTON, P.R.A., R.W.S. (English 1830–96) – Dante in exile – oil on canvas –
152.5 x 254cm.
(Sotheby's) $2,009,100   £1,110,000

FREDERIC, LORD LEIGHTON, P.R.A. (1830–1896) –
Portrait of Henry Evans Gordon – oil on canvas –
61 x 50.8cm.
(Christie's)   **$21,230   £11,000**

FREDERIC, LORD LEIGHTON (English 1830–96) –
Sisters – oil on canvas – 76 x 38cm.
(Sotheby's)   **$955,680   £528,000**

FREDERIC, LORD LEIGHTON, P.R.A. (1830–1896) –
Portrait of Miss Pullen (Dorothy Dene), shoulder length –
black and white chalks, vignette, on pale-blue paper –
9¼in x 6⅝in.
(Christie's)   **$3,184   £1,650**

HARRY LEITH-ROSS (1886–1973) – Photographing
the hunter – oil on board – signed with initials –
8¼ x 10⅜in.
(Bruce D. Collins)   **$1,870   £1,011**

331

LELOIR

MAURICE LELOIR (1853–1940) – The pumpkin lover
– signed – oil on panel – 32.4 x 22.9cm.
(Christie's)   **$10,780 £5,500**

SCHOOL OF SIR PETER LELY – Portrait of Elizabeth
Hamilton, Countess of Grammont – oil on canvas –
128 x 100cm.
(Finarte Casa d'Aste)   **$10,302 £5,374**

Follower of SIR PETER LELY – Portrait of Charles II,
standing three-quarter length, wearing coronation robes –
127 x 101.6cm.
(Christie's)   **$4,617 £2,530**

FRANZ VON LENBACH (1836–1904) – Portrait of the
Bohemian politician Joseph Maria Baernreither
(1845–1925) – bust length facing right – signed and dated
1899 – oil on board – 57 x 49.5cm.
(Lempertz)   **$6,084 £3,477**

GIRALT LERIN (Spanish, b. 1906) – Alter boy – oil on board – 13³/₄ x 10³/₄in.
(Du Mouchelles)   **$350   £188**

BERNARD LENS III (1682–1740) – The Cascade, Bushey Park – inscribed in the margin – pen and grey ink, grey wash – 9 x 12³/₄in.
(Christie's)   **$1,287   £660**

J. LEPAGE (French School, 19th Century) – It's Your Move/A Genre Scene – signed and inscribed – oil on canvas – 12¹/₄ x 16¹/₄in.
(Skinner)   **$1,400   £722**

JEAN-BAPTISTE LEPRINCE (1733–1781) – The dunce's cap – black chalk, gouache on paper – 304 x 245mm.
(Christie's)   **$13,222   £6,790**

E. LERMONTOFF (late 19th Century) – A noble family leaving their palace in winter; and Sportsmen returning to their palace in winter – both signed – 100 x 75cm. – a pair
(Christie's)   **$10,058   £5,029**

LESSORE

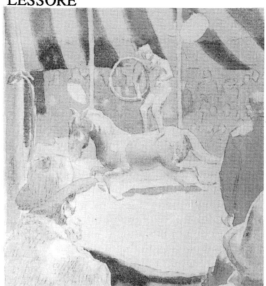

RICHARD HAYLEY LEVER (1876–1955) –
Harbourside, Gloucester – oil on masonite –
50.8 x 60.5cm.
(Christie's)   **$9,900   £5,247**

THERESE LESSORE – Circus performer – watercolour
and pencil – unframed – 21 x 17cm.
(Christie's)   **$880   £440**

HENRY VICTOR LESUR (French b. 1863) – The
introduction – signed – oil on panel – 45 x 55cm.
(Sotheby's)   **$8,052   £4,400**

MAX LEVIS (German b. 1863) – Sleeping beauty –
signed and dated – oil on canvas laid down on board –
23.5 x 35.5cm.
(Sotheby's)   **$13,084   £7,150**

GUILLAUME GUILLON LETHIERE (1760–1832) –
The Judgement of Paris – signed and dated 1812 – oil on
canvas – 198 x 279.4cm.
(Christie's)   **$154,258   £79,286**

ROBERT LEVRAC-TOURNIERES (1667–1752) -
Portrait of a lady – oil on canvas – 129.5 x 97.5cm.
(Sotheby's)   **$24,264   £13,945**

EMILE LEVY (1826–1890) – A little girl in red – signed and dated 1876 – 45.7 x 27.9cm.
(Christie's)   **$4,448**   **£2,640**

JOHN FREDERICK LEWIS, R.A. (1805–1876) – A Suliote soldier – signed and inscribed – pencil, watercolour and bodycolour, on buff paper – 14¹/₄ x 9³/₄in.
(Christie's)   **$9,009**   **£4,620**

JOHN FREDERICK LEWIS, R.A. (1805–1876) – The door of a cafe at Cairo – signed and dated 1866 – oil on panel – 30.5 x 20.3cm.
(Christie's)   **$168,300**   **£99,000**

PERCY WYNDHAM LEWIS, A.R.A. (1889–1949) – Edward Wadsworth – pencil – 44.5 x 30.5cm.
(Christie's)   **$13,299**   **£6,820**

LEYENDECKER

JOSEPH CHRISTIAN LEYENDECKER (1874–1951)
– The homecoming – oil on canvas – 71.6 x 107.5cm.
(Christie's) **$19,800 £10,296**

JUDITH LEYSTER (1600–1660) – The lute player – oil
on panel – 50 x 37.7cm.
(Phillips) **$71,712 £36,000**

ANDRE LHOTE – Nu égyptien – signed – oil on canvas
– 55 x 45.5cm.
(Sotheby's) **$31,790 £18,700**

ROY LICHTENSTEIN – "Crak!" – poster – coloured
offset litho – 47 x 68.5cm.
(AB Stockholms Auktionsverket) **$519 £273**

MAX LIEBERMANN (1847–1935) – Spielende Kinder
im Park – signed lower right M. Liebermann – oil on
canvas – 51 x 69cm.
(Christie's) **$822,360 £462,000**

CHARLES SILLEM LIDDERDALE (1831–1895) –
Coming from the warren – signed with monogram – oil on
canvas – 61 x 50.8cm.
(Christie's) **$7,436 £4,400**

MAX LIEBERMANN (German 1847–1935) – Boys at
the beach – signed – pastel – 22 x 29cm.
(Sotheby's) **$10,467 £5,720**

JONAS LIE (1880–1940) – View of the Seine – signed
and dated 1909 – oil on canvas – 76.5 x 101.7cm.
(Christie's) **$82,500 £42,900**

MAX LIEBERMANN (1847–1935) – Altmännerhaus –
signed – dated and inscribed – oil on canvas –
53.5 x 71.5cm.
(Christie's) **$861,520 £484,000**

LIEVENS

JAN LIEVENS (1607–1674) – Attributed to – Portrait of
an elderly bearded man with beret – signed with
monogram and dated 1631 – oil on wood – 48.7 x 40.3cm.
(Lempertz) **$13,907 £7,947**

Attributed to JEAN ANTOINE LINCK – Swiss
peasants – a pair – watercolour – inscribed 'Grison', 'Glaris'
– both 7¹/₂ x 7³/₄in.
(Bearne's) **$993 £520**

Attributed to JEAN ANTOINE LINCK – Swiss peasant
costumes – a pair – watercolour – inscribed on reverse –
both 7 x 5in.
(Bearne's) **$993 £520**

PAR LINDBLAD (b. 1907) – Girl in white hat – signed –
oil on panel – 38 x 31cm.
(AB Stockholms Auktionsverk) **$888 £465**

RICHARD LINDNER (American, 1901–1978) – Profile
from 'Afternoon' – signed and numbered – colour
lithograph – 71 x 54cm.
(germann Auktionshaus) **$711 £418**

TOD LINDENMUTH (American, 1885–1976) – On
open water, moonlight – signed – oil on masonite –
12 x 13³/₄in.
(Skinner Inc.) **$550 £295**

TOD LINDENMUTH (American, 1885–1976) – In
Harbour – signed – oil on Masonite – 21¹/₂ x 36in.
(Skinner) **$650 £335**

RICHARD LINDNER (1901–1978) – Man with cockerel
– colour litho on blue paper – 63.3 x 50cm.
(AB Stockholms Auktionsverk) **$1,297 £669**

339

RICHARD LINDERUM (German, b. 1851) – The botanist – oil on panel – signed – and companion piece: The cartographer – a pair – one illustrated – 19 x 25.4cm. *(Bonhams)* **$2,984 £1,700**

BENGT LINDSTROM (b. 1925) – Figure in yellow and green – signed – oil on canvas – 73 x 60cm. *(AB Stockholms Auktionsverk)* **$5,331 £2,791**

JOHN LINNELL (1792–1882) – Portrait of Nina as a child, bust length, in profile to the left – signed – inscribed and dated – coloured chalks, on buff card – 18³/4 x 14¹/2in. *(Christie's)* **$898 £495**

LOUIS VAN LINT (1909–1987) – Still life – oil on canvas – signed and dated 45 – 54 x 67cm.
(Hôtel de Ventes Horta) **$9,312 £4,800**

JOHN LINNELL (1792–1852) – Portrait of Thomas Chevalier (1767–1824), seated quarter-length – inscribed and dated Dec. 1816 - watercolour – 20.3 x 13.9cm.
(Lawrence) **$307 £160**

JOHN GEOFFREY CARRUTHERS LITTLE (b. 1928) – Springtime, Quebec, corner of Mazenod et Christophe Colomb – signed and dated 73 – oil on canvas – 30.5 x 40.6cm.
(Pinney's) **$2,551 £1,523**

EDWARD BERNARD LINTOTT (American, 1875–1951) – Dancer Fastening Her Dress – signed – oil on canvas – 24 x 20in.
(Skinner) **$300 £155**

RICHARD LIVESAY (1753–circa 1823) – Portrait of Sir Robert Martin, Bt., small half length, in a dark coat and a white stock – signed and dated 1791 – 22.8 x 20.3cm.
(Christie's) **$703 £385**

LIVESAY

Circle of RICHARD LIVESAY (1733–circa 1825) –
Portrait of a young girl, bust length, in a blue dress
trimmed with lace – 45 x 36cm.
(Christie's) **$1,205 £660**

ANGEL LIZCANO (1846–1929) – The fair of San Isidro
– oil on canvas – signed and dated 1908 – 30.5 x 53cm.
(Duran) **$8,083 £4,188**

SVEN LJUNGBERG (b. 1913) – Bus station – winter
scene – signed – oil on canvas – 61 x 74cm.
(AB Stockholms Auktionsverk) **$7,818 £4,093**

REINHOLD LJUNGGREN (b. 1920) – Auction, Trosa –
signed and numbered 141/260 – colour litho – 35 x 51cm.
(AB Stockholms Auktionsverk) **$648 £334**

JOSE NAVARRO Y LLORENS (Spanish 1867–1923) –
A caravan in a storm – signed – oil on canvas –
36.5 x 54cm.
(Sotheby's) **$12,078 £6,600**

ROBERT MALCOLM LLOYD – Extensive view of an
estuary town – signed and dated 1893 – 13 x 23in.
(Tennants) **$1,700 £850**

GEORGE E. LODGE (1860–1954) - Peregrine Falcon – signed – 8³/₄ x 11in.
(GA Canterbury Auction Galleries) **$1,630 £980**

THOMAS IVESTER LLOYD – Forrard away; and The first flight – signed – pencil and watercolour heightened with white – a pair – 9 x 13¹/₄in.
(Christie's) **$1,333 £715**

GEORGE EDWARD LODGE (1860–1954) – Lesser spotted woodpeckers – signed – watercolour – 9¹/₄ x 5⁷/₈in.
(Christie's) **$4,268 £2,200**

JAMES LODER – Portrait of a hunter standing outside a building, a landscape beyond – signed and dated 1847 – oil on canvas – 16 x 20in.
(Russell, Baldwin & Bright) **$1,343 £750**

JACOB-GERRITZ LOEFF, (active mid 17th Century) – Vessels in the Enkhuizen Roads – signed with monogram – oil on panel – 75 x 105cm.
(Sotheby's) **$34,939 £20,080**

343

LOG

LOG - In the park – signed and dated '48 – 70 x 80cm.
(Christie's) $1,668 £990

DAVID LOGGAN (1635–1692) – Portrait of a gentleman bust length, in ceremonial robes – signed on reverse – pencil, on vellum – oval – 5³/₈ x 4¹/₂in.
(Christie's) $1,792 £990

LOMBARD SCHOOL, 17th Century – The Adoration of the Magi – oil on canvas – 200 x 150cm.
(Finarte Casa d'Aste) $14,304 £7,373

GUSTAVE LOISEAU – Le Pont Tournant à Dieppe – signed and dated '03 – oil on canvas – 55 x 46.5cm.
(Sotheby's) $102,850 £60,500

Attributed to LAMBERT LOMBARD and STUDIO (circa 1506–1566) – The Holy Family – oil on panel – 113.5 x 83.5cm.
(Phillips) $7,160 £4,000

PHILIP ALEXIUS DE LASZLO DE LOMBOS
(1869–1937) – A group portrait of a family with a
gentleman seated half length, his sister seated to his left
and his younger brother standing to his right – signed and
dated 1920 May - 91.5 x 84cm.
(Christie's) $10,058   £5,029

ALESSANDRO LONGHI (1733-1813) – Portrait of
Reverendo Piccardi – signed – oil on canvas – 115 x 98cm.
(Finarte Casa d'Aste) $25,977   £13,551

EDWIN LONG (1829–1891) – A young peasant girl at
her devotions – signed with monogram and dated 1870 –
91.3 x 60.9cm.
(Christie's) $3,814   £2,090

Follower of CARLE VAN LOO – The painters – pastel –
an oval – 900 x 710mm.
(Phillips) $1,534   £800

LOO

JEAN-BAPTISTE VAN LOO, Circle of (1684–1745) –
Double portrait of Monsieur and Madame de Malherbe –
oil on canvas – 81.5 x 107.5cm.
(Sotheby's)   **$9,706   £5,578**

JACOB VAN LOO, (Follower of) – Woman bathers on a
wooded shore – 46.7 x 38.1cm.
(Christie's)   **$6,565   £3,520**

BASILE DE LOOSE (1809–1885) – The school room –
signed and dated 1862 – oil on canvas – 72.4 x 57cm.
(Christie's)   **$26,180   £15,400**

JEAN BAPTISTE VAN LOO (French 1684–1745) –
Manner of – Portrait of Henrietta, Baroness Abergavenny –
oil on canvas – 125 x 100cm.
(AB Stockholms Auktionsverk)   **$3,762   £1,939**

RICARDO LOPEZ-CABRERA (1866–1950) – Rambla
de Mar del Plata – signed and inscribed – oil on paper laid
down on board – 18.4 x 23.5cm.
(Christie's)   **$5,170   £2,750**

WALDEMAR LORENTZON (1899–1982) – The band –
signed – oil on canvas – 38 x 55cm.
(AB Stockholms Auktionsverk) **$5,686 £2,977**

**JOSE RODRIGUEZ DE LOSADA (Spanish, 19th
Century)** – St Francis (after Zurbarán) – signed – oil on
canvas – 64 x 47cm.
(Duran) **$2,128 £1,111**

E. AUGUST LOVATTI (b. 1816) – A water carrier,
Capri – signed – oil on panel – 34.3 x 24.2cm.
(Christie's) **$9,702 £4,950**

LOWCOCK

ALAN LOWNDES (1921–1978) – A Memorial Tree –
signed and dated 1976 – oil on canvas – 51 x 76cm.
(*Christie's*)   **$10,103   £6,050**

CHARLES FREDERICK LOWCOCK (fl. 1878–1922)
– In the temple – signed and dated 81 – oil on panel –
46 x 21.5cm.
(*Christie's*)   **$3,184   £1,650**

ALAN LOWNDES (1921–1978) – Curious Cat – signed –
dated 1964 – oil on board – 26 x 39.5cm.
(*Christie's*)   **$4,776   £2,860**

ORSON BYRON LOWELL (1871-1956) – The
immodesty of the sheath skirt is repellant to American
women – signed and inscribed – pen and black ink on board
– 53.4 x 79.4cm.
(*Christie's*)   **$2,090   £1,240**

ALAN LOWNDES (1921–1978) – Salvation Army –
signed and dated 1965 – oil on board – 24.5 x 30cm.
(*Christie's*)   **$1,707   £880**

LAURENCE STEPHEN LOWRY, R.A. (1887–1976) –
Black bird on a branch – signed and dated 1964 – oil on
board – 17 x 26cm.
(Christie's)   **$17,499   £9,020**

ALAN LOWNDES (1921–1978) – The quarrel – signed
and dated – oil on board – 51 x 36cm.
(Christie's)   **$3,478   £1,870**

LAURENCE STEPHEN LOWRY, R.A. (1887–1976) –
A Footbridge, Stockport Steps – signed and dated 1971 –
oil on canvas – 49.5 x 39.5cm.
(Christie's)   **$51,436   £30,800**

LAURENCE STEPHEN LOWRY, R.A. (1887–1976) –
The Family – signed and dated 1957 – oil on panel –
21.5 x 14.5cm.
(Christie's)   **$22,044   £13,200**

LOZOWICK

LOUIS LOZOWICK (American, 1893–1973) – Still Life #2 (Still Life with apples) – total edition about 75, (Flint, 36) – signed and dated – lithograph on wove paper – unframed – 10³/₈ x 13¹/₈in.
(Skinner Inc.) $5,500   £2,949

MAXIMILIEN LUCE – Notre Dame de Paris, vue du Quai Saint Michel – signed and dated 1901–04 – oil on canvas – 100 x 119cm.
(Sotheby's) $897,600   £528,000

JOHN TEMPLETON LUCAS – Squaring accounts – signed and dated 1877 – 45 x 55cm.
(Spencer's) $4,040   £2,000

MAXIMILIEN LUCE – Coup de vent d'est, St. Claire – signed and dated 1903–4– oil on canvas – 60 x 73cm.
(Sotheby's) $158,950   £93,500

MAXIMILIEN LUCE – Moulineux, Paysage avec maisons – signed and dated '07 – oil on canvas – 49.5 x 63.5cm.
(Sotheby's) $149,600   £88,000

MAXIMILIEN LUCE (French, 1858–1941) – Factory by a canal – signed and dated 1896 – oil on canvas – 61.5 x 82.5cm.
(Galerie Koller Zürich) $158,265   £82,645

ALBERT LUDOVICI Jnr. – Elegant figures in Kensington Gardens – signed – oil on panel – 9 x 13in.
(Tennants)   **$7,800 £3,900**

WILLIAM LUKER, Snr (1851–1889) – Camel and rider – oil on board – signed and dated 1869 – 6 x 9in.
(David Lay)   **$900 £450**

EVARISTE-VITAL LUMINAIS (1822–1896) – The seamstress in the undergrowth – signed – oil on canvas – 24.5 x 19.5cm.
(Sotheby's)   **$3,124 £1,785**

BIRGER LUNDQVIST – Charlie Rivel – signed and dated 1934 – gouache – 17 x 16cm.
(AB Stockholms Auktionsverket)   **$982 £517**

GEORGE BENJAMIN LUKS (1867–1933) – The fly in the ointment – signed – pen and black ink on board - 29.2 x 23.5cm.
(Christie's)   **$1,210 £718**

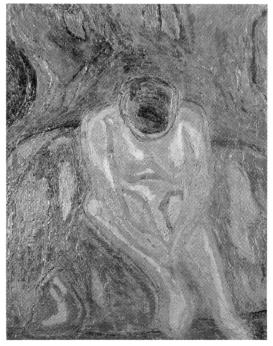

EVERT LUNDQUIST (b. 1904) – Woman – signed – oil on canvas – 102 x 73cm.
(AB Stockholms Auktionsverk)   **$14,214 £7,442**

LUNDQVIST

LUTZ – Study of young girl seated in meadow – signed – oil on canvas – 40 x 30in.
(Du Mouchelles)   **$1,500 £804**

GUSTAF LEONARD LUNDQVIST (1827–1905) – The painter outside with his easel – signed and dated 1898 – oil on canvas – 23.5 x 17.5cm.
(AB Stockholms Auktionsverk)   **$825 £425**

OTTO LUSSI (Swiss, 1883–1942) – Woman of Ticino – bears estate stamp – oil on canvas – 61 x 50cm.
(germann Auktionshaus)   **$533 £314**

JUAN RAMON LUZURIAGA (b. 1938) – Old man with guitar – watercolour – signed - 32.5 x 25cm.
(Duran)   **$425 £220**

ALBERT LYNCH – Portrait of a young lady in a straw
hat – signed and inscribed – pastel – 11 x 8¹/₄in.
(Christie's) **$821 £440**

ROBERT WALKER MACBETH, R.A. (1848–1910) –
Coming from St Ives market – signed with initials and
dated 1878 – oil on canvas – 94.5 x 175cm.
(Christie's) **$8,712 £4,400**

THOMAS MACKAY (1851–1909) - Feeding the Ducks
– signed – watercolour heightened with white –
6¹/₂ x 9³/₄in.
(Christie's) **$3,841 £1,980**

AUGUST MACKE (1887-1914) – Yellow trees – charcoal
drawing – with estate stamp – 20 x 26cm.
(Galerie Koller Zürich) **$11,078 £5,785**

ADOLF MACKEPRANG (Danish 1833–1911) – Italian
peasants on the way to market – signed – oil on canvas –
70 x 83cm.
(AB Stockholms Auktionsverk) **$6,807 £3,509**

EMMA F. MACRAE, A.N.A. (1887–1974) – Flowers in
Zuni pot – oil on panel – signed – 16 x 12in.
(Bruce D. Collins) **$2,640 £1,427**

JEAN BAPTISTE MADOU (Belgian, 1796–1877) –
Pipe smoking – signed and dated 1867 – watercolour and
gouache on paper – 11¹/₂ x 13³/₄in.
(Skinner Inc.) **$500 £268**

MAES

EUGENIE R. MAES – Feeding Time – signed –
50 x 65cm.
(Spencer's)   **$8,592   £4,800**

J. BAPTISTE MAES (1794–1850) – A young Roman
woman at her toilet on a carnival day – oil on canvas –
signed and dated – 97 x 134cm.
(Hôtel de Ventes Horta)   **$43,456   £22,400**

NICOLAES MAES (1634–1693) – Portrait of a young
man, bust length, wearing a long wig – oil on canvas laid
down on board – 35.6 x 27.3cm.
(Christie's)   **$10,019   £5,060**

JOHN CHARLES MAGGS – Coach and four in the snow
with figures – oil on canvas – 17½ x 24½in.
(Hobbs & Chambers)   **$1,945   £1,000**

RENE MAGRITTE (1898–1967) – The storm – signed –
gouache on paper – 40 x 55cm.
(Christie's)   **$173,360   £88,000**

GIAN-FRANCESCO DE MAINERI (circa 1504/05) –
The Madonna and child – on panel – 52.5 x 38cm.
(Phillips)   **$125,300   £70,000**

MARTIN MAINGAUD (1692–1725) – Equestrian portrait of a gentleman, probably Mr Glover, dancing master in London, 1725 – bears signature and inscription l.r. – oil on canvas – 125 x 100.3cm.
(Sotheby's)   **$24,035**   **£12,650**

SCHOOL OF MALTA, Circa 1700 – The Immaculate Conception – 117.5 x 77.5cm.
(Christie's)   **$6,600**   **£3,300**

AUGUST MALMSTROM (1829–1901) – Brother and sister – signed with monogram – oil on canvas – 45 x 33cm.
(AB Stockholms Auktionsverk)   **$6,807**   **£3,509**

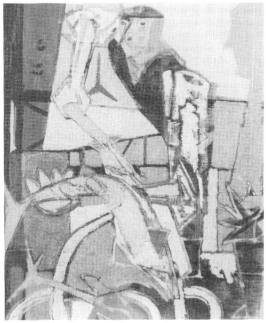

ERIC MALTHOUSE – Sorting fish – signed, inscribed and dated 19.1.57 – unframed – 76.2 x 55.3cm.
(Christie's)   **$616**   **£308**

MANCENELLI

GUSTAVO MANCINELLI (1842–1906) – The odalisque – signed and dated 1875 – oil on canvas – 92.7 x 66cm.
(Christie's) $28,050 £16,500

FRANCESCO MANCINI (1830–1905) – A Neapolitan coastal road – signed – oil on canvas – 43.8 x 76.2cm.
(Christie's) $15,092 £7,700

JOSEF MANGOLD (1884–1937) – Poppies in a grey ceramic jug – signed and dated 1931 – oil on canvas – 53 x 43cm.
(Lempertz) $18,861 £9,722

ANTONIO MANCINI (1852–1930) – Tempo di Carnevale – signed – oil on canvas – 153.6 x 59.4cm.
(Christie's) $199,364 £101,200

HENRI MANGUIN (1874–1949) – Jeanne à la Fontaine, Villa Demière – signed – oil on canvas – 116 x 89cm.
(Christie's) $376,200 £220,000

POL MARA – Portrait of a woman – signed on reverse –
mixed media
(Galerie Moderne) **$3,270   £1,712**

HARRINGTON MANN – Portrait of a young girl in blue
– signed – oil on canvas – 111.8 x 66cm.
(Ritchie's) **$1,470   £762**

L H S MANN – Young lady in black shawl, poised under
tree – oil on panel – 11 x 9in.
(Jacobs & Hunt) **$2,000   £1,000**

SCHOOL OF THE MARCHES – Sacra Conversazione
with Saint Catherine and a Bishop Saint – oil on panel –
38.1 x 49.5cm.
(Christie's) **$5,720   £2,860**

R. MANN (19th Century) – A Blenheim Cavalier King
Charles spaniel on a red cushion – signed and indistinctly
dated 1866 – oil on canvas – 35.6 x 45.7cm.
(Christie's) **$2,926   £1,540**

M. MARESCA (Italian, 19th/20th Century) – Open air
market – signed – 24 x 32in.
(Du Mouchelles) **$1,800   £965**

MARGETSON

WILLIAM HENRY MARGETSON (English, 1861–1940) – Love's Talisman – oil on canvas – signed with initials – 86.3 x 55.8cm.
(Bonhams) **$2,282 £1,300**

FRANCESCO DI MARIA – The tambourine girl – signed – pencil and watercolour – 20½ x 10¾in.
(Christie's) **$1,744 £935**

JOSEPH MARGULIES (American, 1896–1984) – The Cars in the Yard/A Gloucester Scene – unsigned – artist's estate stamp on the reverse – oil on canvas – 19½ x 24in.
(Skinner) **$1,000 £515**

MARIANI (19th Century) – The pet pigeon; and The pet kitten – both signed – in carved Florentine frames – 29.2 x 24.2cm.: one illustrated.
(Christie's) **$2,965 £1,760**

Attributed to ONORIO MARINARI (1687–1715) –
Christ in the Garden of Gethsemane – inscribed with
artist's name and dated 1659 on reverse – oil on panel –
42.5 x 32cm.
(Phillips) $1,900 £950

YOSHIO MARKINO - Evening scene at Piccadilly near
Hyde Park Corner – signed and titled in pencil to margin –
wood block print – 12³/₄ x 9¹/₄in.
(Hy. Duke & Son) $1,416 £800

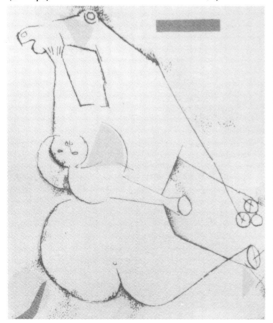

MARINO MARINI (Italian, 1901–1980) – Gioco
Perfetto, 1972 – from the album Marino to Strawinsky –
total edition of 110 – signed and numbered 26/75 – etching
with colours on wove paper - 15³/₈ x 12⁵/₈in.
(Skinner Inc.) $1,600 £858

HENRY STACY MARKS, R.A. (1829–1898) – Portrait
of E.B.S. Montefiore – signed with initials and dated 1873
– oil on canvas laid down on panel – 29.2 x 22.5cm.
(Christie's) $4,670 £2,420

MARNY

PAUL MARNY (1829–1914) – Cologne from the river, Germany – signed – pencil and watercolour heightened with white – 21½ x 29½in.
(Christie's)   **$2,347**   **£1,210**

ALBERT MARQUET – La Cité sous la neige – signed – oil on canvas – 73 x 92cm.
(Sotheby's)   **$523,600**   **£308,000**

ALBERT MARQUET – Les Sables-d'Olonne – signed – oil on canvas – 65 x 81cm.
(Sotheby's)   **$569,500**   **£335,000**

FRANCISCO DOMINGO MARQUES (1842–1920) – The violinist – oil on panel – signed and dated 93 – 61 x 46cm.
(Duran)   **$3,032**   **£1,571**

REGINALD MARSH (American, 1898–1954) – Girl
with umbrella – edition of 100 - signed and numbered –
engraving on paper – unframed – 5^{13}/$_{16}$ x 3^{15}/$_{16}$in.
(Skinner Inc.) $200 £107

REGINALD MARSH (1898–1954) - Two young women
walking and two young women: a double-sided
watercolour – signed and dated 44 – recto and verso –
brush and ink wash and watercolour on paper –
78 x 56.8cm.
(Christie's) **$44,000 £22,880**

REGINALD MARSH (1889–1954) – On the carousel –
signed – black ink on paper – 25.5 x 20cm.
(Christie's) **$3,080 £1,632**

REGINALD MARSH (1898-1954) – Tattoo-Shave-
Haircut (Sasowsky 140) – etching – 1932 – on wove paper
– signed in pencil – numbered 19, from the edition of 31 -
250 x 250mm.
(Christie's) **$22,000 £13,056**

REGINALD MARSH (1889–1954) – Out for a stroll –
signed and dated 1952 – oil on masonite – 40.6 x 30cm.
(Christie's) **$12,100 £6,413**

MARTENS

CONRAD MARTENS (English, 1801–1878) – A view of Sydney Harbour – watercolour and bodycolour over lithographic base – 14.6 x 21.6cm.
(Bonhams)   **$2,022 £1,000**

ANSON A. MARTIN (fl. 1840–1861) – Portrait of a horse – signed – oil on canvas – 16 x 20in.
(David Lay)   **$437 £230**

EDITH MARTINEAU (1842–1909) – A young girl seated on a wheelbarrow in a wood – signed and dated 1884 – pencil and watercolour – 10 x 13¼in.
(Christie's)   **$3,684 £1,870**

EDITH MARTINEAU (1842–1909) – The milkmaid – signed and dated 1882 – pencil and watercolour heightened with white – 9 x 6½in.
(Christie's)   **$1,387 £715**

F.E. MARTINEZ – The present – signed – pencil and watercolour – 13 x 8½in.
(Christie's)   **$1,067 £572**

GONZALO BILBAO Y MARTINEZ – Calle de las
Cruces, Toledo – signed and dated – oil on board –
41.5 x 33cm.
(Sothebys)   **$6,301   £3,520**

FONCO MASAT – In the tentadero – signed – oil on
canvas – 50 x 61cm.
(Duran)   **$836   £420**

FRANS MASEREEL (1889–1972) – On the banks of the
Rhone – signed with monogram – indian ink and
watercolour on ivory paper – 30.5 x 23cm.
(Lempertz)   **$2,829   £1,458**

JACQUELINE MARVAL – Spring adorned – signed –
oil on canvas – 111 x 80cm.
(Jean-Claude Anaf)   **$69,421   £36,157**

FRANS MASEREEL (1885–1972) – The pulled up skirt
– signed with monogram – oil on board – 63.2 x 68.4cm.
(Hôtel de Ventes Horta)   **$2,007   £1,147**

MASOLLE

Circle of **QUENTIN MASSYS (c. 1465–1530)** – St. Jerome in his study – oil on panel – 66.5 x 50.5cm.
(Phillips)   **$4,781   £2,400**

HELMER MASOLLE (1884–1969) – Man standing smoking a pipe – signed and dated 26 – oil on panel – 34 x 20cm.
(AB Stockholms Auktionsverk)   **$1,701   £877**

POMPEO MASSANI (Italian, 1850–1920) – Blind man's buff – signed – oil on canvas – 48.3 x 69.8cm.
(Bonhams)   **$12,132   £6,000**

AGOSTINO MASUCCI (1691–1758) – The presentation in the temple – oil on canvas – 168.3 x 123cm.
(Phillips)   **$19,920   £10,000**

FORTUNINO MATANIA, R.I. – An Italian dandy with his lady in a Venetian square – signed – watercolour – 20½ x 16in.
(Geering & Colyer) **$1,144** **£625**

FORTUNIO MATANIA (b. 1881) – Aqua Santa – signed – signed and inscribed on an attached label on the reverse – on board – 43.3 x 24.2cm.
(Christie's) **$4,819** **£2,860**

FORTUNINO MATANIA, R.I. – Being led a merry dance – signed – oil on panel – 9¾ x 14in.
(Geering & Colyer) **$1,235** **£675**

FORTUNINO MATANIA – The Three Arts Ball at the Royal Albert Hall, 1921 – monochrome watercolour – signed unframed – 39.4 x 26.7cm.
(Bonhams) **$370** **£220**

MATEOS

FRANCISCO MATEOS (1897–1976) – Traditional festival – oil on canvas - signed – signed, titled and dated 1964 on reverse – 100 x 81cm.
(Duran) **$14,147 £7,330**

F.C. MATHEWSON – Hollyhocks – signed and dated 1904 – watercolour – 14^1/$_2$ x 10^1/$_2$in.
(Christie's) **$697 £396**

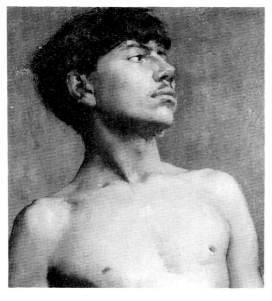

ARTHUR FRANK MATHEWS (1860–1945) - Portrait of Xavier Martinez – signed – oil on canvas laid down on panel – 23.2 x 21cm.
(Christie's) **$15,400 £8,008**

HENRI MATISSE (1869–1954) – Young woman – signed and dated 36 – pen and black ink on paper – 58 x 47cm.
(Christie's) **$368,390 £187,000**

MAX

ROBERTO ECHAURREN MATTA (Chilean, b. 1912) – Les Helvements – edition of 100 – signed and numbered "76/100" - coloured etching and aquatint on paper (full sheet) – framed – 16³/₈ x 22in.
(Skinner Inc.) **$650 £348**

HENRI MATISSE – Visage - signed and dated with dedication 51 – brush and indian ink – 44 x 33.4cm.
(Sotheby's) **$67,320 £39,600**

ALFRED HENRY MAURER (1868–1932) – Flappers – signed – tempera on gessoed board – 55.3 x 46.5cm.
(Christie's) **$19,800 £10,296**

HENRI MATISSE (French, 1869–1954) – Danseuse assise (en hauteur), 1927 – signed and numbered – lithograph on wove paper – unframed – 19 x 13in.
(Skinner Inc.) **$19,000 £10,188**

GABRIEL CORNELIS VON MAX (1840–1915) – An ourang-outang sleeping in a barn – signed – 94 x 79cm.
(Christie's) **$4,359 £2,179**

JEAN A. LE MAYEUR (1844–1923) – Resting in the inner courtyard of a Marrakesh harem - mixed media on paper
(Hôtel de Ventes Horta)   **$12,416 £6,400**

ROGER MAXIMILIEN (1894–1918) - Seated nude – signed – oil on canvas laid down on board
(Hôtel de Ventes Horta)   **$2,725 £1,557**

M.B. (19th Century) – Numerous villagers in a street – signed with initials and dated 18/12/8 63 - oil on panel – 39.5 x 30cm.
(Christie's)   **$2,347 £1,173**

PHILIP WILLIAM MAY (1864–1903) – Study of Joseph Chamberlain, full length, in a frock coat and top hat – signed and dated – pen and black ink on Bristol board – 10¹/₂ x 7³/₈in.
(Christie's)   **$1,083 £605**

ILA MAE MCAFEE (American, b. 1897/1900) – The Combat Zone – signed and titled – lithograph on paper – unframed – 13⁵/₈ x 17¹/₂in.
(Skinner Inc.)   **$50 £27**

EVELYN MCCORMICK (1869–1948) – Monterey houses – signed – oil on canvas – 81 x 96.5cm.
(Butterfield & Butterfield) $5,225   £2,561

MARY McCROSSAN – The Rialto Bridge, Venice – signed and dated 1923 – watercolour and pencil – 25.4 x 35.5cm.
(Christie's) $878   £462

J. MCCOLVIN (late 19th century) – The fruit girl; and The harvester – signed – 60.9 x 30.5cm. – a pair – one illustrated
(Christie's) $2,208   £1,100

FRANCIS MCCOMAS (1875–1938) – English farmhouse – signed and dated 1908 – watercolour on paper – 42 x 55cm.
(Butterfield & Butterfield) $4,950   £2,426

AMBROSE MCEVOY – Marie R. Scott – signed – unframed – 76 x 63cm.
(Christie's) $1,650   £825

MCGILL

DONALD MCGILL – 'My Girl's name is Gertrude ...' –
signed and typed inscription – watercolour and bodycolour
– 20.3 x 15.3cm.
(Bonhams) **$517 £300**

E.L. MCLOY (circa 1850–circa 1920) – Daydreams –
signed – pencil and watercolour heightened with white –
23 x 18in.
(Christie's) **$2,600 £1,320**

SAMUEL MCLOY (1831–1904) – Children playing with
shells on the beach – signed – pencil and watercolour –
10¼ x 13½in.
(Christie's) **$6,501 £3,300**

ROBERT MCGREGOR, R.S.A. (1848–1922) - Mending
the fence – signed – oil on canvas – 33.5 x 24cm.
(Christie's) **$15,614 £9,350**

ARTHUR JOSEPH MEADOWS (1843–1907) – Verona
on the Adige – signed and dated 1892 – oil on canvas –
61 x 91.5cm.
(Christie's) **$11,979 £6,050**

JOHN MELVILLE (b. 1902) – Reclining nude – signed and dated 1934 – oil on board – 46 x 57cm.
(Christie's) $4,776 £2,860

JAMES EDWIN MEADOWS (1828–1888) – A rural cottage – signed and dated 1863 – 40.6 x 35.6cm.
(Christie's) $5,621 £3,080

HANS MEMLING, (Follower of) – Portrait of a man, head and shoulders, in a black hat – on panel – 29.5 x 21.8cm.
(Christie's) $6,564 £3,520

JOHAN MEKKINK (born 1904) – A portrait of Mrs. J.C. Brugman-Dreckschmidt – signed and dated 40 – oil on panel – 38 x 28cm.
(Christie's) $2,412 £1,258

Studio of ANTON RAPHAEL MENGS (1728–1779) – Portrait of the Elector Frederick Christian of Saxony (1706–1763) – oil on canvas – 53.5 x 41.5cm.
(Sotheby's) $10,450 £5,500

MENINSKY

BERNARD MENINSKY – Maternity – signed – gouache, brush and black ink – 50.8 x 40cm.
(Christie's) **$7,733 £4,070**

ADOLPH VON MENZEL (1815–1905) – Man in frock coat wirh top hat – signed and dated 67 – pencil drawing on paper – 23 x 17.3cm.
(Lempertz) **$5,389 £2,778**

SIGMUND JOSEPH MENKES (1896–) – Girl with flowers – signed – watercolour and gouache on paper – 60.3 x 45.7cm.
(Christie's) **$1,760 £933**

JOHANNES MERTZ (1918–1891) – The beloved cavalier – signed and dated 1857 – oil on panel – 53 x 41cm.
(Christie's) **$3,353 £1,676**

CONRADO MESEGUER – At the fountain – signed –
oil on canvas – 50 x 65cm.
(Duran) **$5,320 £2,778**

Ascribed to HENDRIK WILLEM MESDAG (Dutch) –
Fisherman and boats along the coast – signed – oil on
canvas – 12 x 16in.
(Selkirk's) **$300 £147**

SIDNEY HAROLD METEYARD (English 1868–1947)
– Venus and Adonis – oil on canvas –
105.5 x 110.5cm.
(Sotheby's) **$119,460 £66,000**

METZINGER

JEAN METZINGER – Femme à sa toilette – signed – oil
on canvas – 92 x 65cm.
(Sotheby's) **$158,950 £93,500**

C. MEUNIER (Belgian, 1831–1905) – The water carrier
– signed – watercolour on paper – 62 x 32cm.
(Hôtel de Ventes Horta) **$1,451 £754**

Follower of ADAM FRANS VAN DER MEULEN –
Equestrian portait of Louis XIV – oil on canvas –
114 x 98cm.
(Sotheby's) **$14,630 £7,700**

EMILE MEYER (19th Century) – Girl in hammock –
signed and dated 1889 – oil on canvas – 206 x 270cm.
(Sotheby's) **$11,245 £6,693**

HENDRICK DE MEYER (circa 1620–1690) – Snowy landscape – oil on canvas – 99.5 x 125.5cm.
(Jean-Claude Anaf) $37,079   £19,212

FRIEDRICH EDOUARD MEYERHEIM (1808–1879) – Family chores - signed and dated 1859 – oil on canvas – 46.5 x 39.7cm.
(Christie's) $47,674   £24,200

ROLF MEYER (Swiss, b. 1913) – Armando Spaccanapoli, the Florentine dwarf – signed on reverse – oil on canvas – 160 x 80cm.
(germann Auktionshaus)   **$1,849   £1,088**

LOPEZ MEZQUITA – Lady – signed – oil on canvas – 76 x 62cm.
(Duran)   **$678   £341**

MICHONZE

GREGOIRE MICHONZE – Figures in a French village –
signed and dated '52 – on board – 33 x 40.6cm.
(Christie's) **$2,508 £1,320**

WILLIAM VAN MIERIS THE YOUNGER
(1662–1747) – Portrait of a lady, standing three-quarter
length, on a balcony – signed and dated – on panel –
22 x 17cm.
(Phillips) **$7,160 £4,000**

HELMUT MIDDENDORF (b. 1953) – "Guitar" – signed
and dated 80 – gouache, watercolour and coloured chalks –
61.5 x 87cm.
(AB Stockholms Auktionsverk) **$2,162 £1,114**

JAN MIEL (1599–1664) – A rest during the hunt – oil on
canvas – 54 x 75cm.
(Finarte Casa d'Aste) **$26,874 £14,019**

MICHIEL VAN MIEREVELT, (Manner of) – Portrait
of a gentleman, head and shoulders, wearing a ruff collar –
on panel – 43.2 x 29.8cm.
(Christie's) **$1,949 £1,045**

GIOVANNI MIGLIARA (1785–1837) – The interior of Milan Cathedral with a procession and numerous figures – signed and dated 1816 – oil on canvas – 61 x 52cm.
(Phillips) $63,744   £32,000

MARTIN MIJTENS (1648–1736) – Attributed to – Portrait of Maria Teresa of Austria – half length – oil on canvas laid down on board – 73 x 59cm.
(AB Stockholms Auktionsverk) $5,164   £2,662

Manner of ABRAHAM MIGNON – Tulips, roses, lilies, convolvuli, a dahlia and other flowers and fruit in a glass vase on a stone ledge before a niche – unframed – 93 x 70.2cm.
(Christie's) $50,094   £25,300

AURELIANO MILANI (1675–1749) – The tribute – oil on canvas – 62.5 x 40.5cm.
(Finarte Casa d'Aste) $25,977   £13,551

MILEY

R.A. MILEY – A jockey up on a bay racehorse – oil on canvas – 27½ x 35in.
(Hy. Duke & Son) $3,009 £1,700

ADOLPHE MILICH (Swiss, 1884–1964) – Nude – signed – oil on canvas – 92 x 73.5cm.
(germann Auktionshaus) $5,490 £2,823

SIR JOHN EVERETT MILLAIS, P.R.A. (1829–1896) – Portrait of Mrs. Charles Wertheimer – signed and dated 1891 – oil on canvas – 127.6 x 83.9cm.
(Christie's) $42,460 £22,000

ADOLPHE MILICH (Swiss, 1884–1964) – Portrait of a young woman – signed – oil on canvas – 55 x 46cm.
(germann Auktionshaus) $2,672 £1,399

SIR JOHN EVERETT MILLAIS (English 1829–96) – signed with monogram - oil on canvas - 105.5 x 75cm.
(Sotheby's) $298,650 £165,000

ROY MILLER "They're off" – signed and dated 1975 –
24 x 30in.
(Tennants) $1,300   £650

SIR JOHN EVERETT MILLAIS, Bt., P.R.A. (English
1829–96) – A huguenot – signed with monogram – oil on
board – arched top – 24 x 18cm.
(Sotheby's) $408,155   £225,500

ROY MILLER – Berganza, Tartarelle and other mares
and foals at Phil Bull's Sezincote Stud, Glos. – Phil Bull
observing from the fence – inscribed on reverse –
24 x 36in.
(Tennants) $2,400   £1,200

RAOUL MILLAIS (b. 1901) – Huntsman and Hounds –
signed – oil on canvas – 49.5 x 60cm.
(Christie's) $6,402   £3,300

JOHN MILLER (19th Century) – The Dittisham ferry on
the River Dart, Sth Devon – signed – 55 x 90cm.
(Christie's) $3,688   £1,844

WILLIAM WATT MILNE (1873–1951) – The Harbour
– signed and dated 99 – oil on canvas – 24.5 x 35cm.
(Christie's) $3,201   £1,650

MILNE

JOHN MACLAUCHLAN MILNE, R.S.A. – A glimpse of the Firth – oil on canvas – signed - 51 x 61cm.
(Bonhams) **$8,800 £4,400**

A. MININO (late 19th century) – Boating in the Bay of Naples – signed – oil on canvas – 27.2 x 45cm.
(Christie's) **$4,312 £2,200**

JOAQUIN MIRO (Spanish, 1875–1941) – A busy street scene – signed – oil on board – unframed – 15.9 x 21cm.
(Bonhams) **$1,213 £600**

ALFRED R. MITCHELL (1888–1972) – The white barn – signed – oil on board – 41 x 51cm.
(Butterfield & Butterfield) **$6,600 £3,235**

GEORGE B. MITCHELL (1872–1966) – The hoop dance – watercolour heightened with gouache – signed and dated '52 – 7¹/₄ x 14¹/₄in.
(Bruce D. Collins) **$330 £178**

THEO MODESPACHER (Swiss, 1897–1955) – In the café – signed and dated 46 – watercolour – 19 x 17.7cm.
(germann Auktionshaus) **$668 £350**

LOUIS CHARLES MOELLER (1855–1930) – A difficult play – signed – oil on canvas – 46 x 61cm.
(Christie's) $11,000 £5,830

LOUIS CHARLES MOELLER (1855–1930) – Life's small pleasures – signed – oil on canvas – 40.5 x 30.4cm.
(Christie's) $8,800 £4,664

H.A.J.M. MOERKERK – Village scene – signed – oil on canvas – 71 x 101cm.
(Glerum) $543 £273

MOES

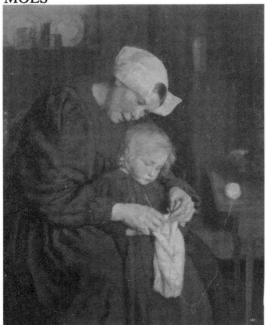

JOHN HENRY MOLE (1814–1886) – Near Tummel Bridge, Perthshire – signed and dated 1858 – pencil and watercolour heightened with white – 7⅝ x 11¾in.
(Christie's) $2,059   £1,045

WALLY MOES (1856–1918) – Eerste Breiles – signed – 57 x 43.5cm.
(Christie's) $16,764   £8,382

JOHN HENRY MOLE – Wrack gatherers on the Devonshire coast – signed – pencil and watercolour – 13½ x 20in.
(Christie's) $1,093   £572

MARCEL EMMANUEL MOISAND (1874–1903) – Jeune Femme disant au Revoir – signed – oil on panel – 34.8 x 26.8cm.
(Christie's) $5,790   £3,080

JULIO MOISES (Spanish 19th/20th Century) – A nude before the mirror – signed and dated – oil on canvas – 115 x 147cm.
(Sotheby's) $16,104   £8,800

JAN MIENSE MOLENAER (Dutch 1630–76) – Manner of – Interior with men playing cards – signed with monogram – oil on panel – 29 x 28cm.
(AB Stockholms Auktionsverk) $2,239   £1,154

– Via Appia, Rome – signed and dated 1929 – oil on canvas – 89 x 130.8cm.
(Christie's) **$26,004 £13,200**

JEAN FERDINAND MONCHABLON (French, 1855–1904) – The River Saone, near Grignancourt – signed – oil on canvas – 46.3 x 61.6cm.
(Bonhams) **$6,066 £3,000**

CLAUDE MONET – Les deux pêcheurs – signed – oil on canvas – 38 x 52.5cm.
(Sotheby's) **$2,805,000 £1,650,000**

PEDER MØNSTED (Danish 1859–1941) – Farmyard scene in summer – signed and dated 1938 – oil on canvas – 41 x 63cm.
(AB Stockholms Auktionsverk) **$8,777 £4,524**

MARTIN MONNICKENDAM (1874–1943) – A pineapple, a pear, an apple and an orange on a dish – signed and dated 1930 – 55.5 x 41.5cm.
(Christie's) **$2,012 £1,006**

PEDER MØNSTED (Danish 1859–1941) – Interior with girl crocheting – signed and dated 1905 – oil on canvas – 79 x 55cm.
(AB Stockholms Auktionsverk) **$35,826 £18,467**

MONTEZIN

PIERRE-EUGENE MONTEZIN – Marais de la Somme
– signed – oil on canvas – oval: 70 x 83cm.
(Sotheby's) **$140,250 £82,500**

Circle of KAREL DE MOOR (1695–?) – A lace maker
seated in an interior observed by a couple – oil on panel –
39.8 x 30.4cm.
(Phillips) **$3,456 £1,800**

JULES MONTIGNY (1847–1900) – The harvest 1883 –
signed – oil on canvas – 155 x 215cm.
(Hôtel de Ventes Horta) **$8,258 £4,088**

FANNIE MOODY, S.W.A. (fl. 1885–1897) – Jack
Russell pups and a tabby kitten – signed – oil on board –
38.1 x 52.1cm.
(Christie's) **$3,344 £1,760**

PIETER CORNELIS DE MOOR (1866–1953) – A siren
– signed – oil on panel – 34 x 30cm.
(Christie's) **$2,816 £1,408**

384

HENRY MOORE, O.M., C.H. – Three women and child – signed and dated '44 – watercolour, pen and indian ink, wax crayon and pastel over pencil – 37 x 48cm.
(Sotheby's) $168,300   £99,000

HENRY MOORE, O.M., C.H. (1898–1986) – Recumbent woman – signed and dated 35 – brush, black ink and grey wash – 38.5 x 56cm.
(Christie's) $11,097   £5,720

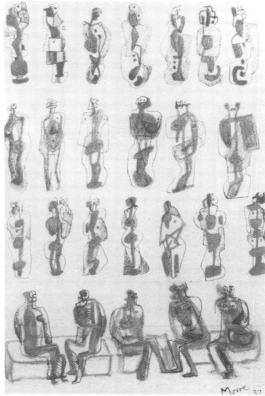

ALBERT JOSEPH MOORE (English 1841–93) – End of the story – signed with anthemion – oil on canvas laid on board – 86 x 30.5cm.
(Sotheby's) $248,875   £137,500

HENRY MOORE, O.M., C.H. (1898–1986) – Studies for sculpture – signed and dated – watercolour, pencil, pen and black ink on paper – 27 x 18.5cm.
(Christie's) $25,393   £14,850

MOORE

JOHN COLLINGHAM MOORE (1829–1880) – Portrait of a young girl, said to be Rosalie, Daughter of Guillaume Coster, Esq. – signed and dated 1875 – pencil and watercolour heightened with white – 28³/₄ x 16in.
(Christie's) **$3,414 £1,760**

FRANCESCO MORANDINI called Il Poppi (1544–1597) - Portrait of a lady, bust-length in profile to the left, wearing a pink dress – oil on panel - 66.7 x 51.7cm.
(Phillips) **$21,912 £11,000**

THOMAS MORAN (1837–1926) – Mist in the canyon – signed and dated 1914 – oil on canvas – 68.5 x 56cm.
(Christie's) **$385,000 £200,200**

GUSTAVE MOREAU (French 1826–98) – L'ibis rose – signed – watercolour and bodycolour – 36 x 24cm.
(Sotheby's) **$547,525 £302,500**

HENRY MORET – Pêcheurs sur la Plage de Larmour –
signed and dated 1883 – oil on canvas – 61 x 103cm.
(Sotheby's) $46,750 £27,500

PAULUS DE MOREELSE (1571–1638), Circle of –
Portrait of a woman – oil on panel – 118 x 91cm.
(Sotheby's) $21,352 £12,271

ALFRED MORGAN (English fl. 1862–1917) – An
omnibus ride to Piccadilly Circus – Mr Gladstone travelling
with ordinary passengers – signed and dated 1885 – oil on
canvas – 81 x 110.5cm.
(Sotheby's) $179,190 £99,000

Probably JOHN MORGAN (English 1823–86) –
Toothache – indistinctly signed – oil on canvas –
35 x 30cm.
(AB Stockholms Auktionsverk)   **$6,270   £3,232**

FRED MORGAN – The ugly bug ball – signed –
inscribed and dated 1916 – oil on canvas laid on board –
unframed – 45 x 28cm.
(Sotheby's)   **$4,978   £2,750**

BERTHE MORISOT (1841–1895) – Jeune Femme se
levant (Mlle. Euphrasie) – the studio stamp lower left (L.
1826) – oil on canvas – 67.9 x 64.8cm.
(Christie's)   **$881,100   £495,000**

FREDERICK MORGAN (1856–1927) – Feeding the
ducks – signed – oil on canvas – 40.7 x 48.2cm.
(Christie's)   **$25,476   £13,200**

Circle of GEORGE MORLAND (1763–1804) – A
spaniel in a woodland – signed with initials 'G. Md.' –
28.5 x 36.7cm.
(Christie's)   **$2,409   £1,320**

HARRY MORLEY, A.R.A. (1881–1943) – The Sea Race – signed – oil on canvas – 85 x 134.5cm.
(Christie's) $18,370 £11,000

HARRY MORLEY, A.R.A. (1881–1943) – The girl by
the window – signed – oil on canvas – 91.5 x 76cm.
(Christie's) $3,306 £1,980

STELLAN MORNER (1896–1979) – Landscape with
figures and old lady with photograph – signed – oil on
canvas – 38 x 46cm.
(AB Stockholms Auktionsverk) $2,932 £1,535

Circle of **FRANCESCO TORBIDO, IL MORO** (active
in Venice circa 1562) – The Madonna appearing to St.
Bernard – oil on canvas – 67 x 56cm.
(Phillips) $2,500 £1,250

MORRIS

SIR CEDRIC MORRIS (1889–1982) – Worms Head, Gower Peninsula – signed and dated 28 – oil on canvas – 56 x 68.5cm.
(Christie's)   **$18,232   £9,350**

R.S. MOSELEY (fl. 1862–1893) – A Mastiff, Bloodhound and a Collie – signed – oil on canvas – 40.7 x 55.9cm.
(Christie's)   **$5,434   £2,860**

SIR CEDRIC MORRIS, Bt. (1889–1982) – Landscape in Herefordshire – signed – oil on canvas – 66 x 76cm.
(Phillips)   **$2,328   £1,400**

ALBERTO MORROCCO (b. 1917) – Portrait of Lauri Morrocco – signed – oil on canvas – 96.5 x 77.5cm.
(Christie's)   **$6,829   £3,520**

KOLOMAN MOSER (Austrian 1868–1918) – An illustration for a poem, Ein Wunder – signed – pen and brush and ink – 32 x 17cm.
(Sotheby's)   **$2,417   £1,320**

OTTO MUELLER (1874–1930) – Girl on the sofa –
signed – original lithograph – 29 x 39.7cm.
(Lempertz) **$11,452   £5,903**

WILLIAM JAMES MULLER (1812–1845) – The
Temple of Baaldeack, Bekka Valley – signed –
29.2 x 52.1cm.
(Christie's) **$2,208   £1,210**

KOLOMAN MOSER (Austrian 1868–1918) – A portrait
of Sylvia Koller – signed and dedicated to the sitter –
pencil – unframed – 48 x 35cm.
(Sotheby's) **$10,065   £5,500**

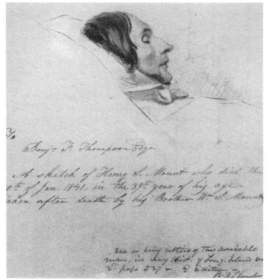

WILLIAM SIDNEY MOUNT (1807–1868) – Henry
Smith Mount on his death bed – signed and inscribed – pen
and ink and watercolour on paper – 19 x 19.7cm.
(Christie's) **$16,500   £8,580**

AUGUSTUS E. MULREADY (fl. 1863–1905) – The maid
of all work – signed and dated 1879 – watercolour – 28 x
20cm.
(Phillips) **$2,685   £1,500**

MUNCH

SIR ALFRED MUNNINGS, P.R.A. (1878–1959) – Sybil Harker with the Norfolk Hunt at Wymondham – signed – oil on canvas – 86.5 x 100.5cm.
(Christie's)   **$171,600   £88,000**

EDVARD MUNCH – Self portrait 1895 – signed – lithograph on vellum – 45.6 x 31.7cm.
(AB Stockholms Auktionsverk)   **$9,367   £4,828**

EDVARD MUNCH (1863–1944) – Moonrise – signed – original lithograph on vellum – 20.5 x 43cm.
(Lempertz)   **$6,063   £3,125**

SIR ALFRED MUNNINGS, P.R.A. (1878–1959) – A young lady – signed and dated 01 – oil on canvas – 33 x 24cm.
(Christie's)   **$9,552   £5,720**

EDVARD MUNCH (1863–1944) – House on the knoll – signed – wax crayon on paper – 17.2 x 19.1cm.
(Christie's)   **$20,587   £10,450**

Circle of FRANCESCO DE MURA – Flora handed a basket of flowers by two putti – oil on panel – 62.2 x 109.2cm.
(Christie's)   **$52,800   £26,400**

BARTOLOME ESTEBAN MURILLO, **Follower of** – A woman en déshabille (Susannah?) – 20.3 x 15.2cm.
(Christie's) **$2,653** **£1,320**

FRANCOIS ETIENNE MUSIN (1820–1888) – Hove-to for a pilot – signed – 122 x 183cm.
(Christie's) **$21,776** **£10,780**

GIOVANNI MUZZIOLI (1854–1894) – In the fields – signed – 87 x 115cm.
(Christie's) **$79,700** **£47,300**

After **BARTOLOMEO ESTEBAN MURILLO** – The Madonna of the Mantle – oil on canvas – 82 x 72.5cm.
(Phillips) **$1,300** **£650**

H. MURRAY (circa 1850–circa 1920) – Drawing a covert; The chase; In the ditch; and The kill – signed 'H. Murray' – pencil and watercolour heightened with white on card – 11⁷/₈ x 17⁷/₈in.
(Christie's) **$2,362** **£1,320**

JEROME MYERS (1867–1940) – Self-portrait – bears signature and signed with initials – pastel on paper – framed – 40.6 x 31.2cm.
(Christie's) **$6,600** **£3,916**

MYN

HERMAN VAN DER MYN (1684–1741) – Danaë – oil
on canvas – 156 x 192cm.
(Phillips) **$13,425 £7,500**

PETER NASON (circa 1612–1688/9) – Portrait of an
elegant woman, standing three-quarter length before a
parapet, wearing a white satin dress and ribbons in her hair
– on canvas – 96 x 80.5cm.
(Phillips) **$21,480 £12,000**

WILLIAM HENRY EDWARD NAPIER (1830–1894) –
Resident – watercolour – 14 x 14.5cm.
(Pinney's) **$1,105 £660**

WILLIAM EDWARD NARRAWAY (b. 1915) – The
Coffee Shop – signed - oil on canvas – 58 x 74cm.
(Christie's) **$5,878 £3,520**

THOMAS NAST (1840–1902) – Boss Tweed – signed and
dated 1890 – pen and black ink on board –
44.3 x 32.3cm.
(Christie's) **$2,090 £1,087**

NEAPOLITAN SCHOOL (late 19th century) – Torro del Greco – with inscription – oil on panel – 23 x 38.5cm.
(Christie's)   **$17,248   £8,800**

PIETRO NEGRI, (Attributed to) – A youth drawing a sculpted head watched by an old man – 101.5 x 83.5cm.
(Christie's)   **$9,847   £5,280**

CHARLES-JOSEPH NATOIRE (1700–1777) - Moses, after Michaelangelo – red chalk – 505 x 292mm.
(Sotheby's)   **$11,156   £5,5'**

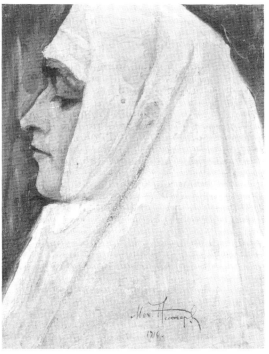

NEAPOLITAN SCHOOL, 19th century – The Bay of Naples with Vesuvius erupting at night – gouache – 40.7 x 55.9cm. – and another of the Bay of Naples by day – a pair
(Bonhams)   **$4,853   £2,400**

MIKHAIL VASIL'EVICH NESTEROV (1862-1942) – Portrait of a novice – signed and dated 1916 – oil on canvas – 24.9 x 19.5cm.
(Christie's)   **$7,507   £3,850**

NETSCHER

ALBERT NEUHUYS (1844-1914) – An interior with a peasant woman sewing, her child in a cradle nearby – signed – 39.5 x 28.5cm.
(Christie's) $4,359 £2,179

Circle of CONSTANTINE NETSCHER (1668–1723) – Portrait of a lady, said to be Marie Adelaide de Savoie, Duchess of Burgundy, three-quarter length, standing on a balcony – oil on canvas – 47.5 x 38cm.
(Phillips) $3,072 £1,600

JOHN ALBERTUS NEUHUYS (Dutch, 1844-1914) – Child's play/An interior genre scene – signed and dated – oil on panel – 6 x 7½in.
(Skinner Inc.) $2,000 £1,072

ABRAHAM CORNELIS NEUFVILLE (d. 1869) – An odalisque playing a harp in a palatial interior, Egypt – 60 x 74cm.
(Christie's) $9,387 £4,694

KARL EUGEN NEUHAUS (1879–1963) – Monterey coastline – signed – oil on canvas – 76 x 102cm.
(Butterfield & Butterfield) $3,575 £1,752

HUGH NEWELL (1830–1915) – A soldier with a gun and A soldier: Two drawings – both signed and dated 1878 – charcoal on paper – the first 45.2 x 27.9cm. – the second 49 x 31.8cm.: one illustrated.
(Christie's) $3,520 £2,089

BEN NICHOLSON (1884–1982) – House, Castagnola –
oil on canvas laid over board – 46 x 55.3cm.
(Christie's) $25,718 £15,400

PETER NEWELL (1862–1924) – "Will you tell me if it's
straight?" – signed and dated 1900 - gouache en grisaille,
pen and black and white ink on paper – 29.2 x 21cm.
(Christie's) $1,650 £979

ERSKINE NICOL (British, 1825–1904) – A willing
pupil – signed and dated 1878 – oil on board –
27 x 20½in.
(Du Mouchelles) $3,250 £1,743

CHARLES WYNNE NICHOLLS (1831–1903) – Elfin
haunts – signed – oil on panel – 28 x 20.5cm.
(Christie's) $2,614 £1,320

EDMUND JOHN NIEMANN (1813–1876) – Boats on
the Medway – signed – 50.5 x 91cm.
(Christie's) $3,413 £1,870

HENRI DE NOBELE (Belgian 1820–70) – Follower of – Home from the hunt, an interior with a family – oil on canvas – 65 x 55cm.
(AB Stockholms Auktionsverk)   **$2,150 £1,108**

JULES ACHILLE NOEL (1815–1881) – A street scene, Brittany; and Unloading the catch – both signed and dated 1872 – oil on canvas – 38.5 x 27.4cm. – a pair
(Christie's)   **$14,014 £7,150**

CEJUDO NOGALES – "Preparing for the boat trip" – signed – oil on canvas – 24 x 27in.
(Spencer's)   **$2,562 £1,400**

GIUSEPPE NOGARI (1699–1763) – Girl with dove – oil on canvas – 60 x 46.5cm.
(Sotheby's)   **$19,411 £11,156**

GIUSEPPE NOGARI (1699–1763) – Portrait – oil on canvas – 62 x 48cm.
(Finarte Casa d'Aste)   **$7,599 £3,917**

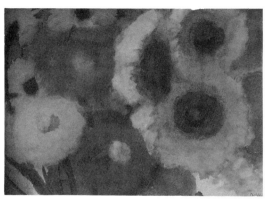

EMILE NOLDE (1867–1956) – Sonnenblumen – signed
– watercolour on Japan paper – 34 x 45cm.
(Christie's)   **$169,290   £99,000**

BENGT NORDENBERG (1822–1902) – Sleigh on the ice
– signed and dated 1891 – oil on canvas – 72 x 62cm.
(AB Stockholms Auktionsverk)   **$17,018   £8,772**

EMIL NOLDE (1867–1956) – Young woman – signed –
watercolour and indian ink on japan paper –
15.8 x 14.2cm.
(Lempertz)   **$70,729   £36,458**

EMIL NOLDE (1867–1956) – Houses by the shallows –
signed – watercolour on paper – 35 x 41cm.
(Christie's)   **$117,018   £59,400**

ANNA NORDGREN (1847–1916) – Interior with a boy
feeding a baby – signed – oil on canvas – 94 x 74cm.
(AB Stockholms Auktionsverk)   **$3,583   £1,847**

ANNA NORDGREN (1847–1916) – Interior with girl
writing a letter before a window – signed – oil on canvas –
77 x 102cm.
(AB Stockholms Auktionsverk)   **$22,391   £11,542**

NORDSTROM

CARL HAROLD NORDSTROM (American, 1876–1934) – At The Pier After Yachting – signed – autumn landscape in oil on the reverse – oil on board – 11 x 14in.
(Skinner)   **$600 £309**

ANDRE NORMIL (Haitian, 20th Century) – Paradise – signed and dated 67 – oil on masonite – 20 x 24in.
(Skinner Inc.)   **$750 £402**

HANS NORSBO – Southern street scene – signed and dated 1943 – pencil and coloured chalks – 23 x 31cm.
(AB Stockholms Auktionsverket)   **$268 £141**

J W NORTH (19th Century) – Olive press in a landscape, Algiers – signed and dated 1880 – oil on panel – 24½ x 29½in.
(Jacobs & Hunt)   **$800 £400**

NORTH ITALIAN SCHOOL, 17th Century – Portrait of a man with a violin – oil on canvas, in a painted oval – 93 x 72cm.
(Sotheby's)   **$8,360 £4,400**

NORTH ITALIAN SCHOOL – Christ the Man of Sorrows – oil on panel – unframed – 53.3 x 40.5cm.
(Christie's)   **$3,098 £1,540**

ELIZABETH NOURSE (1859–1938) – Among neighbours – signed and dated 1889 – oil on canvas – 113 x 117cm.
(Christie's) $35,200 £18,304

DAVID EMIL JOSEPH DE NOTER (Belgian, b. 1825) – In the kitchen – signed and dated '50 – oil on panel – 86.3 x 66cm.
(Bonhams) $14,154 £7,000

WILLIAM DEGOUVE DE NUNCQUES (Belgian 1867–1935) – La Place du Warichet – signed and dated – oil on canvas – 41 x 61cm.
(Sotheby's) $44,286 £24,200

ELIZABETH NOURSE (1859–1938) – The older sister – signed and dated 1901 – pastel on board – 60 x 42.5cm.
(Christie's) $13,200 £6,864

FELIX NUSSBAUM (1904–1944) – At the harbour – signed and indistinctly dated 1935 – oil on board – 49 x 63.5cm.
(Christie's) $48,225 £25,156

NUREMBERG SCHOOL

NUREMBERG SCHOOL, 16th Century – Portrait of Abbess Pirkheimer, bust-length, wearing the habit of her order, the Franciscan Cloister of St. Clara – inscribed – tempera on linen – 47 x 37.5cm.
(Phillips) **$87,648 £44,000**

JENNY NYSTROM (1854–1946) – Interior with couple seated before a window – signed – 21.5 x 13.5cm.
(AB Stockholms Auktionsverk) **$1,253 £646**

JENNY NYSTROM (1854–1946) – Eventide peace – signed and dated 1896 – pastel – 79 x 60cm.
(AB Stockholms Auktionsverk) **$32,243 £16,620**

JENNY NYSTROM (1854–1946) – Portrait of an actress – signed and dated 1914 – oil on canvas laid down on board – 44 x 53cm.
(AB Stockholms Auktionsverk) **$10,748 £5,540**

JENNY NYSTROM (1854–1946) – Portrait of a man – signed and dated 1879 – oil on canvas – 64 x 50cm.
(AB Stockholms Auktionsverk) **$5,374 £2,770**

ANTHONY OBERMAN (1781–1845) – A black horse in a polder landscape – signed and dated 1814 – on panel – 32 x 32cm.
(Christie's) **$4,023 £2,012**

FLORENCIO OCHOA – Lady by the lake – signed – oil on canvas – 55 x 46cm.
(Duran) **$521 £262**

OCTAVIUS OAKLEY (1800—1867) – A young gypsy girl peeling a vegetable – signed and dated 1854 – watercolour with touches of white heightening – 19 x 13³/₄in.
(Christie's) **$2,123 £1,100**

FLORENCIO OCHOA – Granada – signed – oil on canvas – 50 x 61cm.
(Duran) **$501 £252**

OCHOA

RODERIC O'CONOR, R.H.A. (1860–1940) – The model reading – with the artist's atelier stamp on the reverse – oil on panel – 36 x 42cm.
(Christie's) **$34,320 £17,600**

FLORENCIO OCHOA – Young girl from the beach – signed – oil on canvas – 55 x 46cm.
(Duran) **$398 £200**

RODERICK O'CONOR – The foaming sea – signed and dated '92 – oil on panel – $9\frac{1}{2}$ x $10\frac{3}{4}$in.
(Woolley & Wallis) **$64,185 £33,000**

JOHN O'CONNOR – Bishopsgate; and Swan Yard, Lambeth – a pair (one illustrated) – 23 x 18cm.
(Christie's) **$1,753 £880**

RODERIC O'CONOR (1860–1940) – The bridge at Grez-sur-Loing - signed bottom right with initials (probably at a later date) – oil on canvas – 73 x 91cm.
(Phillips) **$232,820 £140,000**

RODERIC O'CONOR, R.H.A. (1860–1940) – Auto-portrait chez l'atelier – oil on card, laid on panel – 69 x 54cm.
(Christie's) **$31,102   £15,950**

WILLIAM OLIVER (English, 1805–1853) – A young girl wearing a yellow dress, seated in parkland – oil on canvas – signed – 75 x 49.5cm.
(Bonhams) **$9,653   £5,500**

TARO OKAMOTO – Bridge across the Seine – signed – 46.3 x 38cm.
(Christie's) **$7,040   £3,520**

WILLIAM OLIVER – 'Say Yes Or No' – signed and dated 1880 – 50 x 60cm.
(Spencer's) **$2,424   £1,200**

MARGARET OLLEY – Still life, The black kettle – signed – oil on board – 69 x 107cm.
(Australian Art Auctions) **$6,084   £3,012**

OLSON

HUGH O'NEILL (1784–1824) – Figures by the Market Cross, Malmesbury – watercolour over pencil – unframed – 28.5 x 22.5cm.
(Phillips) $969 £480

AXEL OLSON (1899–1986) – Portrait – signed with initials and dated 1923 – watercolour – 14 x 10.5cm.
(AB Stockholms Auktionsverk) $883 £455

AXEL OLSON (1899–1986) – Ploughman and sun – signed and dated 40 – oil on canvas – 33 x 41cm.
(AB Stockholms Auktionsverk) $3,910 £2,047

UMBERTO ONGANIA – Gondolas on the Basin of St. Mark's; and The Piazzetta, Venice – both signed – pencil and watercolour – 7 x 12³/₄in.
(Christie's) **$882 £462**

MAX OPPENHEIMER – Das Kolische Quartett – signed MOPP – oil on canvas – oval: 86 x 104.5cm.
(Sotheby's) **$74,800 £44,000**

CHARLES OPPENHEIMER, R.S.A., R.S.W. – Waterside, Kirkcudbright – signed – oil on canvas – 22¹/₂ x 29¹/₂in.
(Bearne's) **$11,252 £5,800**

ERNST OPPLER (German, b. 1869) – Still Life with Fruit – signed – oil on canvas – 16 x 20in.
(Skinner) **$5,700 £2,829**

CHARLES OPPENHEIMER, R.S.A., R.S.W. – The Tolbooth and Old Town, Kirkcudbright – signed – oil on canvas – 22³/₄ x 29³/₄in.
(Bearne's) **$14,744 £7,600**

JAN VAN OPSTAL, (Follower of) – The Madonna and Child with Saint Anne – 123.2 x 97.2cm.
(Christie's) **$6,154 £3,300**

407

ORCHARDSON

SIR WILLIAM QUILLER ORCHARDSON, R.A.
(1832–1910) – A fisher boy – signed and inscribed – oil on
canvas – 76.8 x 63.5cm.
(Christie's) $15,244   £9,020

SIR WILLIAM ORPEN – Arabian Nights – signed and
dated 1903 – pastel and pencil – 33 x 25cm.
(Christie's) $3,344   £1,760

SIR WILLIAM ORPEN, R.A., R.H.A. (1878–1931) – A
young man from the West, self-portrait – signed – oil on
canvas – 79 x 62cm.
(Christie's) $235,950   £121,000

SIR WILLIAM ORPEN, R.A., R.W.S., R.H.A.
(1878–1931) – The mask - signed and dated '99 –
watercolour over pencil – 29 x 23.5cm.
(Phillips) $5,820   £3,500

SIR WILLIAM ORPEN, R.A., R.W.S., R.H.A.
(1878–1931) – A crisis in the New English Art Club -
signed and dated 1930 for 1904 – pen, ink wash and pencil
on paper – 24.5 x 22cm.
(Phillips) **$14,967 £9,000**

MARTIN RICO Y ORTEGA (1833–1908) – Santa
Maria del Giglio, Venice – signed – oil on canvas –
53.4 x 36.2cm.
(Christie's) **$43,340 £22,000**

FRANCISCO PRADILLA Y ORTIZ (Spanish
1848–1921) – A woman reading; A woman carrying a
basket of flowers – two – both signed – watercolour –
one 30.5 x 18cm., the other 27.5 x 13.5cm.
(Sotheby's) **$8,052 £4,400**

SIR WILLIAM ORPEN, R.H.A., R.A. (1878–1931) –
Mrs. St. George - signed on the canvas overlap – oil on
canvas – 221 x 120cm.
(Christie's) **$367,400 £220,000**

FRIEDRICH ORTLIEB (German, 1839–1909) – The
Lesson of Charity – signed and inscribed – oil on canvas –
26³/₄ x 32¹/₄in.
(Skinner) **$8,000 £4,124**

ORVILLO

K.P.C. ORVILLO - Conversing with the parrot – signed – oil on canvas - 45.8 x 37.5cm.
(Pinney's) **$775 £390**

Follower of JAN VAN OS – A wooded landscape with a herder and cattle on a track – oil on panel – 29.8 x 40.7cm.
(Christie's) **$4,138 £2,090**

FRANK O'SALISBURY (1874–1972) – Portrait in black and gold – signed and dated 1910 – oil on canvas – 160 x 93cm.
(Phillips) **$28,271 £17,000**

BERNHARD OSCARSSON (1894–1971) – Spanish fishermen – signed and dated 1928 – oil on canvas – 46 x 75cm.
(AB Stockholms Auktionsverk) **$2,309 £1,209**

GEORGIUS JACOBUS JOHANNES VAN OS (1782–1861) – Kapitaal Bloemstuk: Roses and other flowers in a terracotta vase on a ledge – signed – oil on panel – 71 x 58cm.
(Christie's) **$274,927 £137,463**

Manner of ISAAK VAN OSTADE – The interior of an inn with peasants carousing – oil on panel – 30 x 27.5cm.
(Christie's) **$1,851 £935**

CARL OSTERSETZER (1850–1914) – A game of cards
– signed and dated 97 – on panel – 22.8 x 17.7cm.
(Christie's)   **$2,409**   **£1,430**

EDMUND HENRY OSTHAUS (1858–1928) – English
Setters on the scent – signed – oil on canvas –
61 x 91.5cm.
(Christie's)   **$17,600**   **£9,328**

EDMUND HENRY OSTHAUS (German/American,
1858–1928) – Setters in an Autumn Landscape – signed –
oil on canvas – 10 x 15½in.
(Skinner)   **$5,000**   **£2,577**

ANGEL CABANAS OTEIZA – Fisherman – oil on
canvas – signed – 55.5 x 54cm.
(Duran)   **$2,274**   **£1,178**

GEORGE DEMONT OTIS (1879–1962) – Steamship
California – signed – oil on canvas – 61 x 76cm.
(Butterfield & Butterfield)   **$14,300**   **£7,010**

P. VAN DER OUDERAA (Belgian 19th C.) – The
cantata – oil on panel – signed – 60 x 82cm.
(Hôtel de Ventes Horta)   **$7,450**   **£3,840**

OUDRY

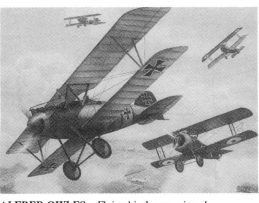

ALFRED OWLES – Flying bi-planes – signed –
watercolour on paper – 40 x 52.7cm.
(Christie's) $385   £204

JEAN-BAPTISTE OUDRY (1686–1755) – Portrait of a
gentleman – oil on canvas – 77 x 63cm.
(Sotheby's) $34,939   £20,080

DAVID OYENS (1842–1902) – A woman preparing a
meal on a stove in an interior – signed – oil on canvas laid
down on panel – 37 x 28cm.
(Christie's) $1,743   £872

JEAN-BAPTISTE OUDRY (1686–1755) – Portrait of a
lady – oil on canvas – 77 x 63cm.
(Sotheby's) $38,823   £22,312

FERENCZ PACZKA (1856–1925) - The dinner party –
signed and dated 1887 – oil on canvas – 124.5 x 207cm.
(Christie's) $44,880   £26,400

BENJAMIN PALENCIA (1900–1980) – Threshing in the country – signed and indistinctly dated – oil on paper – 23 x 29cm.
(Duran) **$5,852 £3,056**

PADUAN SCHOOL, circa 1700 – Saint Nicholas of Bari – 59 x 51.5cm.
(Christie's) **$1,742 £880**

J. FERRER Y PALLOJA (late 19th century) – La Place de la Concorde, Paris – signed and dated 1886 – oil on canvas – 38 x 55cm.
(Christie's) **$7,546 £3,850**

JULES EUGENE PAGES (1867–1946) – Semur in Auxios, Burgundy – signed – oil on canvas – 56 x 46cm.
(Butterfield & Butterfield) **$7,150 £3,505**

MIMMO PALADINO (b. 1948) – Orto di Cacciatore – signed - inscribed and dated 1982 on reverse – oil, charcoal, coloured crayon, papier-mâché and composition on canvas and wooden frame – 160 x 223.5cm.
(Christie's) **$132,440 £77,000**

JOSE PALMEIRO (1901) – Maternal still life – oil on board – signed - 73 x 92cm.
(Duran) **$5,558 £2,880**

413

PALMEIRO

ALFREDO PALMERO (early 20th Century) – A religious festival, Almodovar – signed and inscribed – unframed – 90.2 x 116.2cm.
(Christie's) $3,521   £2,090

JOSE PALMEIRO (b. 1901) – Homage to Gauguin – oil on canvas - signed – 92 x 73cm.
(Duran) $7,073   £3,665

ADELAIDE PALMER (1851–1928) – Pie cherries – oil on canvas – signed and dated – 10 x 14in.
(Bruce D. Collins) $2,420   £1,308

LILI PALMER (Swiss, 1911–1986) – Villa in the park – signed and dated 1969 – oil on artist's board – 55 x 47.5cm.
(germann Auktionshaus) $605   £356

ROMA PANADES – The dodgems – signed and dated 1987 – pastel, watercolour and bodycolour – 132.7 x 67.5cm.
(Christie's) $1,540   £770

ROMA PANADES – "Dance Hall" – signed and dated '86 – signed, inscribed and dated 1986 on the reverse – 130.2 x 80.6cm.
(Christie's) $2,090 £1,045

JULIET PANNETT – Carlo Maria Giulini – charcoal – signed – also signed by Carlo Maria Giulini – 54 x 37.5cm,.
(Bonhams) $440 £220

R.* PANNETT – An elegant lady wearing a bonnet and holding a fur muff – signed – gouache – oval – 74.3 x 48.2cm.
(Bonhams) $724 £360

ROBERT PANITZSCH – Woman seated before a rococo commode with mirror – signed - 66 x 55cm.
(Herholdt Jensens) $890 £476

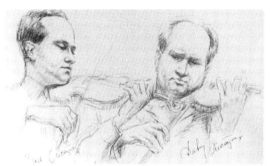

JULIET PANNETT – Igor and David Oistrakh – charcoal – signed in acrylic by Igor and David Oistrakh – 32 x 48cm.
(Bonhams) $640 £320

ANTONIO ERMOLAO PAOLETTI (1834–1912) – The dance – signed and inscribed – oil on canvas – 30 x 40cm.
(Christie's) $13,090 £7,700

PAOLOZZI

SIR EDUARDO PAOLOZZI, R.A. (b. 1924) –
Fishermen – signed and dated 1946 – pen, brush and black
ink – 56 x 76cm.
(Christie's)   **$11,097   £5,720**

HENRY PARK (1816–1871) – The return from rabbiting
– signed and dated 59 – 29.3 x 24.7cm.
(Christie's)   **$843   £462**

FERDINANDO PAPACCENA – Kitchen table with
tureen and fish and Kitchen table with copper pan and
cabbage – a pair – one signed with monogram – oil on
panel and oil on canvas – 8.6 x 14.8cm.
(Sotheby's)   **$5,076   £2,900**

JOHN ANTHONY PARK - Mevagissey Harbour – signed
– 7³/₄ x 11¹/₂in.
(Andrew Hartley)   **$1,769   £1,050**

ROGER PARENT – Reclining nude – signed and dated –
oil on canvas – 54 x 65cm.
(Hôtel de Ventes Horta)   **$3,155   £1,803**

JOHN ANTHONY PARK – Summer, St. Ives Harbour –
signed – on board – unframed – 33 x 40.6cm.
(Christie's)   **$3,520   £1,760**

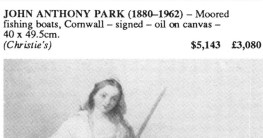

JOHN ANTHONY PARK (1880–1962) – Moored fishing boats, Cornwall – signed – oil on canvas – 40 x 49.5cm.
(Christie's) **$5,143 £3,080**

HENRY H. PARKER (1858–1930) – Bringing the new calf home – signed – oil on canvas – 79.4 x 61.3cm.
(Christie's) **$5,019 £2,970**

HENRY PERLEE PARKER – A fisher courtship – signed and dated 1866 – 44 x 34cm.
(Anderson & Garland) **$7,958 £4,600**

PARKER

ARTHUR WILDE PARSONS – Rocky cove with two fishermen in a moored row boat – signed and dated 1899 – oil on canvas – 50 x 75cm.
(Allen & Harris) $1,953 £1,050

HENRY PERLEE PARKER – Awaiting the return of the fishing fleet – signed and dated 1868 – 44 x 34cm.
(Anderson & Garland) $7,958 £4,600

BEATRICE PARSONS (1870–1955) – Doves at a fountain – signed – watercolour heightened with bodycolour – 28 x 38cm.
(Phillips) $4,848 £2,400

MAXFIELD PARRISH (1870–1966) – Thy rocks and rills – signed with initials and dated 1942 on the reverse – watercolour on paper – 20.2 x 16.5cm.
(Christie's) $12,100 £6,292

CONSTANTIN PARTHENIS (b. 1878) – A sunlit courtyard – signed – oil on canvas – 75.5 x 56.2cm.
(Christie's) $28,171 £14,300

ALF PARTRIDGE – 'Cardinal', study of a horse – signed
– oil on canvas – 17½ x 23½in.
(Hobbs & Chambers)   **$1,362**   **£700**

JULES PASCIN (JULIUS MORDECAI PINCAS)
(1885–1930) – The homecoming – watercolour on paper –
10.5 x 15.3cm.
(Lempertz)   **$3,166**   **£1,632**

JULES PASCIN – La petite actrice – stamped with the
signature – oil on canvas – 73 x 92cm.
(Sotheby's)   **$467,500**   **£275,000**

J. PARTRIDGE – Italian peasants at the steps of a shrine
– signed – pencil and watercolour – 10 x 9½in.
(Christie's)   **$348**   **£198**

LORENS PASCH (1702–66) – Portrait of Engel Cronhiort
in green hunting coat with his dog – inscribed and dated 7
May 1729 on reverse – oil on canvas –
145 x 115cm.
(AB Stockholms Auktionsverk)   **$10,748**   **£5,540**

LUDWIG PASSINI (Austrian, 1832–1903) – A young
Venetian water-carrier – signed and dated 1870 –
watercolour and bodycolour – 35.6 x 24.2cm.
(Bonhams)   **$3,640**   **£1,800**

PATER

CHARLES JOHNSON PAYNE (SNAFFLES) – 'Me Two Feet in a Bog' (Red Letter Days) – watercolour heightened with bodycolour – signed and inscribed on mount – 12 x 10¼in.
(Bearne's) $3,820 £2,000

Follower of PIERRE PATER, the Elder – The finding of Moses – oil on panel – circular – 30.5cm. diameter
(Christie's) $3,267 £1,650

EDGAR PAYNE (1883–1947) – Riders in Canyon de Chelley – signed – oil on canvas – 74 x 89cm.
(Butterfield & Butterfield) $35,750 £17,524

FRITZ PAULI (1891–1968) – Self portrait – etching – signed – 25 x 18.5cm.
(Galerie Koller Zürich) $515 £269

EDGAR PAYNE (1883–1947) – Mediterranean skies – signed – oil on canvas – 51 x 61cm.
(Butterfield & Butterfield) $9,900 £4,853

EDGAR PAYNE (1883–1947) – Chateau town – signed –
oil on canvas laid down – 25.5 x 30.5cm.
(Butterfield & Butterfield)   **$4,400 £2,157**

RUBENS PEALE* (1784–1864) – Still life with crystal
compote – signed and dated – oil on canvas – 52 x 61.3cm.
(Christie's)   **$8,800 £4,664**

PD (early 19th Century) – An artist at a window – signed
with initials and dated 1837 – 43.2 x 40cm.
(Christie's)   **$6,672 £3,960**

BRYAN PEARCE – Village by moonlight – signed – on
masonite – 45 x 57.2cm.
(Christie's)   **$627 £330**

JAMES PEALE (1749–1831) – Portrait of Ann Emily
Rush – oil on canvas laid down on panel – 74.6 x 63.5cm.
(Christie's)   **$14,300 £7,436**

MARGUERITE STUBER PEARSON (1898–1978) –
The open door – signed – oil on canvas – 76.5 x 91.8cm.
(Christie's)   **$22,000 £11,440**

PEARSON

W.H. PEARSON – "The Pier Head" – watercolour
(Greenslades) $955   £500

CHARLES FRANCOIS PECRUS – Lady in lace reading
– signed – oil on panel – 15.2 x 12cm.
(Ritchie's) $1,379   £714

HENRIK PECZ (1813–1868) – Portrait of a girl standing
three-quarter length, wearing a white dress, holding a straw
hat and a camellia – signed and dated 1849 – oil on canvas
– 100.5 x 80.3cm.
(Christie's) $7,762   £3,960

OLE PEDERSEN (1856–1898) – Wash day – signed and
dated 80 – 44.4 x 55.8cm.
(Christie's) $2,965   £1,760

JAMES PEEL (1811–1906) – Bridge in Glenrhydding,
Westmoreland – signed on the reverse – 45.7 x 68cm.
(Christie's) $1,907   £1,045

JOHN THOMAS PEELE – Little children, love one
another – signed and dated 1873 – oil on canvas –
76 x 63cm.
(Sotheby's) $4,978   £2,750

KARL AXEL PEHRSON (b. 1921) – "Stora Fallet –
Attoitto" – signed – oil on canvas – 38 x 58cm.
(AB Stockholms Auktionsverk)   **$7,462   £3,907**

WALDO PEIRCE (1884–1970) – Anna painting Waldo's
portrait – oil on canvas – signed with initials and dated '39
– 20 x 22³/₄in.
(Bruce D. Collins)   **$3,025   £1,635**

ALFRED PELLAN (1906–1988) – Dark eyed woman –
signed and dated 1925 – charcoal – 47 x 29.8cm.
(Pinney's)   **$3,963   £1,991**

WALDO PEIRCE (1884–1970) – Swan boats – oil on
canvas – signed with initials and dated – 27¹/₂ x 39¹/₂in.
(Bruce D. Collins)   **$8,800   £4,757**

HONORE PELLEGRIN (1793–1869) – The vessel
'Prosper', commanded by Captain Guinemont – signed and
dated 1852 – pencil, pen and black ink, grey wash,
watercolour – 435 x 582mm.
(Christie's)   **$4,187   £2,152**

PELLEGRINI

GIOVANNI ANTONIO PELLEGRINI, Follower of –
Diana and Endymion – 94 x 129.6cm.
(Christie's)   **$8,410 £4,180**

RAFAEL PENAGOS (1899–1954) – Coquetry –
watercolour – signed – 53 x 39cm.
(Duran)   **$1,170 £579**

OLIVIER DE PENNE (1831–1897) – Spaniels on a river
bank – signed – oil on panel – 40.7 x 31.7cm.
(Christie's)   **$3,722 £1,980**

PAUL EMILE LEON PERBOYRE (French, 19th/20th Century) – Cavalry galloping up a road – signed – oil on board – 8 x 13in.
(Du Mouchelles) $1,100 £590

CHRISTIAN JOHANN GEORG PERLBERG (German, 1806–84) – View in Seville – signed – oil on canvas – 74 x 52cm.
(Auktionshaus Arnold) $558 £336

ARTHUR PERCY (1886–1976) – Girl bathing – signed and dated 1916 – oil on canvas – 31 x 23cm.
(AB Stockholms Auktionsverk) $2,309 £1,209

SIDNEY RICHARD PERCY (1821–1886) – Llyn Ddinas near Beddgelert, North Wales – signed and dated 1871 – oil on canvas – 46 x 76.5cm.
(Christie's) $28,314 £14,300

CHARLES PERRET – Still life with roses, cherries and peaches – signed – oil on canvas – 121 x 101cm.
(Jean-Claude Anaf) $7,933 £4,132

PERRIN

Circle of JEAN-CHARLES-NICOISE PERRIN (1754–1831) – Hector's farewell to Andromache – paper laid down on panel – 26.5 x 21.5cm.
(Phillips)   **$4,582 £2,300**

GEZA PESKE (b. 1859) – Temptation – signed – oil on canvas – 107.3 x 100.3cm.
(Christie's)   **$9,306 £4,950**

CHARLES EDWARD PERUGINI (1839–1918) – Portrait of Miss Helen Lindsay, half length – signed with monogram, and inscribed on label on reverse – oil on canvas – 71.1 x 48.9cm.
(Christie's)   **$19,107 £9,900**

JANE PETERSON (1876–1965) – Still life with flowers – watercolour – unsigned – 27 x 21in.
(Bruce D. Collins)   **$3,740 £2,022**

JANE PETERSON (1876–1965) – Blue morning glories – oil on canvas – signed – 24 x 24in.
(Bruce D. Collins)   **$7,700 £4,162**

ROY PETLEY – Figures in the park, midsummer –
signed – on board – 22.9 x 34.3cm.
(Christie's)   **$7,315   £3,850**

ROY PETLEY (b. 1951) – On the beach Norfolk – signed
– oil on board – 50 x 75.5cm.
(Phillips)   **$4,989   £3,000**
ROY PETLEY (b. 1951) – Afternoon in the park – signed
– oil on board – 41 x 61cm.
(Christie's)   **$3,628   £1,870**

F X PETTER (Circa 1800) – Still life with fruit, flowers
and parrot – signed and dated 1845 – oil on canvas –
105 x 75cm.
(AB Stockholms Auktionsverk)   **$40,573   £20,914**

PFEIFFER

GLYN WARREN PHILPOT, R.A. (1884–1937) – Three studies of a standing male nude – oil on canvas laid down on board – 80 x 67cm.
(Christie's) $11,022 £6,600

Studio of GIOVANNI BATTISTA PIAZZETTA (1682-1754) – A reclining nude – red chalk heightened with white – 408 x 565mm.
(Phillips) $2,068 £1,200

WILHELM PFEIFFER (German 1822–91) – The young water carrier – signed – oil on canvas – 66 x 56cm.
(Sotheby's) $12,078 £6,600

CAESAR PHILIPP (b. 1859) – Idle hours – signed – oil on canvas – 95.2 x 162.5cm.
(Christie's) $16,544 £8,800

FRANCIS PICABIA (1879–1953) – La Ville de New York aperçue à Travers de Corps – signed and dated 1912 – gouache, watercolour and pencil on paper laid down on board – 54.6 x 74.3cm.
(Christie's) $216,700 £110,000

KAREL FRANS PHILIPPEAU (1825–1897) – Serenading the baby – signed and dated 1866 – oil on panel – unframed – 37.2 x 47cm.
(Christie's) $10,780 £5,500

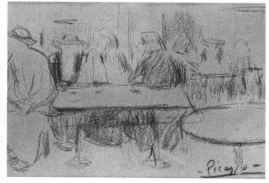

PABLO PICASSO – Café-concert de Malaga – signed at a later date (?) – blue conté crayon on buff paper – 15 x 23.5cm.
(Sotheby's) $130,900 £77,000

PABLO PICASSO (1881–1973) – Les Tuileries – signed –
oil on board – 52 x 66.7cm.
(Christie's)   **$24,475,000**   **£13,750,000**

PABLO PICASSO – Nature morte à la théière – signed on
the reverse – mosaic – 60 x 59.7cm.
(Sotheby's)   **$280,500**   **£165,000**

PABLO PICASSO (1881–1973) – Femme au Fauteuil –
dated on the reverse – oil on canvas – 60.7 x 50.2cm.
(Christie's)   **$1,527,240**   **£858,000**

PICASSO

PABLO PICASSO (1881–1973) – Homme à la sauterelle et Nu Couché – signed and dated 17.11.69. - pencil on paper – 54 x 71cm.
(Christie's)   **$188,100   £110,000**

PABLO PICASSO (1881–1973) – La Balustrade – signed and dated – oil on canvas – 50 x 61cm.
(Christie's)   **$626,560   £352,000**

PABLO PICASSO (1881–1973) – Deux Garçons – soft pencil on paper laid down on board – 38 x 47.5cm.
(Christie's)   **$65,835   £38,500**

Studio of ANDREA PICCINELLI DA BRESCIA, called Brescianino (1485–1525) – The Madonna and Child, accompanied by Saint John – oil on panel – 87.7 x 68.5cm.
(Phillips)   **$19,200   £10,000**

Circle of NICKOLAS ELIAS PICKENOY (1590/1–1653/6) – Portrait of a lady, three-quarter length, wearing a black dress – oil on panel – 81.5 x 59cm.
(Christie's)   **$2,614   £1,320**

FREDERICK RICHARD PICKERSGILL, R.A.
(1820–1900) – Britomart unarming – signed on the
backing board – oil on canvas – 127 x 106.7cm.
(Christie's) $50,952   £26,400

FREDERICK RICHARD PICKERSGILL, R.A.
(1820–1900) – The pleasure boat – signed – oil on board –
63.5 x 76cm.
(Christie's) $15,246   £7,700

PERE CREIXAMS PICO (1893-1965) – Nude – oil on
canvas – signed – 65 x 54cm.
(Duran) $2,526   £1,309

PICOU

SIMONE PIGNONI (1614–1698) – Saint Catherine – on canvas – an oval – 83 x 64cm.
(Phillips)   **$26,850**   **£15,000**

HENRI PIERRE PICOU (1824–1895) – A water nymph and a cherub on a riverbank – signed – on panel – 29.3 x 20.9cm.
(Christie's)   **$1,390**   **£825**

JAZEPS PIGOZNIS (b. 1934) – Reclining nude – signed and dated 76 – oil on canvas – 65 x 73cm.
(Jean-Claude Anaf)   **$787**   **£411**

SANO DI PIETRO (1406–1481) – The Madonna and Child with St Bernardino of Siena, a male saint and two angels – oil on panel – 49.7 x 38.7cm.
(Sotheby's)   **$135,850**   **£71,500**

WILLIAM HENRY PIKE (1846–1908) – A Westcountry harbour – watercolour – signed and dated '91 – 13½ x 25½in.
(David Lay)   **$1,240**   **£620**

V. PILLACE (19th Century) – Feeding the chickens –
signed – unframed – 33 x 44.5cm.
(Christie's) **$1,668   £990**

BARTOLOMEO PINELLI (Italian 1781–1835) – The
first steps – signed and dated 1820 – pencil and
watercolour – 25 x 30cm.
(Sotheby's) **$1,610   £880**

GIULIO SOUZA PINTO (b. 1855), (Attributed to) – A
young girl – 25 x 18cm.
(Christie's) **$1,760   £1,045**

JOHN PIPER, C.H. (b. 1903) – Ruined abbey – signed –
pen, brush, black ink and watercolour – 38 x 51cm.
(Christie's) **$7,469   £3,850**

GIOVANNI BATTISTA PIRANESI (1720–1778) –
Veduta del Ponte salario – etching – 40.6 x 61.7cm.
(AB Stockholms Auktionsverk) **$757   £390**

ALBERTO PISA (Italian, 1864–1931) – Continental
back street – signed – watercolour – 26 x 39.5cm.
(Phillips) **$2,011   £1,050**

CAMILLE PISSARRO (1830–1903) – The hay harvest,
Eragny – signed and dated 1887 – oil on canvas –
51 x 66cm.
(Christie's) **$2,167,000   £1,100,000**

PISSARRO

CAMILLE PISSARRO – Les baigneuses – signed and dated '95 – oil on canvas – 35 x 27cm.
(Sotheby's) **$617,100 £363,000**

FRANZ PITNER (1826–1892) – Santuario di Loreto –
signed and dated 86 – pencil and watercolour heightened
with white – 76 x 111.4cm.
(Christie's) **$6,204 £3,300**

ANTOINE EMILE PLASSAN (1817–1903) – An
elegant company in an interior – signed and dated 68 –oil
on panel – 11 x 13.5cm.
(Christie's) **$2,017 £1,006**

CLAUDE PISSARRO – Clown accordeonist – oil on
polyester – signed and dated 1955
(Hôtel de Ventes Horta) **$5,432 £2,800**

Attributed to NICOLAS DE PLATTEMONTAGNE
(1631–1706) – Seated nude, facing right – red and white
chalk on beige paper – 396 x 262mm.
(Christie's) **$3,306 £1,699**

ANDRE PLUMOT (1829–1906) – Grandparents' duties –
signed – oil on panel – 55.5 x 45cm.
(Christie's)   **$4,694   £2,347**

JOSEF PLATZER (1751–1806) – The interior of a cave
with a loving couple attended by angels – signed – oil on
panel – 40.6 x 30.2cm.
(Phillips)   **$3,586   £1,800**

JOHANN GEORG PLATZER (1704–1761) - Attributed
to – In the sculptor's studio – oil on copper – 47 x 60cm.
(Lempertz)   **$37,666   £21,523**

OGDEN MINTON PLEISSNER (1905–1983) – On the
Western Slope, Wind River, Wyoming – signed – oil on
canvas – 56.3 x 71cm.
(Christie's)   **$18,700   £9,724**

WJATSCHESLAV POBOGENSKIJ (Russian, b. 1943)
– Nude with sword – signed and dated 1988 – acrylic on
canvas – 120 x 95cm.
(germann Auktionshaus)   **$13,333   £6,855**

POLLITT

ALBERT POLLITT (19th Century) – Landscape with
sheep and figures – signed and dated 1897 – watercolour –
20 x 29½in.
(Jacobs & Hunt) $1,000 £500

W* J* POPHAM (English, 20th century) – The three-
masted Barque The High Flyer' – signed – bears
inscription – oil on canvas – 61 x 91.4cm.
(Bonhams) $2,730 £1,350

DEBAT PONSAN – Working in the fields – signed – oil
on canvas – 64 x 91cm.
(Hôtel de Ventes Horta) $7,623 £3,774

EDWARD PORTIELJE (1861–1949) – Good news –
signed – oil on canvas – 49 x 41.5cm.
(Hôtel de Ventes Horta) $10,615 £6,066

WILLEM DE POORTER (1608-after 1648) – Achilles
amongst the daughters of Lycomedes – strengthened
initials W.D.P. and dated 1640 – oil on panel – circular –
71cm. diam.
(Phillips) $17,928 £9,000

GERARD PORTIELJE (Belgian, 1856–1929) – The
boon companions – signed – oil on panel – 30 x 38.5cm.
(Hôtel de Ventes Horta) $7,889 £4,098

JAN PORTIELJE (1829–1908) – Waiting for the rendez-vous – signed and inscribed – oil on panel – 75 x 59.5cm.
(Christie's) **$46,939 £23,469**

BERNARD POTHAST (1882–1966) – The New Arrival – signed – oil on canvas – 40 x 50cm.
(Christie's) **$15,169 £7,700**

Follower of PIETER POURBUS – Portrait of a Lady, bust length, wearing a black embroidered dress, a white ruff and headdress – 42.3 x 30cm.
(Christie's) **$2,420 £1,210**

MICHEL-MARIE POULAIN (French, b. 1906) – Four women – signed – oil on canvas – 65 x 81cm.
(AB Stockholms Auktionsverk) **$1,635 £856**

SIR EDWARD JOHN POYNTER (English, 1836–1919) – Portrait of a young woman – black and white chalk on brown paper – 18.7 x 17.5cm.
(Christie's) **$1,320 £686**

POYNTER

SIR EDWARD JOHN POYNTER (English 1836–1919)
– Adoration to Ra – signed with monogram and dated
1867– oil on canvas - 73 x 42cm.
(Sotheby's) $99,550 £55,000

GIUSEPPE DA POZZO (late 19th Century) – The maid
– signed and inscribed Italy – on panel – 40.7 x 25.4cm.
(Christie's) $2,780 £1,650

ATTILIO PRATELLA – Fishing boats in the Bay of
Naples – signed – oil on canvas – 14½ x 25¼in. –
unframed
(Bearne's) $19,400 £10,000

Manner of SIR EDWARD JOHN POYNTER –
Fairhaired beauty holding a jewellery casket – oil on
canvas on panel – circa 1890 – 70.5 x 58.7cm.
(Ritchie's) $1,101 £571

CAROLINE STIENON DU PRE (1883–1979) – The
Promenade des Anglais at Nice – signed – oil on board –
16 x 24cm.
(Hôtel de Ventes Horta) $9,758 £4,831

MAURICE BRAZIL PRENDERGAST (1859–1924) –
Still life with apples – signed – oil on canvas –
35.8 x 46cm.
(Christie's)   **$275,000   £143,000**

HERMANN PREDIGER (early 20th Century) – A
Parisian cabaret - signed and dated 1908 – 70 x 113cm.
(Christie's)   **$8,340   £4,950**

MATTIA PRETI, il CAVALIERE CALABRESE,
(Follower of) – Christ before Pilate – unframed –
97.8 x 133.3cm.
(Christie's)   **$2,462   £1,320**

MANUEL JIMENEZ PRIETO – In the farmyard –
signed and dated 1889 – oil on canvas – 92 x 60cm.
(Duran)   **$12,767   £6,667**

PRINSEP

VALENTINE CAMERON PRINSEP, R.A.
(1838–1904) – Emily Mary (May) Prinsep, Lady
Tennyson, reading on Afton Downs, near Freshwater Bay,
Isle of Wight – oil on canvas – 87.6 x 66cm.
(Christie's) $33,462 £19,800

DOD PROCTOR, R.A. (1892–1972) – Head of a black
boy – signed – oil on panel – 30 x 24cm.
(Christie's) $7,348 £4,400

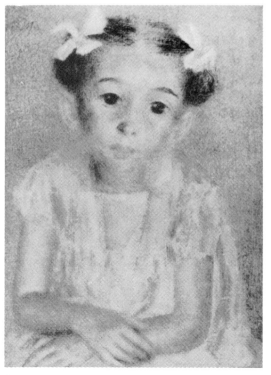

VALENTINE CAMERON PRINSEP, R.A.
(1838–1904) – Study of a girl reading – signed and
inscribed on reverse – oil on panel – 87.6 x 44.5cm.
(Christie's) $13,384 £7,920

DOD PROCTOR, R.A., N.E.A.C. (1892–1972) – The
party frock – oil on canvas – signed and dated 1948 –
20 x 16in.
(David Lay) $6,845 £3,700

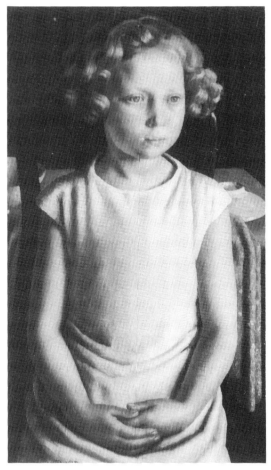

PERE PRUNA (1904) – At the circus – signed –
watercolour – 40.5 x 32.5cm.
(Duran) $5,320 £2,778

DOD PROCTOR, R.A. (1892–1972) – The little girl –
signed and dated 1928 – oil on canvas – 71.1 x 43.2cm.
(Christie's) $56,947 £34,100

DOD PROCTER, R.A. - Hibiscus on a table – signed – oil
on canvas – 14 x 17in.
(Bearne's) $8,148 £4,200

ERNEST PROCTOR, A.R.A. (1886–1935) – Crossing a
waterfall, Burma – signed - oil on canvas – 60 x 75cm.
(Christie's) $9,009 £4,620

PERE PRUNA (b. 1904) – Girl seated – watercolour –
signed – 30 x 23cm.
(Duran) $2,526 £1,309

PUIGAUDEAU

FERDINAND DU PUIGAUDEAU – Champs de
Cocquelicots en fleurs – signed and dated '01 – oil on
canvas – 46 x 55cm.
(Sothebys) **$102,850 £60,500**

FERDINAND DU PUIGAUDEAU – The artist's garden
– oil on canvas – signed – 60 x 50cm.
(Jean Claude Anaf) **$62,953 £36,180**

ALEXANDRE-DENIS-ABEL DE PUJOL (1787–1861)
– Mirabeau before Dreux-Brézé – signed and dated 1832 –
oil on canvas – 70 x 110cm.
(Christie's) **$24,241 £12,459**

HOVSEP PUSHMAN (1877–1966) – Oriental inspiration
– signed – oil on panel – 52.7 x 41.2cm.
(Christie's) **$9,900 £5,148**

LEO PUTZ (1869–1940) – Toni in the wood – signed –
oil on canvas – 37 x 27cm.
(Auktionshaus Arnold) **$20,645 £12,437**

HOWARD PYLE (1853–1911) – The Connecticut Settlers Entering The Western Reserve – signed – oil on canvas – 41 x 61cm.
(Christie's)   **$66,000 £34,320**

JEAN PUY – Nude in the artist's studio – signed and dated 02 – oil on canvas – 79 x 59cm.
(Jean-Claude Anaf)   **$10,744 £5,567**

JEAN PUY – Siesta in the clearing – signed and illegibly dated (1911?) – oil on canvas – 65 x 93cm.
(Jean-Claude Anaf)   **$19,834 £10,330**

GEORGE PYNE (1800–1884) – Oxford: St John's College from St Giles; and Oriel College from Oriel Square – both signed and dated 1870 – pencil and watercolour – $5^7/8$ x $8^1/2$in. and slightly smaller – a pair – one illustrated
(Christie's)   **$1,734 £880**

QUAEDVLIEG

CAREL-MAX-GERLACH-ANTON QUAEDVLIEG
(1823–1874) – Italian woman with letter – signed and
dated 1860 – oil on canvas – oval – 28 x 22cm.
(Sotheby's) $2,147   £1,227

DOMENICO QUAGLIO (1786–1837) – Kipfenburg
castle in the Altmühltal – signed – oil on canvas –
40 x 47cm.
(Lempertz) $554,925   £317,100

FRANZ QUAGLIO (German, 1844–1920) – Itinerants
resting – signed and dated 1886 – oil on wood –
23 x 31cm.
(Auktionshaus Arnold) $3,906   £2,353

Circle of PIETER JANSZ. QUAST (1606–1647) – The
Five Senses – 36.8 x 54.6cm.
(Christie's) $11,979   £6,050

W W QUATREMAIN – View of Broadway High Street,
Worcestershire – signed and dated 1898 – watercolour –
9 x 16in.
(Bigwood) $2,865   £1,500

FRANCOIS QUESNEL (1543–1619) - Portrait of a lady,
believed to be the daughter of the Consul of France –
coloured chalks – 204 x 170mm.
(Phillips) $2,843   £1,650

PIERRE-ANTOINE QUILLARD (1701–1733) –
Elegant company – red chalk – 168 x 274mm.
(Sotheby's) $56,894   £28,447

ALPHONSE QUIZET – Quatorze Juillet, Boulevard
Serrurier – signed – inscribed on reverse – oil on board –
8½ x 10½in.
(Tennants) $3,200   £1,600

JEAN-FRANCOIS RAFFAELLI (French 1850–1924) –
Les vieux officiers – signed – oil on panel – 57 x 40cm.
(Sotheby's) $119,460   £66,000

MAX RABES (1878–1944) – Portrait of a lady – signed
and dated 1908 – oil on canvas – 91 x 76cm.
(Auktionshaus Arnold) $1,092   £584

THEODORE JACQUES RALLI (1852-1909) – The
seamstress – signed and dated 95 – oil on canvas –
36.9 x 28.3cm.
(Christie's) $16,544   £8,800

RANSON

PAUL RANSON (1864–1909) – Les deux Graces –
signed and dated – oil on canvas – 84 x 71cm.
(Christie's) $141,075 £82,500

After **RAPHAEL** – The Betrothal of the Virgin - oil on
panel – arched top – 173.4 x 117.5cm.
(Christie's) $5,533 £2,750

A. **RATY (1889–1970)** – Spring – signed – oil on panel –
36 x 45cm.
(Hôtel de Ventes Horta) $2,725 £1,557

After **RAPHAEL** – The Holy Family with the Infant Saint
John – 143.4 x 101.6cm.
(Christie's) $8,853 £4,400

ALBERT RATY (1889–1970) – Motherhood – signed –
oil on canvas – 60 x 72cm.
(Hôtel de Ventes Horta) $5,855 £2,898

ALBERT RATY – Vresse sur Semois – signed – oil on canvas – 46 x 54cm.
(Hôtel de Ventes Horta) **$4,734 £2,459**

MAN RAY (1890–1976) – Composition – signed and dated 52 – oil on panel – 26 x 35cm.
(Christie's) **$26,179 £13,656**

A. RAUFER – Little Dutch girl eating an apple – signed – oil on canvas – 51.5 x 41.2cm.
(Ritchie's) **$1,011 £524**

LOUISE RAYNER (1829–1924) – The Household Cavalry in Peascod Street, Windsor – signed – watercolour and bodycolour over pencil – 36 x 54cm.
(Phillips) **$19,332 £10,800**

ERIC RAVILIOUS (1903–1942) – Paddle steamer – signed – inscribed with artist's notes – watercolour over pencil – 44 x 52cm.
(Phillips) **$27,439 £16,500**

LOUISE J. RAYNER (1832–1924) – The High Street from the West Bow, Edinburgh – signed – watercolour heightened with bodycolour – 57.2 x 46.3cm.
(Christie's) **$30,880 £16,000**

REAL

RAFAEL DEL REAL (b. 1932) – View of Madrid – oil on canvas – signed – 73 x 100cm.
(Duran) $3,536 £1,832

EDWARD WILLIS REDFIELD (1869–1965) – Snowy lane to the river – signed – oil on canvas – 71.8 x 82cm.
(Christie's) $57,200 £29,744

MORSTON C. REAM (1840–1898) – The dessert table – signed and dated 1873 – oil on canvas – 66 x 81.5cm.
(Christie's) $16,500 £8,580

ARTHUR W. REDGATE (1860–1906) – Wilford, near Nottingham – signed – oil on canvas – 51 x 76cm.
(Christie's) $16,335 £8,250

EDWARD W. REDFIELD (1869–1965) – Cottages at Ocean Point, Boothbay – oil on canvas – signed – 20 x 24in.
(Bruce D. Collins) $13,200 £7,135

GRANVILLE REDMOND (1871–1935) – Early morning, Pacific Park – signed and dated 08 – oil on canvas – 52 x 77.5cm.
(Butterfield & Butterfield) $12,100 £5,931

ODILON REDON – Tête de femme couchée – signed –
oil on paper laid down on canvas – 49 x 49cm.
(Sotheby's) $374,000 £220,000

HENDRIK REEKERS (1815–1854) – Fruit and flowers
on a marble ledge with a partridge hanging from a rope
above – signed and dated 1844 – 62 x 45.5cm.
(Christie's) $25,481 £12,740

ANNE REDPATH (1895–1965) – The white Cineraria –
oil on canvas – 63.5 x 77.5cm.
(Christie's) $27,020 £14,000

ANNE REDPATH (1895–1965) – Summer Afternoon,
Concarneau – signed – oil on board – 50.8 x 76.2cm.
(Christie's) $38,600 £20,000

VITTORIO REGGIANINI (b. 1858) – Reading an Art
Journal – signed – oil on canvas – 46 x 36cm.
(Christie's) $27,087 £13,750

JEAN-BAPTISTE REGNAULT (1754–1829) – Lovers entwined – signed – pen and brown ink with wash – a delineated oval – 210 x 310mm.
(Phillips)   **$2,876   £1,500**

JEAN-BAPTISTE, BARON REGNAULT (1754–1829) – The three Graces, Aglaia, Thalia and Euphrosyne – oil on panel in painted oval – 29 x 23.5cm.
(Sotheby's)   **$81,995   £46,854**

DAVID MORRISON REID-HENRY (1919–1977) – An Indian black-headed oriole or Mango Bird; and A superb tanager – both signed – watercolour heightened with bodycolour – one illustrated – 10 x 7in. and 10 x 7³/₈in.
(Christie's)   **$3,201   £1,650**

RENOIR

STEPHEN J. RENARD (20th Century) – Cetonia racing Meteor IV – signed – 61 x 91.5cm.
(Christie's)   **$11,110**   **£5,500**

ROBERT PAYTON REID, A.R.S.A. (1859–1945) – signed and dated 1908 — oil on canvas – 76.2 x 50.7cm.
(Christie's)   **$27,885**   **£16,500**

GUIDO RENI, 17th Century Italian School – Flight into Egypt – red chalk drawing – unsigned – 42 x 33.5cm.
(Allen & Harris)   **$614**   **£330**

STEPHEN REID (born 1873) – The appeal for mercy – signed – 121 x 183cm.
(Christie's)   **$11,400**   **£5,700**

After REMBRANDT – The Jewish Bride – 124.5 x 165.2cm.
(Christie's)   **$1,980**   **£990**

PIERRE-AUGUSTE RENOIR – Coco jouant aux constructions – stamped with the signature – oil on canvas – 26 x 22cm.
(Sotheby's)   **$476,850**   **£280,500**

RENOIR

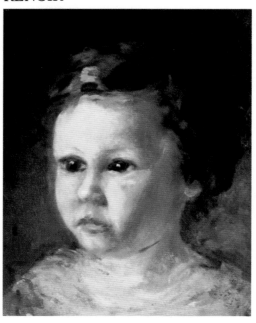

PIERRE-AUGUSTE RENOIR – Baigneuse – signed – oil on canvas – 27.3 x 23cm.
(Sotheby's) $486,200 £286,000

PIERRE-AUGUSTE RENOIR – Portrait de Pierre Sisley – oil on canvas – 27.5 x 22cm.
(Sotheby's) $374,000 £220,000

PIERRE-AUGUSTE RENOIR – Tête de jeune fille – signed – oil on canvas – 31 x 28cm.
(Sotheby's) $841,500 £495,000

PIERRE AUGUSTE RENOIR (1841–1919) – Baigneuses – signed – oil on canvas – 46 x 38cm.
(Christie's) $7,048,800 £3,960,000

PIERRE AUGUSTE RENOIR (1841–1919) – Portait de Jeanne Samary – signed - pastel on paper – 58 x 43cm.
(Christie's) $2,153,800 £1,210,000

PIERRE-AUGUSTE RENOIR – Deux femmes dans l'herbe – signed – oil on canvas – 47 x 56.5cm.
(Sotheby's)   **$1,870,000   £1,100,000**

IL'IA EFIMOVICH REPIN (1844–1930) – Portrait of a bearded man – the reverse with authentification signed by the artist's son – oil on canvas – 55 x 49cm.
(Christie's)   **$12,870   £6,600**

HELGA REUSCH (Norwegian 1865–1944) – Summer scene with woman in traditional costume by a fence – signed and dated 1890 – oil on panel – 40.5 x 33cm.
(AB Stockholms Auktionsverk)   **$896   £462**

REUTERSWARD

JUSEPE DE RIBERA, called LO SPAGNOLETTO
(1591–1652) – The Martyrdom of St Bartholomew –
signed and dated – oil on canvas – 104 x 113cm.
(Sotheby's)   **$5,225,000**   **£2,750,000**

CARL FREDRIK REUTERSWARD (b. 1934) – 'Game'
– signed – dated 1962 on reverse – lacquer-tempera on
canvas – 27 x 22cm.
(AB Stockholms Auktionsverk)   **$1,635**   **£856**

ANGELO RIBOSSI (1822–1886) – The young musicians
– signed – oil on canvas – oval – 60 x 50cm.
(Christie's)   **$12,822**   **£6,820**

LUIS RIBACOA – Basque sailors – oil on canvas – signed with initials and indistinctly dated – 100 x 150cm.
(Duran)   **$4,041**   **£2,094**

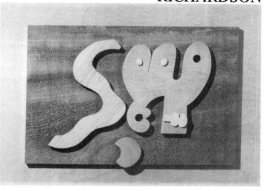

OSCAR RICCIARDI (b. 1864) – Marina Piccola, Capri – signed and inscribed – oil on canvas – 50 x 104cm.
(Christie's) $20,680 £11,000

CERI RICHARDS (1903–1971) – Adam's apple – signed, inscribed and dated on the backboard 1962 – wood relief – 63.5 x 86.5cm.
(Christie's) $10,243 £5,280

CERI RICHARDS (1903–1971) – Interior with piano – signed and dated 1950 – oil on canvas – 29 x 39.5cm.
(Christie's) $5,975 £3,080

FREDERICK STUART RICHARDSON, R.I. (1855–1934) – Cronies – signed – watercolour and bodycolour – 44 x 60cm.
(Phillips) $1,521 £850

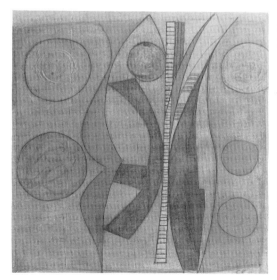

CERI RICHARDS (1903–1971) – Gothic curves – signed with initials – oil on canvas – 40.5 x 40.5cm.
(Christie's) $5,327 £3,190

THOMAS MILES RICHARDSON, Jnr., R.W.S. (1813–1890) – Near Puzzuoli, Gulf of Naples - signed and dated 1867 – watercolour heightened with white – 64.5 x 99cm.
(Phillips) $8,055 £4,500

RICKMAN

PHILIP RICKMAN (1891–1982) – Kingfishers on a branch – signed and indistinctly dated – pencil, watercolour and bodycolour – 22³/₄ x 16³/₄in.
(Christie's)   **$5,122**   **£2,640**

Circle of HYACINTHE RIGAUD – Portrait of a gentleman, possibly a self portrait – oil on canvas laid down on panel – oval – in a carved wood frame – 65 x 55cm.
(Sotheby's)   **$19,855**   **£10,450**

Manner of REMBRANDT HARMENSZ VAN RIJN – The good Samaritan – 39.4 x 32.4cm.
(Christie's)   **$2,877**   **£1,430**

HENRY-FRANÇOIS RIESENER (1767–1828) – Portrait of the sister of Princess de Ponte-Corvo – signed – oil on canvas – 100 x 80cm.
(Sotheby's)   **$9,761**   **£5,578**

LAURITS ANDERSEN RING (Danish 1854–1933) – Beach scene with artists caravan and tent near Enö – signed and dated 1913 – oil on canvas – 40 x 60cm.
(AB Stockholms Auktionsverk)   **$14,331**   **£7,387**

LOUIS RITMAN (1889–1963) – Spring in the valley –
signed – oil on canvas – 66 x 89cm.
(Christie's)   **$33,000 £17,160**

RAMON RIBAS RIUS (b. 1930) – Ballerina – signed –
oil on canvas – 41 x 33cm.
(Duran)   **$521 £262**

BRITON RIVIERE, R.A. (English 1840–1920) –
Aphrodite – signed with monogram and dated 1902 – oil
on canvas – 186 x 158cm.
(Sotheby's)   **$149,325 £82,500**

ANTONIO RIVAS (Italian, 19/20th century) – Roman
scene – signed – oil on bevelled wood panel – 10 x 22^{1}/4in.
(Du Mouchelles)   **$4,000 £1,960**

MANUEL PARRENO RIVERA – View of the river –
signed – gouache – 38 x 46cm.
(Duran)   **$84 £42**

JACQUES RIZO (Greek 19th Century) – A portrait of a
woman – signed – oil on canvas – 34 x 26cm.
(Sotheby's)   **$12,078 £6,600**

ROBERT

DAVID ROBERTS, R.A. (1794–1864) – The Temple of Philae, Egypt – signed and dated 1846 – pencil, pen and ink and watercolour heightened with white, on buff paper – 13¼ x 18¾in.
(Christie's) $33,847 £18,700

HUBERT ROBERT (1733–1808) – The Tivoli Falls seen from a cave – oil on panel – 41 x 34cm.
(Sotheby's) $77,644 £44,463

THOMAS WILLIAM ROBERTS (Australian, 1856–1931) – A bust portrait of Mabel Persis Thompson, aged 36 – signed and dated 1912 – oil on board – 57.2 x 47cm.
(Bonhams) $15,165 £7,500

DAVID ROBERTS – The Silk-Mercers' Bazaar of El-Ghooreeyeh, Cairo – pencil, water and bodycolour – signed and dated 1838 – 53.3 x 33cm.
(Bonhams) $32,015 £19,000

THOMAS WILLIAM ROBERTS (Australian, 1856–1931) – The Bridge at Dinant – signed – oil on board – 13.3 x 21cm.
(Bonhams) $13,143 £6,500

WILLIAM ROBERTS, R.A. (1895–1980) – Pleasure
cruise – signed and dated 1975 – watercolour, bodycolour
and pencil – squared for transfer – 41.5 x 33cm.
(Christie's) $7,715 £4,620

WILLIAM ROBERTS, R.A. (1895–1980) – The dove –
signed – oil on canvas – 182 x 117cm.
(Christie's) $58,784 £35,200

WILLIAM ROBERTS, R.A. (1895–1980) – Portrait of a
boy wearing a blue scarf – signed – watercolour, pencil
and blue crayon – 26.5 x 22cm.
(Christie's) $3,627 £1,870

WILLIAM ROBERTS, R.A. (1895–1980) – Masked
Revels – signed – watercolour and pencil, squared for
transfer – 37 x 30.5cm.
(Christie's) $7,469 £3,850

ROBERTSON

ANNA MARY ROBERTSON (GRANDMA) MOSES
(1860–1961) – The Old Church Yard on Sunday Morning
– signed – tempera on board – 35.5 x 45.7cm.
(Christie's)   **$19,800   £10,296**

Circle of MICHELE ROCCA – Flora receiving offerings
– 34.3 x 43.8cm.
(Christie's)   **$2,530   £1,265**

NORMAN ROCKWELL (1894–1978) – The sleepy
scholar – signed – oil on canvas – 35.6 x 28.5cm.
(Christie's)   **$71,500   £37,895**

**MANUEL GARCIA Y RODRIGUEZ (Spanish
1863–1925)** – Washerwomen by the Alcalá River – signed
and inscribed – oil on canvas – 42 x 48cm.
(Sotheby's)   **$40,260   £22,000**

SEVERIN ROESEN (active 1848–1871) – Nature's
bounty – oil on canvas – 76.3 x 63.5cm.
(Christie's)   **$16,500   £8,580**

SEVERIN ROESEN (active 1848–1871) – Bountiful
harvest – signed – oil on canvas – 73.9 x 92cm.
(Christie's)   **$41,800   £21,736**

CHRISTIAN ROHLFS (1849–1938) – The return of the
prodigal – signed with monogram and dated 1916 –
tempera overpainting of the woodcut – 48.2 x 34.4cm.
(Lempertz)   **$19,534   £10,069**

HENRY LEONIDAS ROLFE (fl. 1847–1881) – A pike chasing rudd – signed and dated 1865 – oil on canvas – 61 x 91.4cm.
(Christie's)   **$6,098   £3,080**

ROMAN SCHOOL, circa 1700 – The return from Egypt – oil on canvas – 118 x 90cm.
(Sotheby's)   **$13,588   £7,809**

Follower of SALOMON ROMBOUTS (active 1652–died before 1702) – A winter landscape with kolf players, skaters and other townsfolk on a frozen town moat – with signature 'SR (linked) onbouts' – on panel – 36.6 x 49.5cm.
(Christie's)   **$11,326   £5,720**

GEORGE ROMNEY, Circle of – Portrait of a lady as Venus with Cupid as a child – 76.8 x 62.8cm.
(Christie's)   **$8,410   £4,180**

JOSEF RONAI (1861–1927) – Elegant lady in a hat – pastel on card – signed
(Hôtel de Ventes Horta)   **$5,587   £2,880**

461

RONNER

HENRIETTE RONNER (1821–1909) – A Kitten by a cloisonné jardiniere – signed – oil on panel – 22.8 x 19.1cm.
(Christie's) **$6,270 £3,300**

HENRIETTE RONNER (1821–1909) – The red basket – signed – oil on panel – 24.5 x 32.5cm.
(Hôtel de Ventes Horta) **$21,460 £11,148**

THOMAS MATTHEWS ROOKE (1842–1942) – Apollo and the Muses – inscribed on the backing – in a painted roundel – oil on canvas – 52 x 52cm.
(Christie's) **$46,475 £27,500**

A. ROOSENBOOM (1845–1875) – First meeting – signed – oil on canvas – 24 x 19cm.
(Hôtel de Ventes Horta) **$3,578 £1,771**

GIULIO ROSATI (1858–1917) – The brass beater – signed – pencil and watercolour – 38.1 x 55.5cm.
(Christie's) **$6,204 £3,300**

GUY ROSE (1867–1925) – French poppies – signed – oil on canvas – 60 x 73cm.
(Butterfield & Butterfield) **$110,000 £53,921**

GUY ROSE (1867–1925) – Near Arch Beach, Laguna – signed – oil on canvas – 54 x 61cm.
(Butterfield & Butterfield)   **$88,000 £43,137**

LEONARD ROSOMAN, R.A. (b. 1913) – A burnt-out fire appliance – signed – oil on canvas – 75 x 100cm.
(Christie's)   **$33,068 £19,800**

PIETRO ROTARI (1707–1762) – The Penitent Magdalen – bears inscription and date 1757 – oil on canvas – unstretched and unframed – 46 x 35.2cm.
(Phillips)   **$9,562 £4,800**

GEORGES ROUAULT (1871–1958) – Von Krapot, Philosophe – signed and dated 1915 – gouache and coloured chalk on paper – 28.9 x 19cm.
(Christie's)   **$18,810 £11,000**

DANTE GABRIEL ROSSETTI (English 1828–82) – A Christmas carol – signed with monogram and dated 1867 – red and white chalk – 45 x 37.5cm.
(Sotheby's)   **$99,550 £55,000**

GEORGES ROUAULT (1871–1958) – Dancer and Monsieur Loyal – signed and dated 1905 – watercolour, gouache, pastel and black ink on paper – 28 x 36.5cm.
(Christie's)   **$86,680 £44,000**

ROUAULT

GEORGES ROUAULT (1871–1958) - Maria Lani (en Pierrette) - signed and dated 1929 – gouache and pastel on paper – 51.1 x 37cm.
(Christie's)   **$112,860 £66,000**

ANNE-LOUIS GIRODET DE ROUCY-TRIOSON (1767–1824), Attributed to – The Turk's head – oil on canvas – unframed – 60 x 49.5cm.
(Sotheby's)   **$11,713 £6,693**

HENRI ROUSSEAU (1844–1910) – Rounding up the cattle – signed – oil on canvas – unframed – 54.6 x 68.9cm.
(Christie's)   **$6,617 £3,520**

GEORGES ROUAULT (1871–1958) – Portrait of the poet Paul Verlaine – signed and dated 1914 – oil and tempera on halfboard – 75 x 52cm.
(Lempertz)   **$538,889 £277,778**

PHILIPPE ROUSSEAU (1816–1887) – Still life with fruit – signed – oil on canvas – 33 x 46cm.
(Sotheby's)   **$7,496 £4,462**

THEODORE ROUSSEAU – Tress by a pond, Autumn – signed – oil on panel – 26.6 x 41.2cm.
(Ritchie's)   **$3,492**   **£1,810**

THOMAS ROWLANDSON (1756–1827) – A Dutch Academy – inscribed on the artist's mount – pencil and ink and watercolour – 7³/₈ x 11¹/₄ in.
(Christie's)   **$19,910**   **£11,000**

ANTOINE ROUX (1765–1835) – The great roads at Marseilles in 1823; and a view of the surroundings of Arles – signed and dated 1823 – graphite pen and brown and black ink, brown wash, watercolour – 183 x 252mm and 220 x 310mm. – both on the same mounting
(Christie's)   **$7,052**   **£3,624**

THOMAS ROWLANDSON (1756–1827) – The Comforts of Bath: The concert – pencil, pen and grey ink and watercolour – 4¹/₄ x 7¹/₈in.
(Christie's)   **$19,305**   **£9,900**

ANTOINE ROUX (1765–1835) – The 45 ton 'Le Loyal', captured by Captain François Mordeille – signed – pencil, pen and brown ink, brown wash, watercolour – 460 x 600mm.
(Christie's)   **$4,848**   **£2,492**

STANLEY ROYLE (1888–1961) – Young girl picking roses – signed and dated 1910 – oil on canvas – 81 x 62cm.
(Christie's)   **$5,511**   **£3,300**

RUBENS

After SIR PETER PAUL RUBENS – The Holy Family with Saint Anne – 122 x 94cm.
(Christie's) $3,984 £1,980

After SIR PETER PAUL RUBENS – The Holy Family and the Infant Saint John the Baptist and Saint Anne – 123.8 x 99.6cm.
(Christie's) $8,616 £4,620

Studio of SIR PETER PAUL RUBENS (1577–1640) – Nymphs and satyrs in a landscape – oil on canvas – 274.5 x 329cm.
(Sotheby's) $45,980 £24,200

PETER PAUL RUBENS (Flemish 1577–1640) – Manner of – Lot and his wife led by angels – oil on panel – 29 x 49cm.
(AB Stockholms Auktionsverk) $2,687 £1,385

ENRIQUE MARTINEZ CUBELLS Y RUIZ (1874–1917) – Waiting for the boat – signed – oil on canvas – unframed – 50.2 x 39.7cm.
(Christie's) $24,816 £13,200

466

JOHANN VALENTIN RUTHS (1825–1905) – The Flüela Pass – signed – oil on panel – 35.6 x 52.1cm.
(Christie's) $3,881 £1,980

Manner of RACHEL RUYSCH – Roses, peonies, tulips, convolvuli, a sunflower and other flowers in a sculpted urn – with signature 'Rachel Ruisch f.t.' – 118.2 x 90.3cm.
(Christie's) **$21,780 £11,000**

RUSSIAN SCHOOL, 19th Century – Portrait of the poet Aleksandr Sergeevich Pushkin – inscribed and dated 1835 – oil on canvas – 77 x 62.5cm.
(Christie's) **$8,580 £4,400**

RYBACK

PAUL S*** –Battleships – signed and dated – oil on canvas – 103.5 x 94cm.
(Sotheby's)   **$7,482**   **£4,180**

V. DE SAEDELEER (Belgian 1867–1941) – Winter – oil on canvas – signed – 71 x 85cm.
(Hôtel de Ventes Horta)   **$14,899**   **£7,680**

ISSACHAR BER RYBACK (1897–1935) – Felix, the jolly vagabond – signed – watercolour heightened with white on paper – 44.5 x 28cm.
(Christie's)   **$6,006**   **£3,080**

MARTIN RYCKAERT (1587–1631) – An extensive river landscape, with travellers approaching a chapel on a path – oil on copper – 18.5 x 23.4cm.
(Phillips)   **$29,880**   **£15,000**

OLOF SAGER-NELSON (1868–96) – Portrait of Esther Wallerstedt – signed and dated 89 – oil on canvas – 46 x 32cm.
(AB Stockholms Auktionsverk)   **$2,754**   **£1,442**

EMILIO GRAU SALA (1911–1975) – The harbour entrance at Honfleur - oil on canvas – signed – signed and dated 1961 on reverse – 60 x 73cm.
(Duran)   **$75,785   £39,267**

EMILIO GRAU SALA (1911–1975) – The beach at Deauville – oil on canvas – signed, and dated 70 on reverse – 73 x 92cm.
(Duran)   **$101,047   £52,356**

EMILIO SALA (1850–1910) – Coastal landscape – oil on canvas laid down on board – signed – 25 x 35cm.
(Duran)   **$2,526   £1,309**

CHARLES-LOUIS SALIGO (b. 1804) – Portrait of Jules-Frédéric-Paul of Pontoi Marquis of Pont-Carré – signed and dated 1828 – oil on canvas – 172 x 128cm.
(Sotheby's)   **$26,355   £15,060**

SALIMBENI

FLORENCE A. SALTMER (English, Exh. 1882–1908)
– Cornish wild flowers – signed and dated 1895 – oil on
canvas – 61 x 91.4cm.
(Bonhams) **$11,121 £5,500**

GIOVANNI BATTISTA SALVI called Il Sassoferrato
(1609–1685) – The Penitent Magdalen – oil on canvas –
73 x 59.6cm.
(Phillips) **$6,972 £3,500**

Attributed to VENTURA SALIMBENI (1568–1613) –
The Resurrection – oil on panel – 233.7 x 155cm.
(Phillips) **$69,720 £35,000**

ROBERT SALMON (1775–1842) – The harbour,
Liverpool – signed on reverse – oil on panel –
20.3 x 25.4cm.
(Christie's) **$19,800 £10,296**

Circle of FRANCESCO SALVIATI – Portrait of a Saint,
possibly Saint Bernard – oil on panel – 71.5 x 56cm.
(Sotheby's) **$96,140 £50,600**

RAGNAR SANDBERG (1902–72) – Umbrellas – street scene with women – signed – oil on canvas – 41 x 65cm.
(AB Stockholms Auktionsverk) **$35,536 £18,605**

GOSTA SANDELS (1887–1919) – Reclining woman – signed and dated 1908 – watercolour and pencil – 23.5 x 29cm.
(AB Stockholms Auktionsverk) **$2,577 £1,349**

JAMES SANT, R.A. – Geraldine, daughter of Frederick Massey, Esq. – signed with monogram – oil on canvas – 162 x 77cm.
(Sotheby's) **$27,874 £15,400**

OTTO SANDRECZKI (American, 20th Century) – Resting in the Shade – signed and dated 1915 – gouache on paper – 7 x 8³/₄in.
(Skinner) **$500 £258**

RUBENS SANTORO (1859–1942) – Rio San Trovaso, Venice – signed – oil on panel – unframed – 20 x 25.3cm.
(Christie's) **$30,338 £15,400**

SANTORO

RUBENS SANTORO (1859–1942) – Male figure singing
and playing instrument – signed – oil on mahogany panel –
9¹/₂ x 7¹/₂in.
(Du Mouchelles)   **$4,500   £2,320**

Circle of CARLO SARACENI (1580–1620) – A peasant
woman holding mushrooms – oil on canvas – 56.5 x 44cm.
(Phillips)   **$6,528   £3,400**

RUBENS SANTORO (1859–1942) – Washing day,
Venice – signed – oil on canvas – unframed – 42 x 29cm.
(Christie's)   **$23,716   £12,100**

Circle of ANDREA D'ANGIOLO SARTO called
Andrea del Sarto (1487–1530 or 31) – Saint Catherine –
oil on panel – 106 x 82.5cm.
(Sotheby's)   **$40,763   £23,427**

HUBERT SATTLER (Austrian 1817–1904) – A view of
Burgos – signed and dated – oil on canvas – 103 x 132cm.
(Sotheby's)   **$12,078   £6,600**

SAVERIJS (1866–1964) – Still life – signed and dated 52
– oil on canvas – 105 x 135cm.
(Hôtel de Ventes Horta)   **$15,148   £7,869**

HENDRIK SCHAEFFER – The coal quay at Antwerp –
signed and dated 1882 – oil on canvas – 105 x 183cm.
(Hôtel de Ventes Horta)   **$1,894   £984**

GODFRIED SCHALCKEN (Dutch 1643–1706) –
Manner of – Woman illuminated – oil on canvas –
62 x 44cm.
(AB Stockholms Auktionsverk)   **$1,738   £896**

SCHANTZ

PHILIP VON SCHANTZ (b. 1928) – Heap of currants –
signed, dated 1981 and numbered 133/195 – colour litho –
50 x 74.5cm.
(AB Stockholms Auktionsverk)   **$2,252   £1,161**

BARTOLOMEO SCHEDONE (1578–1615) – The Holy
Family – oil on canvas – 58.5 x 49cm.
(Sotheby's)   **$23,293   £13,387**

ANDRIES SCHEERBOOM (Dutch, 1832–1880) –
Conversation – oil on canvas – 11 x 16½in.
(Du Mouchelles)   **$2,800   £1,501**

JOHAN HENRIK SCHEFFEL (1690–1781) – Attributed
to – Portrait of Cornelia Florentina Hildebrand née von
Düben – oil on canvas – 52 x 44cm.
(AB Stockholms Auktionsverk)   **$1,110   £572**

JOHAN HENRIK SCHEFFEL (1690–1781) – Manner of
– Portrait of the businessman Pehr Reimers – half length –
oil on canvas – 76 x 62cm.
(AB Stockholms Auktionsverk)   **$1,434   £739**

VAN SCHENDEL (1806–1870) – The evening class –
signed – oil on canvas – 51 x 40cm.
(Hôtel de Ventes Horta)   **$8,893   £5,082**

PETRUS VAN SCHENDEL (Flemish, 1806–1870) –
Rotterdam fish market – signed and dated 1840 – oil on
wood – 76 x 87.5cm.
(Kunsthaus am Museum)   **$43,708   £22,530**

PETRUS VAN SCHENDEL (1806–1870) – The
blacksmith's forge – oil on panel – 52.6 x 62.7cm.
(Christie's)   **$22,638   £11,550**

**JOHAN FREDERIK CORNELIS SCHERREWITZ
(1868–1951)** – A drover with cattle in a landscape – signed
– oil on canvas – 70.5 x 101cm.
(Christie's)   **$4,743   £2,420**

EGON SCHIELE (1890–1918) – Portrait of Fräulein
Toni Rieger – signed and dated 1917 – soft pencil and
gouache on buff paper – 44.5 x 29.5cm.
(Christie's)   **$433,400   £220,000**

EGON SCHIELE (1890–1918) – Portrait of a man –
signed and dated 10.1.07 – soft pencil on paper –
49.3 x 34.4cm.
(Christie's)   **$26,004   £13,200**

SCHIELE

EGON SCHIELE (1890–1918) – Child in black clothes – signed and dated 1911 – gouache – 44 x 31cm.
(Galerie Koller Zürich)   **$197,831**   **£103,306**

HERBERT GUSTAVE SCHMATZ (1857–1935) – The awakening of love – signed and dated 1894 – oil on canvas – 110 x 148cm.
(Christie's)   **$28,814**   **£17,050**

EGON SCHIELE – Portrait of the actress Marga Boerner with powder compact – signed and dated 1917 – gouache and black crayon – 48.2 x 30.5cm.
(Sotheby's)   **$822,800**   **£484,000**

KARL SCHMIDT-ROTTLUFF (1884–1976) – Garden in the South – signed and dated 53 on reverse – oil on canvas – 87 x 101cm.
(Lempertz)   **$114,514**   **£59,028**

HEINRICH AUGUST GEORG SCHIOTT (1823–1895) – A father proposing on behalf of his son (Thelemarken, Norway) – signed – oil on canvas – 96.5 x 129.5cm.
(Christie's)   **$20,680**   **£11,000**

KARL SCHMIDT-ROTTLUFF (1884–1976) – Still life with deer – signed – oil on wood – 74 x 66cm.
(Lempertz)   **$60,625**   **£31,250**

FRANK EARLE SCHOONOVER (1877-1972) – The
Pirate – signed and dated 11 – oil on canvas –
56 x 83.8cm.
(Christie's) **$30,800 £16,016**

AERT SCHOUMAN (1710–1792) – A blue and scarlet
macaw in a tree – oil on canvas – 76 x 63.5cm.
(Phillips) **$14,890 £7,475**

HENRY SCHOUTEN (1864–1927) – A sportsman with
his English and Gordon setters; and A sportsman with his
Irish and English setters – both signed – oil on canvas – a
pair (one illustrated) – 81.2 x 63.5cm.
(Christie's) **$5,434 £2,860**

SCHUHMACHER

WIM SCHUHMACHER (1894-1986) – The courtyard of
Auberge de Cervantes, Toledo – signed – oil on canvas –
66 x 80cm.
(Christie's) **$24,112 £12,578**

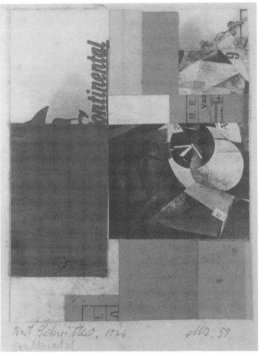

ALEKSANDR PETROVICH SCHWABE (1818–1872)
– Two Life-Guard Cossack soldiers in discussion –
inscribed on reverse – oil on canvas – 57.8 x 46.4cm.
(Christie's) **$17,160 £8,800**

KURT SCHWITTERS (1887–1948) – Continental –
signed, dated and inscribed on mount – collage laid on card
– 13.4 x 9.6cm.
(Christie's) **$324 £190**

Attributed to SINIBALDO SCORZA (1589–1631) – La Piazza del Mercato Vecchio – oil on canvas – 40 x 87cm.
(Phillips) **$15,936 £8,000**

EDWARD SEAGO (1910–1974) – Jeremy Spenser in Terence Rattigan's "The Sleeping Prince" – signed – oil on canvas – 61 x 46cm.
(Christie's) **$14,328 £8,580**

BAUDWYNS ET SCOUVAERT – Landscape with figures – oil on panel – 40 x 35cm.
(Hôtel de Ventes Horta) **$62,080 £32,000**

EDWARD SEAGO (1910-1974) – In the Tuileries Gardens – signed – watercolour – 31.5 x 49cm.
(Christie's) **$14,938 £7,700**

EDWARD SEAGO (1910-1974) – Evening sunlight, Honfleur – signed – pencil and watercolour – 32.5 x 51cm.
(Christie's) **$17,499 £9,020**

EDWARD SEAGO (1910–1974) – Evening sunlight, Honfleur – signed - oil on board – 26.8 x 35.6cm.
(Christie's) **$32,147 £19,250**

479

SEDLACEK

STEPHAN SEDLACEK (late 19th Century) – The harem dancers – signed – 80 x 59cm.
(Christie's) **$10,194 £6,050**

HERMANN SEEGER (German 1857–) – Babes in the woods – signed – oil on canvas – 90 x 71cm.
(AB Stockholms Auktionsverk) **$3,762 £1,939**

DANIEL SEGHERS (1590–1661) – The birth of Christ – oil on wood – 63.5 x 48cm.
(Kunsthaus am Museum) **$4,370 £2,253**

GUILLAUME SEIGNAC (French 19th Century) – The family meal – signed – oil on panel – 36 x 46cm.
(Sotheby's) **$8,052 £4,400**

GUILLAUME SEIGNAC (late 19th Century) –Le Coffret – signed – oil on canvas – 62.5 x 80cm.
(Christie's) **$25,850 £13,750**

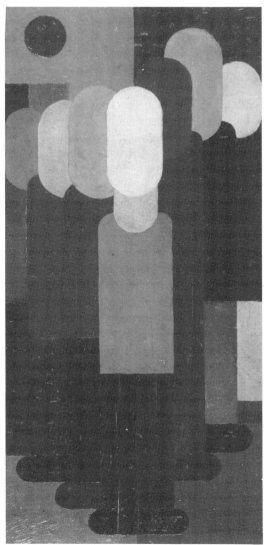

HENRY COURTNEY SELOUS (1811–1890) – A flower market in the Piazzetta San Marco by the Column of St. Theodore, Venice – signed – oil on canvas – 65 x 55cm. *(Christie's)* $9,295 £5,500

LUIS SEOANE (b. 1910) – Nude – signed and dated 79 – wax crayon – 49 x 63cm. *(Duran)* $3,192 £1,667

FRANZ WILHELM SEIWERT (1894–1933) – Mass – signed with monogram and dated 31 – oil on wood – 58 x 28cm. *(Lempertz)* $67,361 £34,722

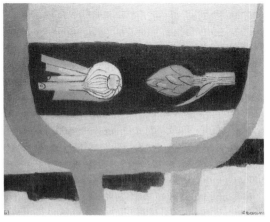

CHRISTIAN SELL – The outpost – signed and dated 81 – oil on panel – 20.5 x 27cm. *(Ritchie's)* $1,470 £762

LUIS SEOANE (1910) – Fennel and artichoke - oil on canvas – signed - 64 x 80cm. *(Duran)* $9,094 £4,712

SEOANE

LUIS SEOANE (b. 1910) – Woman – signed and dated 79
– wax crayon – 62.5 x 48cm.
(Duran)   **$2,926   £1,528**

ISMAEL GONZALEZ DE LA SERNA (1897–1970) –
The Spanish dancer – tempera on board – signed –
117 x 80cm.
(Duran)   **$40,418   £20,942**

ISMAEL GONZALEZ DE LA SERNA (1897–1970) –
Still life with watermelon - oil on tablex – signed –
100 x 125cm.
(Duran)   **$55,576   £28,796**

**VALENTIN ALEKSANDROVICH SEROV
(1865–1911)** – Portrait of Prince Feliks Feliksovich
Iusupov, Count Sumarokov-El'ston – signed and dated 09
– oil on canvas – 90 x 83cm.
(Christie's)   **$117,975   £60,500**

AUGUSTE SERRURE (1825–1903) – The flower market
– signed and dated 1870 – oil on panel – 62 x 89.5cm.
(Christie's)   **$26,004   £13,200**

482

SCHOOL OF SEVILLE, Early 17th Century – Portrait of a gentleman – oil on canvas – 49.5 x 40cm.
(Sotheby's) $18,810   £9,900

GINO SEVERINI (1883–1966) – A pierrot playing a guitar – signed – bodycolour on paper – 17.5 x 12.5cm.
(Christie's) $26,179   £13,656

DOROTHEA SHARP (1874–1955) – Cornish holiday – signed – oil on panel – 36 x 46cm.
(Christie's) $9,002   £4,840

SHARP

WILLIAM SHAYER (1788–1879) – A drover with cattle and a dog in a landscape – signed and dated 1849 – 43.2 x 53.4cm.
(Christie's) $9,034   £4,950

DOROTHEA SHARP (1874–1955) – Girl among blossom – signed – oil on canvas – 75 x 63cm.
(Christie's) $25,718   £15,400

HENRY and CHARLES SHAYER – View on the South Downs – signed – oil on canvas – 50.8 x 40.6cm.
(Pinney's) $2,128   £1,282

WILLIAM SHAYER, SEN. (1787–1879) – Interior of a fisherman's cottage; and The itinerant fishmonger – both inscribed, signed and dated 1830 on labels on reverse – oil on panel – 35 x 44.5cm. – a pair
(Christie's) $12,313   £6,380

MILLARD SHEETS (1907–1989) – Afternoon, Kona Coast – signed and dated 1984 – watercolour on paper
– 55 x 75cm.
(Butterfield & Butterfield) **$11,000 £5,392**

MILLARD SHEETS (1907–1989) – Chululu Hills –
signed – watercolour on paper – 55 x 75cm.
(Butterfield & Butterfield) **$4,950 £2,426**

DAVID SHEPHERD (b. 1931) – Guarding the herd –
signed and dated 80 – oil on canvas – 70 x 151cm.
(Christie's) **$70,785 £36,300**

G. SHERMAN (20th Century) – The exposition – oil on
canvas – signed – 24 x 20in.
(Bruce D. Collins) **$1,320 £714**

SHINN

EVERETT SHINN (1876–1953) – The bright shawl –
signed – dated and inscribed – oil on board – 83 x 63.5cm.
(Christie's) $6,600   £3,498
EVERETT SHINN (1876–1953) – Girl in white on stage
– signed – oil on canvas – 23.2 x 28.2cm.
(Christie's) $24,200   £12,584

WALTER RICHARD SICKERT, A.R.A. (1860–1942)
– Seated woman, Granby Street – signed – oil on canvas –
51 x 40.5cm.
(Christie's) $146,960   £88,000

HENRI LE SIDANER (1862–1939) – Le Goûter sous Bois, Gerberoy – signed – oil on canvas – 150.5 x 126cm.
(Christie's) **$1,279,080 £748,000**

WALTER RICHARD SICKERT, A.R.A. (1860–1942) – Woman seated on a bed – signed – oil on canvas – 45 x 37cm.
(Christie's) **$29,392 £17,600**

HENRI LE SIDANER – Fenêtres sur le Parc, Pavillon Français – signed – oil on canvas – 58.5 x 71.5cm.
(Sotheby's) **$121,550 £71,500**

HENRI LE SIDANER (1862–1939) – Le Pavillon de Musique in the snow, Versailles – signed – oil on canvas – 73 x 60cm.
(Christie's) **$60,676 £30,800**

PAUL SIGNAC (1863–1935) – Le Tréguier, Bateaux à Quai – signed and inscribed – watercolour and pencil on paper – 28 x 46cm.
(Christie's) **$43,263 £25,320**

SIGNAC

PAUL SIGNAC (1863–1935) – Antibes, le Nuage rose – signed and dated lower left P Signac 1916 – oil on canvas – 73 x 92cm.
(Christie's)   **$2,055,900**   **£1,155,000**

LAUMA SIKA – Delilah – signed – oil on canvas – 100 x 100cm.
(Jean-Claude Anaf)   **$590**   **£308**

LOUIS DE SILVESTRE THE YOUNGER (1675–1760) – An allegory of hearing; An allegory of smell – a pair – both oil on canvas – each 130 x 152.5cm.
(Sotheby's)   **$68,970**   **£36,300**

F. SILVANI (late 19th Century) – Venice from the lagoon – signed – 45 x 76cm.
(Christie's)   **$3,521**   **£2,090**

SIMON SIMONSEN (1841–1928) – A Pointer and two Dachshunds hunting a fox – signed and dated 1886 – oil on canvas laid down on panel – 45 x 54cm.
(Christie's)   **$2,926**   **£1,540**

ALFRED SISLEY (1839–1899) – The geese –
indistinctly signed – pastel on paper – 26 x 33cm.
(Christie's) $75,845   £38,500

HENRY SIMPSON – A street, Cairo – signed – oil on
board – 20.9 x 14.6cm.
(Bonhams) $452   £280

CHARLES SIMS, R.A., R.W.S., R.S.W. (1873–1928) –
Young boy fishing – signed – gouache – 39 x 55cm.
(Phillips) $4,157   £2,500

P.G. SJAMAAR (1819–76) – The card players – signed –
oil on panel – 43 x 66cm.
(Hôtel de Ventes Horta) $7,745   £4,426

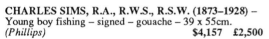

SJOBERG

AXEL SJOBERG (1866–1950) – At the seaside – signed –
pastel – 49 x 64cm.
(AB Stockholms Auktionsverk) **$2,239 £1,154**

FRANZ SKARBINA (1849–1910) – Children skating in a
Berlin street – signed – oil on canvas laid down on board –
65.7 x 51.7cm.
(Christie's) **$14,212 £8,360**

DZEMMA SKULME – Girl in blue – signed – oil on
canvas – 80 x 100cm.
(Jean-Claude Anaf) **$1,180 £616**

HARALD SLOTT-MØLLER (1864–1937) – Georg Brandes at the University in Copenhagen – signed and dated 1889 – oil on canvas – 92 x 81cm.
(Christie's)   **$71,511**   **£36,300**

JAN SLUIJTERS (1881–1957) – A portrait of a lady – signed – oil on canvas – 70 x 59cm.
(Christie's)   **$33,068**   **£17,250**

JAN SLUIJTERS (1881–1957) – Transitoriness – signed and dated 1903 – oil on canvas – 147 x 105cm.
(Christie's)   **$27,557**   **£14,375**

JAN SLUIJTERS (1881–1957) – A flower still life – signed and dated 12 – oil on canvas – 128 x 94cm.
(Christie's)   **$192,898**   **£100,625**

SLUIJTERS

JAN SLUIJTERS (1881–1957) – A view of the sawing-mill, Amsterdam, the new building site of 'De Admiraal de Ruyterweg' in the distance – signed and dated 08 – oil on canvas – 51 x 66cm.
(Christie's) **$51,669 £26,953**

FRANS SMEERS (Belgian 1873–1960) – Harbour scene – oil on panel – signed – 40 x 50cm.
(Hôtel de Ventes Horta) **$3,414 £1,760**

FRANS SMEERS (1873–1960) – The hussy – signed and dated – oil on canvas – 60 x 40cm.
(Hôtel de Ventes Horta) **$5,738 £3,279**

FRANS SMEERS (Belgian School) – By the sea – signed – oil on canvas – 100 x 100cm.
(Galerie Moderne) **$36,071 £18,836**

LEON DE SMET (1881–1966) – Vue sur le jardin, Wingstone – signed and dated 1914 – oil on canvas – 76.8 x 63.5cm.
(Christie's) **$31,845 £16,500**

CARLTON ALFRED SMITH (1853–1946) – The Birthday Book – signed – pencil and watercolour – 21½ x 14½in.
(Christie's)   **$12,570**   **£6,380**

SIR MATTHEW SMITH (1879–1959) – Still life with clay figure – signed with initials – oil on canvas – 76 x 51cm.
(Christie's)   **$19,288**   **£11,550**

LIONEL PERCY SMYTHE (English, 1839–1913) – Young harvesters – oil on canvas – signed – 61 x 106.7cm.
(Bonhams)   **$7,371**   **£4,200**

SNAPE

SNOWMAN - Coming to the river – oil on canvas –
signed and dated 1909 – 66 x 107cm.
(Hôtel de Ventes Horta)   **$7,139**   **£3,680**

WILLIAM H. SNAPE (fl. 1885–1892) – In the studio –
signed – oil on canvas – 61 x 37.5cm.
(Christie's)   **$8,917**   **£4,620**

PIETER SNYERS (1681–1752) – A still life of a glass
vase containing roses, tulips and hydrangeas beside
bunches of asparagus – oil on canvas – 61.5 x 76cm.
(Phillips)   **$13,944**   **£7,000**

ISAAC SNOWMAN – Two children on a rocky shoreline
– signed – oil on board – 32 x 26cm.
(Phillips)   **$4,989**   **£3,000**

RIGOBERTO SOLER (1896–1968) – The water carriers
– signed and dated 1935 – oil on canvas – 60 x 70cm.
(Christie's)   **$16,456**   **£9,680**

FRANCESCO SOLIMENA (1657–1747) – The Martyrdom of St Januarius – oil on canvas – 175 x 145cm. *(Sotheby's)* $41,800   £22,000

Circle of FRANCESCO SOLIMENA (1657–1747) – The Virgin giving suck – 89 x 69.3cm. *(Christie's)* $6,534   £3,300

Follower of FRANCESCO SOLIMENA – Ratchis, King of the Lombards, relinquishing his crown to become a monk on Montecassino – 76.5 x 152.7cm. *(Christie's)* $3,960   £1,980

FRANCESCO SOLIMENA, (Follower of) – Portrait of a noble lady in Turkish costume – unframed – 87.6 x 73cm. *(Christie's)* $2,667   £1,430

SOLOMON J. SOLOMON, R.A. (1860–1927) – Study for 'Eve' – signed with initials – oil on canvas – 69.8 x 56.4cm. *(Christie's)* $8,276   £4,180

SON

JORIS VAN SON (1623–1667) – A still life on a table covered by a green cloth consisting of a silver beaker, glasses of wine, lemon, a shoulder of lamb, shrimps and crab – signed – oil on panel – 57.5 x 90cm.
(Phillips) **$45,816 £23,000**

WILLIAM LOUIS SONNTAG, JR. (1869–1898) – Lady on a hillside – signed – watercolour and gouache on paper laid down on board – 17.2 x 24.2cm.
(Christie's) **$2,420 £1,436**

JOSE-GIULIO or JULIO DE SOUZA-PINTO, (b. 1855), Portuguese school – The torn trousers – signed and dated 1883 – oil on canvas – 76.5 x 60.5cm.
(Sotheby's) **$24,364 £14,502**

JOAQUIN SOROLLA Y BASTIDA (Spanish 1863–1923) – Playa de Valencia (Sol de Tarde) – signed and dated 1908 – oil on canvas – 103.5 x 148cm.
(Sotheby's) **$3,285,150 £1,815,000**

JOSE DE SOUZA-PINTO – Reading in an interior –
signed – oil on panel – 46 x 38cm.
(Sotheby's)   **$23,628   £13,200**

RAPHAEL SOYER (1899–1988) – A model's break –
signed – oil on canvas – 101.3 x 76.2cm.
(Christie's)   **$35,200   £18,304**

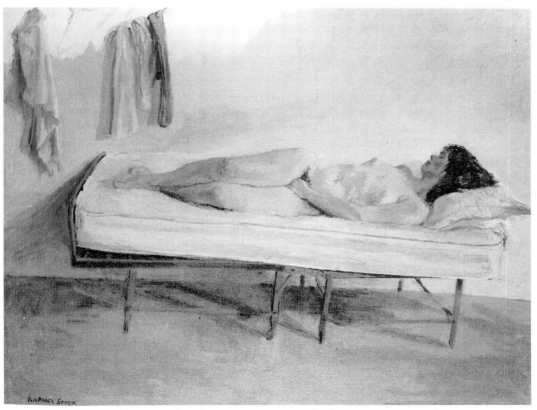

RAPHAEL SOYER (1899–1988) – Young woman on a cot – signed – oil on canvas – 101.6 x 127cm.
(Christie's)   **$55,000   £28,600**

SPANISH SCHOOL

SPANISH SCHOOL (circa 1700) – Portrait of a gentleman with ruff – oil on wood – 77.5 x 60cm. (Auktionshaus Arnold) **$1,943 £1,039**

SPANISH SCHOOL – Portrait of a Grandee – oil on canvas – 72 x 58cm. (Galerie Moderne) **$1,431 £749**

SPANISH SCHOOL, 17th Century – Portrait of a noblewoman – oil on wood – 67 x 56cm. (Galerie Moderne) **$3,250 £1,702**

CORNEL M. SPANYIK (born 1858) – Gentlemanly conduct – signed and dated 1912 – oil on canvas – 119 x 95cm. (Christie's) **$6,618 £3,520**

RUSKIN SPEAR, R.A. (1911–1990) – Public House – signed and dated 1949 – oil on canvas – 61.5 x 73.5cm.
(Christie's)   **$29,392 £17,600**

ROBERT SPENCER (1879–1931) – The peddler's cart on the canal, New Hope – signed – oil on canvas – 51 x 61cm.
(Christie's)   **$50,600 £26,312**

RUSKIN SPEAR, R.A. (1911–1990) - Girl in a Bar – signed – oil on panel – 37 x 47cm.
(Christie's)   **$4,908 £2,530**

CHARLES SPENCELAYH – A meatless day - signed – oil on canvas – 46 x 30.5cm.
(Sotheby's)   **$43,802 £24,200**

SIR STANLEY SPENCER, R.A. (1891–1959) – Portrait of Mrs. Frank, M.D., J.P. - oil on canvas – 90.5 x 70cm.
(Christie's)   **$39,495 £23,650**

SPENCER

SIR STANLEY SPENCER, R.A. (1891–1959) – The harbour, St. Ives – oil on canvas – 71 x 94cm.
(Christie's)   **$220,440**   **£132,000**

HEINRICH SPERLING (1844–1924) – A St. Bernard on the edge of a wood – signed – oil on canvas – 58.3 x 69.8cm.
(Christie's)   **$4,807**   **£2,530**

LEON SPILLIAERT (1881–1946) – Workyard in the port of Ostende – signed and dated 1924 – gouache on thick paper – 38 x 35cm.
(Christie's)   **$11,804**   **£6,116**

CARL SPRINCHORN (American, 1887–1971) – The Dancer – initialled – watercolour and graphite on paper – 10³/₄ x 8³/₈in.
(Skinner Inc.)   **$300**   **£161**

JAN JACOB SPOHLER (1811-1866) – A winter landscape with peasants by an inn and skaters on a frozen river – signed and dated 60 (?) - 59 x 80cm.
(Christie's)   **$53,644**   **£26,822**

HOWARD F. SPRAGUE (American, active 1871–99) – Portrait of the boat, "Livingstone" – signed and dated 1887 – oil on canvas – 17 x 30¹/₂in.
(Du Mouchelles)   **$13,000**   **£6,599**

C. SPRINGER – Morning market – signed – tempera on porcelain – 41 x 31cm.
(Hôtel de Ventes Horta)   **$3,471   £1,803**

HANS LUDWIG STADLER (1605-1660) – Dorothea, patron saint of gardeners with a child – oil on canvas – 139 x 115.5cm.
(Galerie Koller Zürich)   **$10,287   £5,372**

CORNELIS SPRINGER (1817–1891) – A view in Bolsward towards the townhall with townsfolk conversing on a bridge – signed and dated 1872 – oil on panel – 45 x 57cm.
(Christie's)   **$147,522   £73,761**

CLARKSON STANFIELD - 'Oude Scheldt, Texel Island' – signed and dated 1882 – 43.5 x 65cm.
(Anderson & Garland)   **$16,608   £9,600**

JOHANNES SPRUYT, Manner of (16th Century Dutch school) – Study of an ornamental cockerel, hens, rabbits and a guinea pig – 71 x 95cm.
(Spencer's)   **$5,858   £2,900**

LILIAN STANNARD (1884–1944) – Rambler Roses – signed – watercolour – 34.5 x 49.5cm.
(Phillips)   **$8,080   £4,000**

STASSEN

FRANZ STASSEN (b. 1869) – Spring – signed with
initials – oil on canvas – 71.1 x 71.1cm.
(Christie's)   **$5,790**   **£3,080**

PHILIP WILSON STEER (1860–1942) – Portrait of
Edna Waugh – oil on board – 46 x 44cm.
(Phillips)   **$8,315**   **£5,000**

EDWARD BOWRING STEPHENS, A.R.A.
(1815–1882) – Portrait of Jane Harris Stephens, the artist's
wife, seated small full length, with her daughter Jane Helen
Mary, on a terrace – oil on canvas – 91.5 x 71.1cm.
(Christie's)   **$6,506**   **£3,850**

ROMAIN STEPPE (1859–1927) – Sailing boat at dusk –
oil on canvas – signed – 49 x 69cm.
(Hôtel de Ventes Horta)   **$2,483**   **£1,280**

JACQUES STELLA (1596–1657) – Lamentation over
the dead Christ – on amethyst quartz within a lapis
surround – octagonal – 10.5 x 13.8cm.
(Phillips)   **$7,968**   **£4,000**

ALFRED STEVENS (Belgian 1823–1906) – Exchanging
confidences – signed with monogram and dated – pen and
ink and brown wash – 20.5 x 23.5cm.
(Sotheby's)   **$4,026**   **£2,200**

JULIUS LEBLANC STEWART (1855–1919) – Five
o'clock tea – signed and dated 1883-4 – oil on canvas –
167.5 x 231.3cm.
(Christie's) **$847,000 £440,440**

JULIUS LEBLANC STEWART (1855–1919) – Repose
– signed and dated 88 – oil on panel – 73 x 99.8cm.
(Christie's) **$71,500 £37,180**

JULIUS LEBLANC STEWART (1855–1919) – Sarah
Bernhardt and Christine Nilsson – signed – oil on canvas –
96.5 x 130.8cm.
(Christie's) **$187,000 £97,240**

CONSTANTIN STOITZNER (1863-1934) – A draught
of ale; and A good read – both signed – on panel –
unframed – 20.9 x 15.7cm.: one illustrated.
(Christie's) **$1,575 £935**

STOKELD

JAMES STOKELD – 'The Anxious Enquiry' – a shipwreck off Tynemouth – signed and dated 1861 – 40 x 54.5cm.
(Anderson & Garland)   **$32,870**   **£19,000**

J. STOLL – A fruit seller and a gentleman conversing – signed – oil on canvas – 42.8 x 53cm.
(Ritchie's)   **$1,654**   **£857**

MARCUS STONE, R.A. – "Awaiting the verdict" – 60 x 27in.
(Tennants)   **$40,000**   **£20,000**

MOSSE STOOPENDAAL (1901–48) – Fox on wooded slope – signed and dated 1940 – oil on canvas – 40 x 50cm.
(AB Stockholms Auktionsverk)   **$6,270**   **£3,232**

JOHN HENRY BRADLEY STORRS (1885–1956) – Two seated nudes – signed with initials and dated 17/1/24 – pencil and coloured pencil on tan paper – 31.5 x 25.1cm.
(Christie's)   **$4,950**   **£2,574**

Attributed to GEORGE HENRY STORY (American, 1835–1923) – Portrait of a child seated at a writing table, expansive landscape beyond – initialled and dated 1856 – pastel on paper – 12½ x 9½in.
(Skinner)   **$3,500**   **£1,823**

VEIT STOSS (c. 1450–1533) – St Augustine – oil on wood – 96 x 77cm.
(Lempertz) **$46,357 £26,490**

ARTHUR CLAUDE STRACHAN (1865-Circa 1935) – Playing in the wheelbarrow, and a companion – a pair – signed – watercolour heightened with white – 28.5 x 45cm.
(Phillips) **$8,950 £5,000**

Manner of JAN VAN DER STRAET, called Stradanus – A bull and stallion with dogs confronting a lion in a menagerie – 108.3 x 130cm.
(Christie's) **$13,200 £6,600**

TOBIAS STRANOVER (1684–1724) – Two macaws in a tree above a lake with ducks – oil on canvas – 113 x 105.5cm.
(Phillips) **$22,080 £11,500**

Follower of TOBIAS STRANOVER – Fruit in a basket with plums, cherries and peaches – 46.3 x 55.8cm.
(Christie's) **$4,792 £2,420**

STRETTON

PHILIP EUSTACE STRETTON - By the fireside – oil on panel – signed – 29½ x 24in.
(Bearne's)   **$5,820**   **£3,000**

CHARLES STUART (fl. 1880–1904) -- Deer at a Highland Loch – signed – oil on canvas – 76 x 128cm.
(Christie's)   **$13,013**   **£7,700**

WILLIAM HOLMES SULLIVAN (English - 1908) – "Men were deceivers ever" – signed and dated 1889 – oil on canvas – 45 x 30cm.
(AB Stockholms Auktionsverk)   **$3,940**   **£2,031**

HADDON HUBBARD SUNDBLOM (1899–1976) –
Paper dolls - oil on canvas – 76.5 x 96.5cm.
(Christie's)   **$5,500   £2,915**

GRAHAM SUTHERLAND, O.M. – Palm Palisade –
signed and dated 1947 – oil on canvas – 51 x 41cm.
(Sotheby's)   **$74,800   £44,000**

MAX WALTER SVANBERG (b. 1912) – The fair dream
– signed and dated 53 – watercolour – 45 x 37cm.
(AB Stockholms Auktionsverk)   **$5,686   £2,977**

SVANBERG

J. SWINNERTON – Collecting bait – signed – oil on canvas – 76 x 101cm.
(Christie's) $3,069 £1,650

MAX WALTER SVANBERG (b. 1912) – A day in the puppet theatre – signed and dated 46 – gouache – 50 x 64cm.
(AB Stockholms Auktionsverk) $5,331 £2,791

J. SWINNERTON – The fisherman's tale – oil on canvas – 76 x 101cm.
(Christie's) $5,319 £2,860

NICOLAS GREGOROVITCH SVERTSCHKOFF (1817–1898), Russian school – The barouche – signed in Russian and dated 1854 – oil on canvas – 72.5 x 91.5cm.
(Sotheby's) $14,642 £8,367

WALTER HENRY SWEET – Norrad Slip, Newlyn – watercolour – signed – 10 x 14½in.
(David Lay) $1,400 £700

RUDOLF SWOBODA (1859–1914) – Arabs conversing in a village street – signed and dated 1894 – oil on canvas – 110 x 85.5cm.
(Christie's) $18,612 £9,900

DE TAEYE – Nude and waterlilies – signed and dated 81 – mixed media on canvas – 142 x 110cm.
(Galerie Moderne) **$3,576 £1,872**

ANNIE LOUISA SWYNNERTON (née Robinson) (1844–1933) – Portrait of a boy, half length – oil and gold leaf on panel – 43.2 x 28.9cm.
(Christie's) **$7,436 £4,400**

Manner of PEETER SNYERS – A boy buying vegetables at a stall – 52.1 x 61cm.
(Christie's) **$1,948 £1,045**

ALFRED TABOIS (English, 19th century) – 'H.M.S. Royal Alfred, 1869, Halifax' – signed and dated 1870 – oil on canvas – 43.2 x 56.5cm.
(Bonhams) **$506 £250**

ARNALDO TAMBURINI (b. 1843) – The new vintage – signed – oil on canvas – 51 x 39.5cm.
(Christie's) **$3,881 £1,980**

TANKA

N.W. TANKA – Troops returning from battle, World War I – signed and dated 16 – 40.6 x 58.4cm.
(Christie's) $715 £424

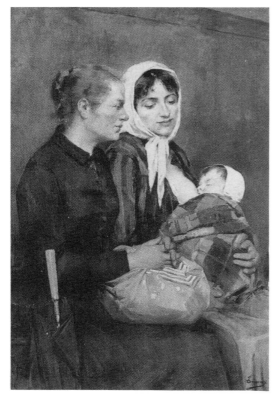

ADRIEN HENRI TANOUX (French 1865–1923) – Two women seated, one with a baby – signed – oil on canvas – 117 x 80cm.
(AB Stockholms Auktionsverk) $8,420 £4,340

ANTONI TAPIES – Catalunya 1972 – signed – colour lithograph – 73 x 57cm.
(AB Stockholms Auktionsverk) $2,252 £1,161

GUILLAUME TARAVAL, Manner of – Pastoral landscape with reclining women – oil on canvas – 81 x 75cm.
(AB Stockholms Auktionsverk)   **$4,119**   **£2,123**

HUGHES TARAVAL (1729–1785) – Two children – oil on canvas – monogrammed and dated 1756 – 43.5 x 53.5cm.
(Sotheby's) $38,823   £22,312

MARGARET WINIFRED TARRANT (1888–1959) – A fairy sitting on a branch of apple blossom with butterflies nearby – watercolour – inscribed – 6¼ x 4¼in.
(Ewbank Auctioneers) $2,325   £1,250

TASSEL

Studio of JEAN TASSEL (1608–1667) – The Madonna and child – oil on canvas – 69 x 57cm.
(Phillips)   **$2,880   £1,500**

NICOLAS-ANTONIE TAUNEY (1755–1830), Attributed to – Market scene with conjurer – oil on canvas – 33.5 x 44cm.
(Sotheby's)   **$7,808   £4,462**

ALBERT CHEVALLIER TAYLER (1862–1925) – Quiet moments – signed and dated 89 – oil on canvas – 60 x 75cm.
(Christie's)   **$20,207   £12,100**

EDWARD TAYLER – A portrait of a young lady, wearing a white decollete blouse with a yellow rose, and a black feathered hat – signed with initials – watercolour heightened with stopping out and touches of bodycolour – mounted in an oval - 33 x 25.5cm.
(Woolley & Wallis)   **$1,974   £1,050**

EDWARD TAYLER (1828–1906) – Day dreams: A girl holding a posy of roses and lilies of the valley – watercolour with touches of white heightening – 17^3/4 x 13^1/2in.
(Christie's)   **$2,757   £1,540**

PAVEL TCHELITCHEV – Costume design for "Prince
Igor" – inscribed – pencil, watercolour, gouache and silver
foil – 15½ x 13in.
(Tennants)   **$5,000   £2,500**

PAVEL TCHELITCHEW (1892–1952) – Portrait of
Ruth Ford – signed and dated – oil on canvas –
100 x 73.8cm.
(Christie's)   **$52,668   £30,800**

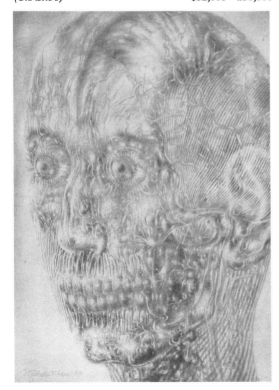

PAVEL TCHELITCHEW (1892–1952) – The Head of
Gold – signed and dated - oil on canvas – 64.7 x 46.1cm.
(Christie's)   **$41,382   £24,200**

JAN TENGNAGEL (1584/85–1635) – The laughing
Democritus and the crying Heraclitus – both signed and
dated 1624 – oil on panel – 57 x 45.5cm.
(Phillips)   **$16,110   £9,000**

TENIERS

DAVID TENIERS (1610–1690), School of – Village fair
– oil on canvas – 50 x 65cm.
(Jean-Claude Anaf) $12,931   £6,700

SIR JOHN TENNIEL (1820–1914) – 'November, Now
Gents 'unt in Gorse' – signed with monogram – pencil and
coloured chalks heightened with white – 15.8 x 23.5cm.
(Lawrence) $383   £200

PABLO SALINAS Y TERUEL (Spanish 1871–1946) –
Flirting with the courtesan – signed and inscribed – oil on
panel – 15 x 24.5cm.
(Sotheby's) $22,143   £12,100

DAVID TENIERS the younger (1610–1690) – The
woodcutters – signed with monogram – oil on panel –
17.5 x 25cm.
(Phillips) $91,632   £46,000

Follower of DAVID TENIERS II – A young nobleman,
bust length, wearing a plumed cap, a brown coat and the
Order of the Golden Fleece – oil on panel – 16 x 21.1cm.
(Christie's) $2,178   £1,100

Circle of AUGUSTIN TERWESTEN, the elder
(1649–1711) – Bathsheba - oil on canvas – 82.5 x 56.5cm.
(Phillips) $7,570   £3,800

P.* TESTU (Continental School, 19th/20th Century) –
Harvesters – oil on canvas – signed – 64.8 x 92.8cm.
(Bonhams) $1,667   £950

HENRY HERBERT LA THANGUE, R.A. (1859–1926)
– The end of the day – signed – oil on canvas –
59.5 x 70cm.
(Christie's) $11,253   £6,050

FRITS THAULOW (1847–1906) – Children playing on a
beach – signed and dated 93 – oil on canvas – 56 x 87.5cm.
(Christie's) $18,326   £9,350

FRITS THAULOW (Norwegian 1847–1906) – Village on
the Channel coast at low tide – signed and dated 1875 – oil
on canvas – 60 x 90cm.
(AB Stockholms Auktionsverk) $23,288   £12,004

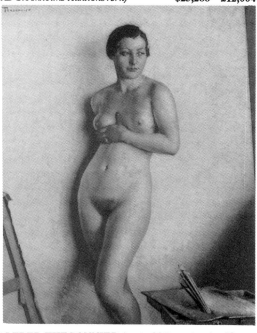

ALFRED THEGONNIER (early 20th century) – Nu
débout – signed – oil on canvas – 146 x 114cm.
(Christie's) $4,312   £2,200

CHARLES JAMES THERIAT (American, b. 1860) –
Middle Eastern Scene – signed, inscribed and dated 89 –
oil on panel – 12½ x 16¼in.
(Skinner) $1,400   £722

THEVENET

PIERRE THEVENET (1870–1937) – Paris - le Pont Neuf
– signed and dated 13.6.27 – watercolour – 40 x 51cm.
(Hôtel de Ventes Horta) **$3,495 £1,730**

HENRI THOMAS (1878–1972) – 'Reverie' – mixed media
on paper – signed – 63 x 77cm.
(Hôtel de Ventes Horta) **$4,877 £2,787**

ANTHONY THIEME (American, 1888–1954) – In the
Harbour, Channel – signed - oil on canvas – 25 x 30in.
(Skinner Inc.) **$5,000 £2,681**

PAUL THOMAS – Sheep and herder – signed and dated
1921 – oil on canvas – 20 x 27in.
(Du Mouchelles) **$500 £245**

HENRI THOMAS (1878–1972) – Sweet sleep – signed –
oil on canvas – 27 x 40cm.
(Hôtel de Ventes Horta) **$1,894 £984**

FATHER M. THOMPSON? – View in the highlands –
inscribed to reverse and dated July 1860 – oil on canvas –
10³/₄ x 13¹/₂in.
(Hobbs & Chambers) **$322 £180**

LESLIE P. THOMPSON (American, 1880–1963) – Girl Reading (Meditation) – signed and dated 1916 – oil on canvas – 34½ x 30¼in.
(Skinner)   **$2,000**   **£1,031**

ARCHIBALD THORBURN (1860–1935) – A long-eared owl – signed and dated 1925 – pencil and watercolour with touches of white heightening – 11 x 7½in.
(Christie's)   **$19,206**   **£9,900**

FRANZ THONE (German, 1851–1906) – The Mischief Makers – signed and dated 1881 – oil on panel – 45.7 x 35.6cm.
(Bonhams)   **$4,246**   **£2,100**

ARCHIBALD THORBURN (1860–1935) – Pink-footed Geese, and a companion, 'Bean Geese' – a pair – signed and dated 1917 – watercolour heightened with bodycolour – 18.5 x 27.5cm.
(Phillips)   **$22,375**   **£12,500**

THORBURN

ARCHIBALD THORBURN – Woodcock in undergrowth
– gouache – signed and dated 1899 – 36.9 x 53.3cm.
(Bonhams) $33,700   £20,000

ARCHIBALD THORBURN (1860–1935) – A woodcock
and chicks – signed and dated 1933 – pencil and
watercolour heightened with white – 11 x 5in.
(Christie's) $59,752   £30,800

ESAIAS THOREN (1901–81) – Ice bird – a surreal
landscape composition – signed and dated 1940 – oil on
canvas – 72 x 91cm.
(AB Stockholms Auktionsverk) $7,995   £4,186

WILLIAM THORNLEY – A Fishing Port at Dawn – one
of a pair – oil on canvas – monogrammed – 11½ x 9in.
(Michael J. Bowman) $4,250   £2,500

Attributed to JOSEPH THORS (fl. 1863–1900) – A river landscape with a figure in a punt; and A figure on a country track at sunset – with signatures – 30.5 x 60.9cm. – a pair – one illustrated
(Christie's) $5,220   £2,860

DOMENICO TIEPOLO (1727–1804) – Head of an oriental man – oil on canvas – 60.5 x 50cm.
(Sotheby's) $428,450   £225,500

PAUL THUMANN (German, 1834–1908) – Portrait of a girl – signed – oil on board – 34 x 27cm.
(Auktionshaus Arnold) $1,032   £552

PELLEGRINO TIBALDI (1527–1596) – The Madonna and child – oil on panel – 64 x 51cm.
(Phillips) $358,560   £180,000

Attributed to LORENZO TIEPOLO (1736–1776) - A young boy wearing a fur cloak and clasping a book in his hands – oil on canvas – 52 x 38cm.
(Phillips) $2,685   £1,500

E. TIKHMENOV (Russian) – Hunter with three dogs and a lynx at bay in a tree – signed and dated 1903 – 58 x 89cm.
(Herholdt Jensens) **$7,149 £3,823**

WALASSE TING (b. 1929) – Female nude – signed – watercolour – 20 x 27.3cm.
(AB Stockholms Auktionsverk) **$883 £455**

Circle of PIETER TILLEMANS – A hunt in full cry in a river landscape – 22 x 35½in.
(Tennants) **$1,300 £650**

Attributed to DOMENICO TINTORETTO - Portrait of a gentleman – oil on canvas – 61 x 51cm.
(Sotheby's) **$10,032 £5,280**

DAVID TINDLE, R.A. (b. 1932) – Sunlight – signed and dated 70 – oil on canvas – 113 x 77.5cm.
(Christie's) **$3,306 £1,980**

W.V. TIPPET (fl. 1866) – Sheep grazing in a landscape – signed – 20.2 x 35.6cm.
(Christie's) **$562 £308**

JOHAN TIREN (1853–1911) – Lapps with shot reindeer –
signed and dated 1891 – oil on canvas – 124 x 166cm.
(AB Stockholms Auktionsverk)   **$134,349   £69,252**

Circle of FRANCESCO TIRONI (18th Century) –
View of the Grand Canal, looking east, from the Campo di
S. Vio – oil on canvas – 63.5 x 101.5cm.
(Phillips)   **$19,920   £10,000**

After TITIAN – A lady in a fur – 76.2 x 61.6cm.
(Christie's)   **$3,077   £1,650**

Manner of TITIAN – The Toilet of Venus –
99.1 x 82.6cm.
(Christie's)   **$4,840   £2,420**

After TITIAN – Portrait of Pope Paul III, seated half
length in a chair – 118.2 x 88.3cm.
(Christie's)   **$2,667   £1,430**

TITIAN (Italian 1485–1576) – Follower of – Salome with the Baptist's head – oil on canvas – 114 x 93cm.
(AB Stockholms Auktionsverk)   **$3,314   £1,708**

FELIX ELIE TOBEEN (1880–1938) – Circus amazon on a horse – signed lower right – oil on canvas – 67 x 88cm.
(Christie's)   **$4,478   £2,336**

F. TITO (late 19th Century) – A good vintage; and A good smoke – signed – 38.2 x 25.4cm. – a pair, one illustrated.
(Christie's)   **$1,390   £825**

BEN TOBIAS – The Rabbis – Frumahs Wedding feast –
oil on canvas – signed and dated 1960 – 40.5 x 51cm.
(Bonhams) $1,600 £800

RALPH TODD, R.A. (1891–1966) – Cornish fishergirl –
signed – watercolour and bodycolour heightened with
white – 37.5 x 26cm.
(Christie's) $1,707 £880

THEO TOBIASSE – Jacob's Well – signed and numbered
87/250 – colour litho, serigraph and relief print –
105 x 70cm.
(AB Stockholms Auktionsverk) $865 £446

RALPH TODD – St. Martin's, summer, picking
blackberries – signed – watercolour – 14 x 10in.
(Christie's) $1,744 £935

RALPH TODD (Exh. 1880–1928) – Departure of the
fishing fleet – watercolour - signed – 15 x 10½in.
(W.H. Lane & Son) $4,608 £2,400

TODESCHINI

Manner of GIACOMO FRANCESCO CIPPER, IL TODESCHINI – A boy holding a hen with a basket of eggs beside him – unframed – 73.7 x 62.2cm.
(Christie's) **$4,840 £2,420**

ANNA TONELLI (circa 1763–1846) - Portrait of a young girl, half length, wearing a white dress edged with lace – pastel – oval – 9³/₄ x 7¹/₄in.
(Christie's) **$1,294 £715**

FRANCIS TODHUNTER (1884–1963) – Houses on Belvedere; The Mission – a pair, each signed – watercolour on paper – 37 x 46cm.
(Butterfield & Butterfield) **$1,320 £647**

CRISTOBAL TOLEDO – Female nude – signed – oil on canvas – 125 x 198cm.
(Duran) **$442 £221**

ANNA TONELLI (circa 1763–1846), after Hugh Douglas Hamilton (1740–1806) – Portrait of John La Touche, full length, with the Amphitheatre at Taormina and Etna behind – signed and inscribed – pastel – 38 x 27in.
(Christie's) **$15,928 £8,800**

HENRY TONKS (1862–1937) – Young woman with black hair – signed – black crayon on buff paper – 23 x 18cm. – and three other drawings by the same artist. (4)
(Christie's) **$4,481 £2,310**

JACOB TOORENVLIET (Dutch 1635–1719) – Woman holding a hare – signed and dated 1675 – oil on copper – 18 x 15cm.
(AB Stockholms Auktionsverk) **$6,270 £3,232**

HENRY TONKS (1862–1937) – Head of a girl – signed – oil on panel – 34 x 24cm.
(Christie's) **$9,821 £5,280**

JACOB TOORENVLIET (Dutch 1635–1719) – Attributed to – Old man writing – oil on panel – 31 x 24cm.
(AB Stockholms Auktionsverk) **$2,687 £1,385**

TOOROP

CHARLEY TOOROP (1891–1955) – A peasant woman
– signed and dated 1915 – oil on canvas – 100 x 81cm.
(Christie's)   **$5,511 £2,875**

JAN TOOROP (1858–1928) – A portrait of Charley
Toorop – signed and dated 97 – pencil and pen and pastel
on paper – 33.5 x 22.5cm.
(Christie's)   **$34,447 £17,969**

JAN TOOROP (1858–1928) – A portrait of Lucie van
Dam van Isselt – signed and dated 1905 – oil on canvas –
91 x 70.5cm.
(Christie's)   **$186,008 £97,031**

FRANK WILLIAM WARWICK TOPHAM
(1838–1924) – The morning of the Festival–Central Italy –
signed and dated 1876 – oil on canvas – 55.3 x 77.5cm.
(Christie's)   **$10,615 £5,500**

FRANCIS WILLIAM TOPHAM (1808–1877) – Italian
peasants resting by a wall – signed with monogram and
dated 1865 – pencil and watercolour heightened with white
– 9½ x 14½in.
(Christie's) $1,870   £1,045

AUGUSTE TOULMOUCHE (French 1829–90) –
Interior with woman in red – signed and dated 1866 – oil
on canvas – 60 x 44cm.
(AB Stockholms Auktionsverk) $16,480   £8,495

GUNNAR TORHAMN (1894–1965) – Fishermen – a
hilly coastal landscape with buildings and figures – signed
– oil on panel – 43 x 60cm.
(AB Stockholms Auktionsverk) $4,443   £2,326

JOSE MONGRELL Y TORRENT (Spanish b. 1870) –
Grape picking – signed and dated and inscribed – oil on
canvas – 74.5 x 98cm.
(Sotheby's) $84,546   £46,200

GIOVANNI BATTISTA TORRIGLIA (b. 1858) – The
See-Saw – signed – oil on canvas – 45 x 59.5cm.
(Christie's) $86,680   £44,000

HENRI DE TOULOUSE-LAUTREC (1864–1901) –
The cat – signed – oil on board – 30.5 x 22.8cm.
(Christie's) $108,350   £55,000

TOULOUSE-LAUTREC

HENRI DE TOULOUSE-LAUTREC (1864–1901) – Original cover of L'Estampe – original colour lithograph on simple ivory paper – numbered 50/100 – 56 x 64cm. *(Lempertz)* $26,945 £13,889

HENRI DE TOULOUSE-LAUTREC (1864–1901) – Mademoiselle Cocyte – signed with studio stamp (L.1338) – sanguine and pencil on paper – 34.5 x 25.3cm. *(Christie's)* $130,020 £66,000

FERNAND TOUSSAINT (1873–1956) – The Belgian Nation – signed – oil on canvas – 57 x 46cm. *(Hôtel de Ventes Horta)* $3,586 £2,049

HENRY SPERNON TOZER (circa 1870–circa 1940) – The tea party – signed and dated 1916 – pencil and watercolour – 9¹/₈ x 13¹/₈in.
(Christie's)   **$2,384   £1,210**

JULIAN TREVELYAN – Street scene – oil on canvas – signed and dated '47 – 49.5 x 65cm.
(Bonhams)   **$6,400   £3,200**

JULIAN TREVELYAN, R.A. (1910–1988) – The little cornfield – signed and dated 44 - oil on canvas – 38.5 x 63.5cm.
(Christie's)   **$9,552   £5,720**

CARL TRAGARDH (1861–99) – Summer landscape with girl and grazing cow – signed – oil on canvas – 64 x 80cm.
(AB Stockholms Auktionsverk)   **$4,656   £2,400**

Attributed to GASPAR TRAVERSI (d. 1769) – Three women holding a cat as they extract its claws – oil on canvas – 110 x 138cm.
(Phillips)   **$16,932   £8,500**

LOUIS-ROLLAND TRINQUESSE (1746–circa 1800) – Portrait of a lady with carnation – signed and dated 1788 – oil on canvas – oval - 72.5 x 59cm.
(Sotheby's)   **$27,175   £15,618**

TRIVETT

JOHN TRIVETT (20th Century) – Black Labradors on a moor – signed – oil on canvas – 76.2 x 91.4cm.
(Christie's) **$4,180   £2,200**

JAN ZOETELIEF TROMP (1872–1947) – Off to work – signed – 38 x 50cm.
(Christie's) **$28,163   £14,082**

Circle of PAUL TROGER (1698–1762) – Saint Nepomuk – 73.7 x 51.4cm.
(Christie's) **$1,307   £660**

JAN ZOETELIEF TROMP (1872–1947) – Countrygirls in a cornfield making garlands of flowers – signed – 40.5 x 50.5cm.
(Christie's) **$20,116   £10,058**

FRANÇOIS DE TROY, Circle of (1645–1730) –
Portraits of the Duke and Duchess of Saint Simon – a pair
– oil on canvas – 89 x 69cm.
(Sotheby's) $7,706   £5,578

HENRY SCOTT TUKE, R.A., R.W.S. – A boy sitting on
rocks – watercolour – signed – 13³/₄ x 9³/₄in.
(Bearne's) $8,148   £4,200

JOHN TUNNARD, R.A. (1900–1971) – Red River –
signed, dated and numbered – oil on gesso prepared board
– 54 x 70cm.
(Christie's) $24,799 £14,850

HENRY SCOTT TUKE, R.A. (1858–1929) – Newporth
Beach, Falmouth – signed and dated 1908 – oil on panel –
33 x 24cm.
(Christie's) $10,243   £5,280

CHARLES FREDERICK TUNNICLIFFE (1901–1979)
– Study of a dove – inscribed with colour notes and dated
Aug. 1959 – pencil and watercolour heightened with white
and gum arabic – 9 x 11³/₄in.
(Christie's) $1,592   £825

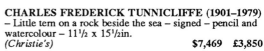

CHARLES FREDERICK TUNNICLIFFE (1901–1979)
– Little tern on a rock beside the sea – signed – pencil and
watercolour – 11¹/₂ x 15¹/₂in.
(Christie's)   **$7,469   £3,850**

CHARLES FREDERICK TUNNICLIFFE (1901–1979)
– Flamingoes tending their young – pencil, watercolour
and bodycolour – paper cut down – 11 x 9in.
(Christie's)   **$1,707   £880**

CHARLES F. TUNNICLIFFE (b. 1901) – A fox in
cover – signed – watercolour on brown paper –
31.7 x 41.9cm.
(Lawrence)   **$728   £380**

CHARLES FREDERICK TUNNICLIFFE – Juvenile blackbacked gulls – signed – pencil and watercolour – 35.6 x 50.8cm.
(Bonhams)   **$3,618**   **£1,800**

KEN TURNER – Four red breasted geese – signed – on masonite – 94 x 125cm.
(Christie's)   **$1,045**   **£550**

GEORGE TURNER – View near Hathersage Derbyshire – signed and dated (18)88 - 60 x 90cm.
(Spencer's)   **$10,100**   **£5,000**

CHARLES FREDERICK TUNNICLIFFE, (1901–1979) – A Seal Point Siamese cat in a blossoming tree – signed – pencil and watercolour – 62.2 x 29.3cm.
(Christie's)   **$3,971**   **£2,090**

LAURA TURNER – Motherhood – signed – oil on canvas – 87 x 67cm.
(Galerie Moderne)   **$1,505**   **£788**

TYTGAT

EDGARD TYTGAT (1879–1957) – La Petite Ouvrière – signed and dated 1922 – oil on canvas – 63.5 x 76.8cm.
(Christie's) **$106,150 £55,000**

MEDARD TYTGAT (1871–1948) – Young woman at her toilet – signed and dated 54 – brush and black ink on paper – 54 x 42cm.
(Christie's) **$1,845 £956**

WALTER UFER (1876–1936) – His wealth – signed – oil on canvas – 63.5 x 76.2cm.
(Christie's) **$110,000 £57,200**

SAM UHRDIN (1886–1964) – Interior with woman and
small child in cradle – signed and dated 1939 – oil on
canvas – 73 x 80cm.
(AB Stockholms Auktionsverk)   **$7,164   £3,693**

SAM UHRDIN (1886–1964) – Girl by fireplace – signed –
oil on canvas – 73 x 93cm.
(AB Stockholms Auktionsverk)   **$5,911   £3,047**

JOSEPH URBACH (1889–1973) – Youths on horseback
and female nudes – signed – oil on canvas –
62.5 x 68.5cm.
(Lempertz)   **$4,379   £2,257**

UTRECHT

Circle of ADRIAEN VAN UTRECHT (1599–1652) – A table laden with fruit and game, a boy looking in through a window to the right – indistinctly signed and dated 1646 – 79 x 129cm.
(Phillips) $6,000 £3,000

SUZANNE VALADON – Nature morte aux groseilles – signed and dated 1917 – oil on board – 38 x 46cm.
(Sotheby's) **$56,100 £33,000**

UTRECHT SCHOOL, 17th Century – Heraclitus and Democritus – oil on canvas – 117.5 x 126cm.
(Phillips) **$4,600 £2,300**

ADOLPHE VALETTE (1876–1942) – Seated girl reading a newspaper – signed – oil on canvas – 54 x 46cm.
(Christie's) **$1,920 £990**

MAURICE UTRILLO – L'église – signed and dated 1922 – gouache – 24.2 x 34cm.
(Sotheby's) **$54,230 £31,900**

VALLIN (HUGO GOLLI) (Continental, 20th century) – A Venetian backwater – signed – oil on canvas – 54 x 65.4cm.
(Bonhams) **$1,618 £800**

FREDERICK E. VALTER – A group in the
Worcestershire meadows – signed and dated 1911 – pencil
and watercolour – 19 x 38in.
(Christie's)   **$968   £550**

**Studio of ALLESSANDRO VAROTARI, called Il
Padovanino (1588–1648)** – Venus and Adonis – oil on
canvas – 145.5 x 115.5cm.
(Phillips)   **$13,944   £7,000**

After **PIETRO VANNUCCI, called Perugino** – The
Madonna adoring the Christ child with an angel in a
landscape, while three other angels sing above – oil on
canvas – 126 x 63.5cm.
(Phillips)   **$2,700   £1,350**

Follower of GIORGIO VASARI – Saint John on Patmos
– oil on panel – unframed – 113.7 x 85.7cm.
(Christie's)   **$4,138   £2,090**

VASARELY

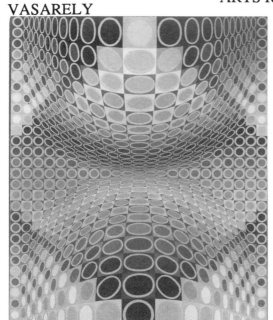

VICTOR VASARELY (b. 1911) – Bisoll – signed – also signed, inscribed with title and dated 1978 on the reverse – acrylic on canvas – 145 x 115cm.
(Christie's)   **$47,300**   **£27,500**

M. VASSELON (19th century French School) – Girl with Tanagra figurine – signed and dated – oil on canvas – 64 x 54cm.
(Hôtel de Ventes Horta)   **$5,738**   **£3,279**

Follower of ANTON MARIA VASSALLO – A boy stealing a goose – oil on canvas – 113.5 x 85.2cm.
(Phillips)   **$2,200**   **£1,100**

MARIE VASSILIEFF (Russian, 1894–1955) – Realisation – signed and dated 1931 – oil on canvas – 73 x 60cm.
(germann Auktionshaus)   **$13,362**   **£6,996**

KEITH VAUGHAN (b. 1912) – Eight figures – signed –
oil on canvas – 24 x 36in.
(David Lay)   **$1,140   £600**

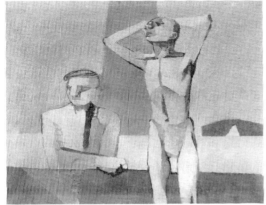

KEITH VAUGHAN (1912–1977) – Urchin – oil on
canvas – 51 x 63.5cm.
(Christie's)   **$20,273   £10,450**

KEITH VAUGHAN (1912–1977) – Study for an
Assembly of Figures (1) - signed – dated and inscribed on
the backboard – gouache – 17 x 13.5cm.
(Christie's)   **$4,592   £2,750**

KEITH VAUGHAN (1912–1977) – Four bathers - oil on
board – 35.5 x 51.5cm.
(Christie's)   **$18,370   £11,000**

VAUTHIER

PIERRE VAUTHIER (1845–1916) – L'Avenue Victoria
– signed – oil on canvas – 125 x 84cm.
(Christie's)   **$26,004**   **£13,200**

ELIHU VEDDER (1836–1923) – Head of a young
woman – signed with monogrammed initials and dated
1898 – pastel on paper laid down on board –
20.3 x 26.7cm.
(Christie's)   **$24,200**   **£14,362**

BAIBA VEGERE (b. 1948) – Angel portrait – pastel on
canvas – 55 x 33cm.
(Jean-Claude Anaf)   **$314**   **£164**

Follower of **WILLEM VAN DE VELDE II** – Fishermen about to beach a smack – 35.9 x 31.8cm.
(Christie's)   **$2,420**   **£1,210**

VENETIAN SCHOOL, 17th Century – Christ among the soldiers – oil on canvas – 99 x 75cm.
(Finarte Casa d'Aste)   **$13,409**   **£6,912**

WILLEM VAN DE VELDE THE YOUNGER
(1633–1707) – Calm: a states yacht, pont and other vessels in a light wind – bears signature and date – oil on canvas – 47.5 x 56.5cm.
(Sotheby's)   **$142,120**   **£74,800**

WILHELM VELTEN (1847–1929) – The attack – signed – oil on wood – 16 x 24cm.
(Auktionshaus Arnold)   **$3,643**   **£1,948**

VENETIAN SCHOOL, late 16th Century - St. Agnes – oil on canvas – 81 x 66cm.
(Sotheby's)   **$5,824**   **£3,347**

VENETIAN SCHOOL

EUGENE VERBOECKHOVEN (Flemish, 1799–1881)
– Landscape with cattle, sheep, ducks and sea view beyond
– signed and dated 1864 – oil on canvas – 145 x 90cm.
(Hôtel de Ventes Horta)   **$12,622   £6,557**

VENETIAN SCHOOL, 16th Century – The Madonna
and Child – oil on panel – 36 x 26cm.
(Phillips)   **$7,296   £3,800**

School of EUGENE JOSEPH VERBOECKHOVEN
(1799–1881) – Study of recumbent sheep with a cockerel
in farm buildings – signed – oil on panel – 8½ x 12in.
(Spencer's)   **$3,294   £1,800**

Attributed to OTTO VENIUS (1556–1629) – Lucretia –
oil on board – 90.2 x 67.3cm.
(Pinney's)   **$4,683   £2,821**

EUGENE-JOSEPH VERBOECKHOVEN (1798–1881)
and JOHANN-BERNARD KLOMBECK (1815–1893) –
A wooded winter landscape with figures – signed and
dated 1863 – oil on canvas – 93.4 x 128.5cm.
(Christie's)   **$95,348   £48,400**

GASPAR PIETER VERBRUGGEN THE YOUNGER (1664–1730) – Flora, with cherubs and garlands of summer flowers resting on a stone plinth – oil on canvas – 135 x 172cm.
(Sotheby's) $52,250 £27,500

DIONYS VERBURGH (died before 1722) – An extensive estuary landscape with travellers at a fountain – signed with initials DVB – 80.4 x 116.4cm.
(Christie's) $9,148 £4,620

H*** DU CHENE DE VERE (French 19th Century) – The travelling salesman; A family by the fireside – a pair – signed and dated – oil on canvas – each 59 x 89cm.
(Sotheby's) $40,260 £22,000

VERHAERT

DIRCK VERHAERT, 18th century – An extensive italianate landscape with travellers crossing a bridge – signed with initials DVH – oil on panel – 46.3 x 39.4cm.
(Christie's) **$6,970 £3,520**

IS. VERHEYDEN (Belgian, 1848–1905) – Child with dolls – signed – oil on canvas – 110 x 86cm.
(Hôtel de Ventes Horta) **$11,361 £5,902**

FRANÇOIS VERHEYDEN (1806–1890) – The artist's lunch – signed and dated 1878 – oil on canvas – 94 x 70.5cm.
(Christie's) **$7,546 £3,850**

IS. VERHEYDEN – The butter churner – signed – oil on canvas – 118 x 96cm.
(Hôtel de Ventes Horta) **$11,059 £5,475**

MATTHEUS VERHEYDEN (1700–1776) – Portraits of
the Voshol children set in an ornamental garden – inscribed
recto and verso – pen and grey ink with wash on blue paper
– 362 x 393mm.
(Phillips) $3,067 £1,600

ALBERTUS VERHOESEN – "Poultry near a ruined
brick building" – a pair – oil on canvas
(Greenslades) $3,151 £1,650

ALBERTUS VERHOESEN – "Cattle in a meadow" – a
pair – oil on canvas
(Greenslades) $2,483 £1,300

ALBERTUS VERHOESEN – "Cockerels fighting" – oil
on canvas
(Greenslades) $2,206 £1,150

VERNER

ELIZABETH O'NEILL VERNER (1883–) – Flower
seller – signed – pastel on canvas – 48.3 x 35.6cm.
(Christie's) $5,720 £3,032

EMILE VERNON (active 1890–1920) – Girl with
flowers – signed – oil on canvas – 61 x 45.8cm.
(Pinney's) $9,353 £5,584

WOUTER VERSCHUUR, JNR. (Dutch, 1841–1936) –
Horses in a stable – oil on panel – signed – and companion
piece – a pair – one illustrated – 15.3 x 21cm.
(Bonhams) $3,861 £2,200

MARCEL VERTES (1895–1961) – A proud father –
signed – gouache and pencil – 14 x 9½in.
(David Lay) $437 £230

ANTOINE VESTIER (1740–1824) – Portrait of
Mademoiselle Rouille at the pianoforte – signed and dated
1792 – oil on canvas – 80 x 64cm.
(Sotheby's) $93,174 £53,548

CORNELIS VETH (1880–1962) – Bremmer has to give
his judgement – signed with initials and dated 1930 –
pencil and watercolour on paper – unframed –
26.5 x 31cm.
(Christie's) $2,893 £1,509

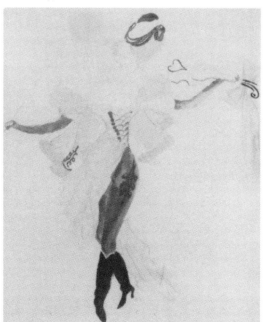

MARCEL VERTES (1895–1961) – A dancing girl with a
violin – signed – gouache and pencil – 11 x 8½in.
(David Lay) $304 £160

JEAN GEORGES VIBERT (1840–1902) – Visiting the
Cardinal – signed – oil on panel – 85 x 105cm.
(Christie's) $17,248 £8,800

VICAJI

DOROTHY VICAJI (d. 1945) – Young girl packing china – signed with monogram – oil on canvas – 122 x 91.5cm.
(Christie's)   **$10,103**   **£6,050**

VICTORIAN SCHOOL – Lady in chair playing with young child – unsigned – oil – 11 x 9in.
(G.A. Key)   **$588**   **£300**

Attributed to EMILY VICKERS – An Irish street on a rainy day – watercolour – 7³/₄ x 6¹/₄in.
(Hy. Duke & Son)   **$336**   **£190**

VICTORIAN SCHOOL – Portrait of a pretty young girl in a red and lace trimmed ball-gown – monogrammed TD – oil – 11 x 9in.
(G.A. Key)   **$470**   **£240**

JAN VICTORS (1620–1676) – The Virgin with the Infant
Christ and John the Baptist – oil on canvas – 128 x 108cm.
(Sotheby's)   **$34,939   £20,080**

JOSEPH-MARIE VIEN, (Follower of) – A young
woman with a dove in a basket, on a velvet cushion – oil on
canvas – 101 x 84cm.
(Phillips)   **$5,400   £3,000**

**After MARIE LOUISE ELISABETH VIGEE-
LEBRUN** – Portrait of the artist, bust-length – inscribed –
oil on canvas – 62 x 50cm.
(Phillips)   **$3,586   £1,800**

VIGNEAU

MARIANO ALONSO-PEREZ VILLAGROSA (1857–1930) – The arrival of the pilgrims in Lourdes – signed – oil on canvas – 150 x 285cm.
(Lempertz) $22,599 £12,914

ALCIDE VIGNEAU (late 19th Century) – A Great Dane in a park – signed and dated 1890 – oil on canvas – 88.9 x 114.3cm.
(Christie's) $836 £440

ISABEL VILLAR (b. 1934) – Maja in a landscape – oil on canvas – signed and dated 1988 – 33 x 46cm.
(Duran) $3,285 £1,702

CLAUDE VIGNON (1593–1670) – St Paul the Hermit – signed and dated 1633 – oil on canvas – 137 x 100cm.
(Christie's) $26,444 £13,592

MARIANO GUTIERREZ VIGUERA – Parisian scene – signed – oil on canvas – 38 x 46cm.
(Duran) $521 £262

RICARDO DE VILLODAS (1846–1904) – Moor's head – oil on canvas – signed – 45 x 29.5cm.
(Duran) $7,073 £3,665

MAURICE DE VLAMINCK – Maison de l'Artiste à
Chatou – signed – oil on canvas – 46 x 55cm.
(Sotheby's) **$280,500 £165,000**

HERNANDO VINES (1904) – "Woman" – oil on canvas
– signed – 46 x 33cm.
(Duran) **$4,041 £2,094**

MAURICE DE VLAMINCK – Marine – signed – oil on
canvas – 61 x 82cm.
(Sotheby's) **$149,600 £88,000**

G. VIVIAN (Italian, 19th/20th century) – A Venetian
canal scene – signed – oil on canvas – 50.8 x 76.2cm.
(Bonhams) **$1,820 £900**

W.E. VIZKELETI (1819–1895) – Market day – signed –
48.3 x 71.1cm.
(Christie's) **$1,668 £990**

JEAN VOILLE (1744–after 1804) – Portrait of Monsieur
de la Guerche – signed and dated 1765 – oil on canvas –
100 x 80cm.
(Sotheby's) **$38,823 £22,312**

VOLLERDT

JOHANN CHRISTIAN VOLLERDT (1708–1769) – A Rheinland landscape with peasants conversing on a hillside path overlooking a river valley – oil on canvas – 62 x 76.5cm.
(Phillips) **$29,880 £15,000**

DAVID DE VOS, Attributed to – Saints Paul the Hermit and Anthony Abbot in a wooded landscape – oil on canvas laid down on board – 108.6 x 142.3cm.
(Christie's) **$2,213 £1,100**

WILHELM VOLTZ (1855–1901) – Symbolist subject – oil on canvas – signed – 50 x 84cm.
(Hôtel de Ventes Horta) **$2,483 £1,280**

VINCENT DE VOS (1829–1875) – A Blenheim and a tricolour King Charles spaniel on a Persian rug – signed – oil on canvas – 50.7 x 64.7cm.
(Christie's) **$15,675 £8,250**

Attributed to CORNELIS DE VOS – Portrait of a gentleman – oil on panel – 49.5 x 41cm.
(Hôtel de Ventes Horta) **$3,414 £1,760**

Circle of SIMON VOUET – Apollo, bust length, holding a lyre – 71.7 x 61cm.
(Christie's) **$8,360 £4,180**

ROELOF JANSZ DE VRIES (1631–1681) – An elegant couple inspecting a horse being led through a gateway – bears initials J.W. – oil on panel – 55.7 x 45cm.
(Phillips) $14,940 £7,500

EDOUARD VUILLARD – Quatre personnages sur un banc – stamped with the signature – oil on card – 47 x 44cm.
(Sotheby's) $168,300 £99,000

EDOUARD VUILLARD (1868–1940) – Self portrait – oil on canvas – 28.6 x 25.1cm.
(Christie's) $119,185 £60,500

EDOUARD VUILLARD – Portrait de Femme – stamped with the signature (Lugt 2497a) – pastel – 53 x 52cm.
(Sotheby's) $121,550 £71,500

NICOLAS VAN DER WAAY (Dutch 1855–1936) – La toilette – signed – watercolour – 56 x 76cm.
(Sotheby's) $5,234 £2,640

WAHLBOM

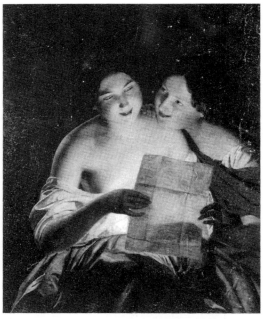

CARL WAHLBOM (1810–58) – Italian girl seated by a ruined temple – signed and dated 1843 – oil on canvas – 64 x 53cm.
(AB Stockholms Auktionsverk)   **$3,046**   **£1,570**

LOUIS WAIN – Which do I love best? – signed – watercolour heightened with white – 8³/₄ x 11in.
(Christie's)   **$2,953**   **£1,650**

FERDINAND GEORG WALDMULLER (Austrian, 1793–1865) – The love letter – signed and dated – oil on canvas – 78 x 64.5cm.
(Galerie Koller Zürich)   **$316,528**   **£165,289**

WILLIAM AIKEN WALKER (1838–1921) – Life in the South – signed – oil on board – 15.5 x 31.3cm.
(Christie's)   **$19,800**   **£10,494**

FREDERICK DUDLEY WALENN (English, Exh. 1894–1930) – 'Frank, son of W. Bell Esq.' – oil on canvas – signed and dated 1905 – 130.8 x 66cm.
(Bonhams)   **$2,984**   **£1,700**

T. DART WALKER (1869–1914) – Home from Europe – signed T. Dart Walker, l.r. – gouache en grisaille and chinese white on board – 33.7 x 54.3cm.
(Christie's)   **$1,760**   **£1,044**

WILLIAM AIKEN WALKER (1838–1921) – The Possum Hunter – signed – oil on board – 31.5 x 15.5cm.
(Christie's)   **$51,700**   **£27,401**

WALKER

WILLIAM AIKEN WALKER* (1838–1921) –
Sheepshead – signed with conjoined initials WAW and
dated 1864 – oil on canvas – 51 x 36cm.
(Christie's)   **$22,000**   **£11,660**

DAVID WALLIN (1876–1957) – On an island in the
archipelago – signed – dated 1940 on reverse – oil on panel
– 42 x 51cm.
(AB Stockholms Auktionsverk)   **$1,635**   **£856**

JOSEF WILHELM WALLANDER (1821–88) – Italian
couple – signed on reverse – oil on canvas – 113 x 80cm.
(AB Stockholms Auktionsverk)   **$4,478**   **£2,308**

ALFRED WALLIS (1855–1942) – Ship entering harbour
– signed – oil, crayon and pencil on yellow card –
26.5 x 33.5cm.
(Christie's) $8,266   £4,950

HENRY WALLIS (1830–1916) – A despatch from
Trebizond; 'Some news is come that turns their
countenances'–Shakespeare – signed with initials – oil on
canvas – 91.5 x 137.8cm.
(Christie's) $33,968   £17,600

JAN WALRAVEN (Dutch, b. 1827) – Children with
their pet goat – signed – oil on panel – 51 x 39.5cm. – and
companion piece, a pair.
(Bonhams) $4,044   £2,000

JAN WALRAVEN (b. 1827) – A mother standing on a
doorstep of a cottage, watching her daughter feeding the
chickens – signed – oil on panel – 42 x 32cm.
(Christie's) $3,353   £1,676

**CHARLES WALTENSPERGER (American,
1871–1931)** – Mother and children – signed – oil on
canvas – 20 x 16in.
(Du Mouchelles) $2,600   £1,320

WALTERS

SAMUEL WALTERS – The 'Mary Anne' and other shipping in a stormy sea – signed and dated 1839 - oil on canvas – 27½ x 41½in.
(Bearne's) **$29,100 £15,000**

JAMES WARD, R.A. (1769–1859) – 'The mousetrap': a study of the artist's son, George Raphael – signed with monogram and inscribed – pencil and watercolour with touches of white heightening – 9⅜ x 7½in.
(Christie's) **$4,290 £2,200**

JAMES WARD, R.A. (1769–1859) – Mr Crooks Chinese Sow – signed with monogram and inscribed – pencil – 3¾ x 6⅞in.
(Christie's) **$15,015 £7,700**

ARTHUR WARDLE (1864–1949) – Walking up –
signed – oil on canvas – 38 x 53.5cm.
(Christie's) $11,979   £6,050

ARTHUR WARDLE (1864–1949) – A Borzoi – signed –
oil on canvas laid down on board – 24 x 30.5cm.
(Christie's) $5,949   £3,520

ARTHUR WARDLE (1864–1949) – Two smooth-haired
and one-wired haired Fox Terrier – signed and dated 1886
– oil on canvas – 91.4 x 71.2cm.
(Christie's) $6,270   £3,300

ARTHUR WARDLE (1864–1949) – Friend or foe –
signed – oil on canvas – 35.6 x 45.7cm.
(Christie's) $24,167   £14,300

WARHOL

ANDY WARHOL (American, 1930–1987) – Karen
Kain, 1980 – signed – colour serigraph – 100 x 80cm.
(germann Auktionshaus) **$7,074   £3,704**

EDMUND GEORGE WARREN, R.I. (1834–1909) –
Harvesters gathering in the wheat sheafs – signed – pencil,
watercolour and bodycolour – 10³/₄ x 18¹/₂in.
(Christie's) **$3,300   £1,650**

EDMUND GEORGE WARREN (1834–1909) – Robin
Hood and his Merry Men in Sherwood Forest – signed and
dated 1859 – mixed media on paper – 61 x 81.9cm.
(Christie's) **$5,663   £2,860**

ANDY WARHOL – Mick Jagger, 1975 – signed and
numbered 110/250 – serigraph – 103 x 73cm.
(AB Stockholms Auktionsverk) **$7,565   £3,900**

**HAROLD BROADFIELD WARREN (American,
1859–1934)** – A plein air/A coastal scene with an artist at
work – signed – watercolour on paper – 7 x 10in.
(Skinner Inc.) **$2,500   £1,340**

ABEL WARSHAWSKY (1883–1962) – Fishing in the
stream – signed and dated 1916 – oil on canvas –
63.5 x 81cm.
(Butterfield & Butterfield)   **$5,500   £2,696**

JAN ABEL VAN WASSENBERG (1689–1750) – A
young girl playing a violin – signed and dated J.
Wassenberg Junior, 1743 – oil on panel – 27.7 x 22.7cm.
(Phillips)   **$2,112   £1,100**

CH. J. WATELET – Lady in a red cape – signed – oil on
canvas – 81 x 65cm.
(Galerie Moderne)   **$1,243   £651**

WATENPHUL

JOHN WILLIAM WATERHOUSE, R.A. (1849–1917)
– Study for 'A Tale from the Decameron' (recto); Studies
for 'Miranda – The Tempest' (verso) – pencil –
8⁷/₈ x 11¹/₂in.
(Christie's)   **$4,117   £2,090**

MAX PEIFFER WATENPHUL (1896–1976) – View of
Lacroma near Ragusa, Dubrovnik – signed and dated
1926 – watercolour on buff paper – 43.5 x 59cm.
(Lempertz)   **$8,084   £4,167**

MARCUS WATERMAN (American, 1834–1914) – A
Middle Eastern genre scene – signed - oil on canvas –
16 x 24in.
(Skinner Inc.)   **$1,800   £965**

**JOHN WILLIAM WATERHOUSE, R.A. (English
1849–1917)** – Pandora – signed and dated 1896 – oil on
canvas – 152 x 91cm.
(Sotheby's)   **$418,110   £231,000**

GEORGE SPENCER WATSON – Portrait of a lady –
signed – oil on canvas – 136 x 70cm.
(Sotheby's)   **$11,946   £6,600**

ANTOINE WATTEAU (1684–1721) – Study for the head of a young woman – colour chalks on paper – 16.4 x 12.8cm.
(Lempertz)   **$26,076   £14,901**

P*** FLETCHER WATSON – The interior of Burgos Cathedral – inscribed and dated 1894 – 13³/₄ x 9¹/₂in.
(Tennants)   **$1,300   £650**

R. WATSON – An extensive highland landscape with sheep and lambs – indistinctly signed – unframed – 65 x 87cm.
(Spencer's)   **$859   £480**

After JEAN ANTOINE WATTEAU – Fetes Champetres
– unframed – 78.7 x 95.7cm.
(Christie's) **$5,560 £3,300**

GEORGE FREDERICK WATTS – My Yorkshire
Terrier – signed – oil on panel – 38 x 30cm.
(Hôtel de Ventes Horta) **$2,210 £1,148**

GEORGE FREDERICK WATTS, R.A., O.M.
(1817–1904) — Portrait of Claude Joseph Goldsmid-
Montefiore, half length – signed and dated 1897 – oil on
canvas – 76.8 x 63.8cm.
(Christie's) **$10,782 £6,380**

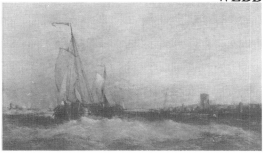

JAMES WEBB – Fishing boats off Dordrecht – signed and dated 1876/77 – oil on canvas – 23½ x 39½in.
(Bearne's) $14,550 £7,500

W. WEBB – Venetian scene with sailing vessels and gondola in foreground – signed – oil on canvas – 19¼ x 29¼in.
(Hobbs & Chambers) $1,712 £880

JAMES WEBB (1825–1895) – Ischia in the Bay of Naples from Castle Rock – signed and dated 76 – oil on canvas – 51 x 76cm.
(Christie's) $8,276 £4,180

W.H. WEATHERHEAD – Girl with a pitcher of water – signed and dated 1886 – water colour drawing – 32 x 22in.
(Austin & Wyatt) $2,888 £1,500

WEBBER

WESLEY WEBBER (American, 1841–1914) – Self Portrait – The Artist Pulling a Sled of Firewood – signed – oil on canvas – 12 x 18¹/₂in.
(Skinner) **$850 £438**

WESLEY WEBBER (American, 1839–1914) – Low Tide and Fog/A Coastal View – signed and dated – oil on canvas – 14 x 22in.
(Skinner Inc.) **$3,938 £2,250**

WALTER E. WEBSTER (1878–1959) – The attentive courtier – signed – 75.6 x 61.6cm.
(Christie's) **$3,413 £1,870**

MAX WEBER (1881–1961) – After the bath – signed – oil on canvas – 45.2 x 76.2cm.
(Christie's) **$19,800 £10,296**

HERBERT WILLIAM WEEKES – The morning mail –
signed – 46.5 x 33.5cm.
(Anderson & Garland) $3,287 £1,900

WALTER ERNEST WEBSTER (1878–1959) –
Ballerina in pink – oil on canvas – 100.5 x 70cm.
(Christie's) $12,491 £7,480

HERBERT WILLIAM WEEKES (fl. 1864–1904) – My
Lady's at Home – signed – oil on artist's board –
29 x 46cm.
(Christie's) $20,691 £10,450

EDWIN LORD WEEKS (American, 1849–1903) – The Courtyard – A Harem Scene – signed – oil on canvas – 26 x 32¼in.
(Skinner Inc.) $17,000 £8,763

EDWIN LORD WEEKS (American, 1849–1903) – Elephants and Camel, Qjmere – signed and inscribed – oil on canvas – 13 x 20in.
(Skinner Inc.) $1,000 £536

Manner of JAN WEENIX – Still life of a hanging hare and grouse and wheel-lock rifle and a blue velvet game bag, a view to a classical garden beyond – oil on canvas – 86.3 x 78.8cm.
(Christie's)   **$5,500   £2,750**

EDWIN LORD WEEKS (American, 1849-1903) – Persian Boy, Bombay – signed and titled – oil on canvas – 19³/₄ x 13¹/₄in.
(Skinner Inc.)   **$2,200   £1,178**

Attributed to EDWIN LORD WEEKS (American, 1849–1903) – Camels Lying Down – unsigned – oil on canvas – 12¹/₄ x 18in.
(Skinner)   **$900   £464**

JAN WEENIX (1640–1719) – Portrait of a lady, seated three-quarter length, wearing a blue dress – with signature – oval – 73 x 61.5cm.
(Christie's)   **$3,703   £1,870**

WEGUELIN

CAREL WEIGHT, R.A. (b. 1908) – Sunday-go-to-
Meeting – oil on canvas – 75 x 62cm.
(Christie's) $53,273 £31,900

JOHN REINHARD WEGUELIN (1849–1927) – "The
bath": green pot, golden hair; brown and grey marble – oil
on canvas – 50.8 x 25.7cm.
(Christie's) $10,615 £5,500

JOHANNES RAPHAEL WEHLE (1848–1936) –
Reflections – signed and dated 1919 – oil on canvas –
39.5 x 55cm.
(Christie's) $15,895 £9,350

CAREL WEIGHT, R.A. (b. 1908) – Three figures in a
country lane – signed – oil on canvas-board –
73.5 x 68.5cm.
(Christie's) $7,715 £4,620

CAREL WEIGHT, R.A. (b. 1908) – Figure in the gardens at Abbotsford – signed – oil on board – 26 x 38cm.
(Christie's) $8,593 £4,620

CAREL WEIGHT, R.A. (b. 1908) – Old woman in a garden – signed – oil on canvas – 91 x 122cm.
(Christie's) $14,938 £7,700

WEIR

JOSE WEISS – An extensive country Landscape – signed – oil on panel – 16.5 x 26.2cm.
(Christie's) **$594 £308**

JOHN FERGUSON WEIR (1841–1926) – Roses of white and pink – signed – oil on canvas – 40.5 x 32.5cm.
(Christie's) **$52,800 £27,456**

HENDRIK JOHANNES WEISSENBRUCH (1824–1903) – A cloudy summer afternoon – signed and dated 71 – on panel – 27.5 x 60.5cm.
(Christie's) **$39,774 £22,471**

ROBERT WALTER WEIR (1803–1889) – The letter – signed and dated 1851 – watercolour and gouache on paper – 34.9 x 27.6cm.
(Christie's) **$24,200 £14,362**

JAN WEISSENBRUCH (1822–1880) – A river landscape with a tow-boat, a couple conversing on a track near a wind-mill beyond – signed on cover of tobacco-box – 7 x 11.5cm.
(Christie's) **$5,849 £3,305**

DENYS GEORGE WELLS – The porcelain Venus – oil on board – signed and dated '61 – 53 x 76cm.
(Bonhams) $3,000 £1,500

HENRY TANWORTH WELLS, R.A. (1828–1903) – A young girl seated beside her basket in a wood – signed – watercolour on ivorine – 22.3 x 17.2cm.
(Christie's) $3,920 £1,980

HENRY TANWORTH WELLS, R.A. (1828–1903) – The bird's nest – signed and dated 1847 – watercolour on ivorine – 40 x 26.6cm.
(Christie's) $6,098 £3,080

JOANNE MARY WELLS, née BOYCE (1831–1861) –
Head of a Mulatto woman – inscribed on reverse – oil on
paper on canvas – 16.5 x 12.7cm.
(Christie's)   **$13,068   £6,600**

ALBERT BECK WENZELL (1864–1917) – Opening
night – signed with initials in monogram and dated 1894 –
watercolour and gouache on board – 80 x 62.2cm.
(Christie's)   **$9,900   £5,875**

CARL WELZ (German 1860–1929) – Village school with teacher and pupils – signed and dated 1891 – oil on
canvas – 63 x 119cm.
(AB Stockholms Auktionsverk)   **$8,957   £4,617**

PIETER VAN DEN WERFF (1665-1722) – A portrait of a lady, half length, wearing a blue dress trimmed with lace and a brown wrap – oval – 87.5 x 72.5cm.
(Christie's) $3,267 £1,650

Circle of PIETER VAN DER WERFF (1665–1722) – Portrait of a lady, half length, wearing a floral brocade dress – oval – 89 x 71.5cm.
(Christie's) $2,069 £1,045

ANTON ALEXANDER VON WERNER (1843–1915) – Don Quixote and the goat herders – signed with initials and dated 1870 – oil on canvas – 99 x 133.5cm.
(Christie's) $26,004 £13,200

BENJAMIN WEST (1738–1820) – Portrait of Cowper Rose, in profile to left – with inscription – pen and brown ink – 187 x 146mm.
(Christie's) $550   £286

BENJAMIN WEST (1738–1820) – An Allegory of Britannia - pen and black ink, brown and grey wash, watercolour, and oil on light brown paper – 337 x 153mm.
(Christie's) $7,700   £4,004

BENJAMIN WEST (1738–1820) – Study of King David rising after the death of his child – signed and inscribed – black chalk, pen and brown ink, brown wash – 244 x 375mm.
(Christie's) $19,800   £10,296

BENJAMIN WEST (1738–1820) - Study of a lion – signed – black and white chalk on blue paper – 175 x 254mm.
(Christie's) $7,150   £3,718

RICHARD WESTALL – Musical Inspiration – bears inscription on old label on reverse – oil on canvas – 82 x 65.5cm.
(Christie's) $3,520   £1,760

MAX WEYL (American, 1837–1914) – Still Life with Summer Fruits and Nuts à plein air – signed and dated "M. Weyl 1870" – oil on board – $13^1/2$ x $10^1/4$in.
(Skinner Inc.) $800   £414

MAX WEYL (American, 1837–1914) – Spring Marshes – signed and dated "Max Weyl 10" – oil on canvas – 25 x 33in.
(Skinner Inc.) $650   £337

WHEELER

ALFRED WHEELER (1852–1898) – Portrait head studies of Fox Hounds, a Dachshund and rough-coated Fox terriers – oil on board – another portrait sketch on the reverse – 30.4 x 46.9cm.
(Christie's)   **$1,881   £990**

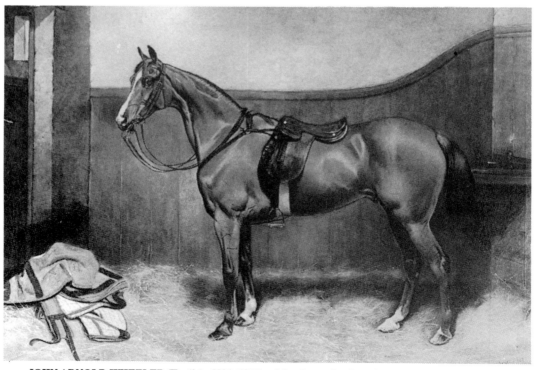

JOHN ARNOLD WHEELER (English, 1821–1877) – A bay hunter in a loose box – signed and dated 1868 – oil on canvas – 71.1 x 91.4cm.
(Bonhams)   **$4,044   £2,000**

ARTHUR WHITE (1865–1953) – Boats leaving harbour,
St. Ives – signed – oil on canvas – 27 x 37cm. – and
another by the same artist, on board – one illustrated
(Christie's) $3,306   £1,980

GWENDOLINE WHICKER (fl. 1940–65) –
Rhododendron – signed – oil on board – 24½ x 19½in.
(David Lay) $722   £380

ETHELBERT WHITE – Children at the duckpond –
signed – 53.3 x 72.4cm.
(Christie's) $2,926   £1,540

GEORGE A. WHITAKER (1841–1916) – Barlett pears
– oil on panel – signed – 12 x 18in.
(Bruce D. Collins) $2,310   £1,249

GEORGE WILLIAM WHITAKER (American,
1841–1916) – "Old Wharf Pawtuxet (sic) R.I." – signed
and dated 1890 – oil on canvas – 18 x 24in.
(Skinner) $1,900   £980

JOHN WHITE (1851–1933) – A time of promise –
signed and dated 1889 – watercolour heightened with
white – 17³/₈ x 25³/₈in.
(Christie's) $5,095   £2,640

WHITE

JOHN WHITE (1851–1933) – The Fountain Head,
Branscombe – signed – watercolour – 35.5 x 53cm.
(Phillips)   **$3,636   £1,800**

FREDERICK WHITEHEAD – A view of Dorchester
with cattle in the foreground – signed – oil on canvas –
19³/₄ x 29¹/₂in.
(Hy. Duke & Son)   **$3,540   £2,000**

OLIVE WHITMORE – The kill – pastel – 11¹/₂ x 21in.
(Christie's)   **$329   £187**

FRANK REED WHITESIDE (American, 1866–1929) –
Altar Rock at Walpi, Arizona – signed and dated on the
reverse – oil on canvas – 12 x 16in.
(Skinner Inc.)   **$1,700   £911**

JOHN WHORF (American, 1903–1959) – Fishing Boats
at the Pier – signed – watercolour and gouache on paper –
15¹/₄ x 21in.
(Skinner)   **$1,600   £825**

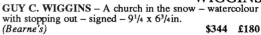

GUY C. WIGGINS – A church in the snow – watercolour with stopping out – signed – 9¹/₄ x 6³/₄in.
(Bearne's) $344 £180

JOHN WHORF, A.N.A. (1903–1959) – Morning wind, Point Genor – watercolour – signed – 14¹/₂ x 21¹/₂in.
(Bruce D. Collins) $3,520 £1,903

GUY CARLETON WIGGINS (1883–1962) – New York Public Library – signed – oil on canvasboard – 30.2 x 40.1cm.
(Christie's) $13,200 £6,996

GUNNAR WIDFORSS – Summer at the boating creek – signed and dated 1913 – watercolour – 26.5 x 45cm.
(AB Stockholms Auktionsverk) $847 £436

GUSTAVE ADOLPH WIEGAND (American, 1870–1957) – Gold and Brown/An Autumn Landscape – signed – oil on canvas – 8 x 10in.
(Skinner Inc.) $300 £155

GUY CARLETON WIGGINS (1883–1962) – Winter at Broadway and Wall Street – signed – oil on canvasboard – 30.5 x 22.5cm.
(Christie's) $8,800 £4,664

WIJDOOGEN

N.M. WIJDOOGEN (19th Century) – Fishermen on the beach by a moored bomschuit, a village beyond – signed – 96.5 x 62cm.
(Christie's) $7,376 £3,688

CARL WILHELMSON (1866–1928) – Portrait of Anna Sehstedt – oil on canvas – 100.4 x 80.9cm.
(Christie's) $40,090 £20,350

AUGUSTE DE WILDE (1819–1886) – Domestic scene – signed – oil on canvas – 72 x 59cm.
(Hôtel de Ventes Horta) $19,517 £9,662

Attributed to JAN WILDENS (1586–1653) – An avenue of trees with elegant figures playing bowls – oil on canvas – 99 x 149cm.
(Phillips) $25,060 £14,000

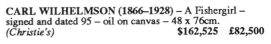

CARL WILHELMSON (1866–1928) – A Fishergirl –
signed and dated 95 – oil on canvas – 48 x 76cm.
(Christie's)   **$162,525   £82,500**

NORMAN WILKINSON, C.B.E., P.R.I., R.O.I.,
R.S.M.A., H.R.W.S. – Discharging cargo – signed – oil on
canvas – 17½ x 23½in.
(Geering & Colyer)   **$5,307   £2,900**

PIERRE-ALEXANDRE WILLE, THE YOUNGER
(1748–1821) – The wedding procession – signed and dated
1809 – coloured crayons on ink washed paper –
670 x 990mm.
(Christie's)   **$55,092   £28,316**

THOMAS WILLEBORTS, called Bosschaert
(1614–1654) – Daedalus and Icarus – oil on canvas –
112 x 89cm.
(Phillips)   **$7,968   £4,000**

WILLEMS

FLORENT WILLEMS (1823–1905) – A young lady showing roses – signed – on panel – 72 x 47cm. *(Christie's)* **$7,604 £4,296**

GEORGE AUGUSTUS WILLIAMS (1814-1901) – The boathouse – oil on board – monogrammed and dated 1879 – 8 x 10in. *(David Lay)* **$600 £300**

FLORENT WILLEMS (1829–1905) – A fresh bouquet for the paintress – signed – on panel – 90 x 64.5cm. *(Christie's)* **$10,528 £5,948**

INA SHELDON WILLIAMS (late 19th Century) – A pug – signed – pencil and watercolour heightened with white – 13.9 x 10.7cm. *(Christie's)* **$1,003 £528**

WARREN WILLIAMS – The Conway River, looking towards Trefriw, Denbyshire side – signed – signed, inscribed and dated July 1915 on the backboard – watercolour heightened with white – 14 x 24½in.
(Christie's) **$2,051 £1,100**

WARREN WILLIAMS – Boats anchored at Morfa Nefyn, the Lyn Peninsula beyond – signed – watercolour heightened with white – 13 x 19¾in.
(Christie's) **$1,641 £880**

JOHN HAYNES WILLIAMS – "The suitor" – signed – inscribed on reverse – 30 x 20½in.
(Tennants) **$2,800 £1,400**

TERRICK JOHN WILLIAMS (1860–1936) – Harbour at dawn – watercolour – 11½ x 14½in.
(David Lay) **$1,800 £900**

WILLISON

T.J. WILLISON (American, 20th century) – Covered Bridge, Winter – signed and dated – oil on canvasboard – 10½ x 16½in.
(Skinner Inc.) **$1,225 £700**

CHARLES EDWARD WILSON (d. circa 1936) – The pet robin – signed – watercolour – 37 x 26.5cm.
(Phillips) **$8,950 £5,000**

CHARLES EDWARD WILSON – Feeding chickens – watercolour heightened with bodycolour – signed and inscribed – 12½ x 8in.
(Bearne's) **$8,148 £4,200**

CHARLES EDWARD WILSON (d. circa 1936) – The pet rabbits - signed – watercolour – 37 x 26.5cm.
(Phillips) **$8,055 £4,500**

CHARLES EDWARD WILSON (d. circa 1936) –
Harvesting – signed and dated 1905 – watercolour –
49 x 74.5cm.
(Phillips) $16,160 £8,000

CHESTER WILSON (English, 19th Century) – Feeding
the rabbit – oil on canvas – signed and dated 1874 –
61 x 50.8cm.
(Bonhams) $6,669 £3,800

JEREMIAS VAN WINGHEN (1578–1645) – A kitchen
scene - on canvas – 128 x 108cm.
(Phillips) $46,540 £26,000

587

Attributed to PETER DE WINT – A rural landscape with figures and animals beside farm buildings –
28 x 37cm.
(Spencer's)   **$3,629   £1,900**

CHARLES ALLEN WINTER (American, 1869–1942) – Nymph – circa 1930 – unsigned – oil on canvas –
20 x 24in.
(Skinner Inc.)   **$1,100   £569**

CHARLES ALLEN WINTER (American, 1869–1942) –
Nude Study – circa 1930 – unsigned – oil on canvas –
24 x 20in.
(Skinner Inc.)   **$1,000   £518**

CHARLES ALLAN WINTER (American, 1869–1942) -
River Nymphs/An allegorical scene – signed – oil on
canvas – 17¼ x 15¼in.
(Skinner Inc.)   **$1,000   £536**

HEINRICH WINTER (1843–1911) – Horse wagons in
the Puszta – signed and dated 1872 – oil on canvas –
19.5 x 34cm.
(Auktionshaus Arnold)   **$6,696   £4,034**

Follower of WILLEM WISSING – Portrait of a girl as
Saint Agnes, small full length, wearing an embroidered
dress and yellow wrap – 124.4 x 100.3cm.
(Christie's)   **$8,800   £4,400**

Circle of JACOB DE WIT (1695–1754) – Putti with
garlands of flowers – feigned bas reliefs – monochrome –
on panel – 58.4 x 165.1cm. – a pair
(Christie's)   **$3,703   £1,870**

WIT

JACOB DE WIT (1695–1754) – An allegory of winter; an allegory of summer – a pair – signed and dated – both oil on canvas in painted cartouches – 46.5 x 143.5cm.
(Sotheby's) $29,260   £15,400

PON DE WIT – Interior of the inn – signed – oil on canvas – 60 x 52cm.
(Galerie Moderne) $1,820   £939

Manner of ALIDA WITHOOS – A vanitas still life with sunflowers, poppies, thistle and flowers, a chart, a set of dividers, a snuffed-out lantern, an hour-glass and skulls – with indistinct signature – oil on canvas – 87 x 71cm.
(Christie's) $6,160   £3,080

W. WITJENS – Ballerina – signed – pastel – 57 x 48cm.
(Glerum)   **$884 £444**

KARL WITKOWSKI (1860–1910) – Playing with fire –
signed – oil on canvas – 51 x 61cm.
(Christie's)   **$22,000 £11,660**

HEINZ WOELCKE (German, 1889–1963) – The green
hat – signed – oil on canvas – 80 x 65cm.
(Auktionshaus Arnold)   **$217 £131**

WOELCKE

HEINZ WOELCKE (German, 1889–1963) – Three girls – signed – oil on canvas – 92 x 61.5cm.
(Auktionshaus Arnold) **$424 £227**

PETRONELLA VAN WOENSEL (The Hague 1785–1839) – A still life of flowers and fruit on a stone ledge – signed – oil on canvas – 42 x 31.5cm.
(Sotheby's) **$10,032 £5,280**

HEINZ WOELCKE (German, 1889–1963) – A pair of circus artistes – signed – oil on canvas – 90 x 60cm.
(Auktionshaus Arnold) **$447 £269**

GUSTAVE VAN DE WOESTIJNE (1881–1947) – Valerius de Saedeleer – signed and dated– oil on canvas – 220 x 140cm.
(Christie's) **$424,600 £220,000**

Circle of ARTUS WOLFAERT (1581–1641) – Saint
Peter – oil on canvas – 89 x 70cm.
(Phillips)   **$1,536**   **£800**

EDWARD WOLFE, A.R.A. (1897–1972) – Moored
yacht, the Lady Anne – oil on canvas-board – 38 x 47cm.
(Christie's)   **$5,878**   **£3,520**

FRANZ XAVIER WOLF (b. 1896) – Poppies,
convolvuli, lilies, delphiniums, roses, dahlias and
carnations in a glass vase on a marble ledge – signed – oil
on panel – 66 x 50.8cm.
(Christie's)   **$12,936**   **£6,600**

WOLFE

GEORGE WOLFE (1834–1890) – View of Scarborough from the beach at low tide, with figures and beached fishing boats – signed – watercolour – 13½ x 20½in.
(Russell, Baldwin & Bright) **$3,133 £1,750**

FRANZ XAVIER WOLFLE (Austrian, b. 1896) – A quiet smoke – oil on panel – signed – 24.2 x 17.8cm.
(Bonhams) **$2,106 £1,200**

PROFESSOR FRANZ XAVIER WOLF (Austrian, 1896–1989) – Gothic Madonna – signed – oil on wood panel – 27 x 23in.
(Du Mouchelles) **$5,000 £2,681**

FRANZ XAVIER WOLF – Connoisseur – signed – oil on board – 20 x 16in.
(Du Mouchelles) **$4,000 £2,145**

GERT WOLLHEIM (1894–1974) – Bedroom gymnastics – signed and dated 24 – watercolour and gouache on paper – 39 x 49cm.
(Christie's) **$11,804 £6,116**

GARNET RUSKIN WOLSELEY (b. 1884–1967) – A nude young girl at the water's edge – watercolour – signed – 11½ x 14¾in.
(W.H. Lane & Son) **$1,229 £640**

CHRISTOPHER WOOD – "Drop curtain" – watercolour heightened with white – 12¹/₂ x 13¹/₂in.
(Tennants)   **$5,600   £2,800**

P.M. WOOD – Herzogin Cecile – oil on canvas – 26 x 30in.
(G.E. Sworder & Sons)   **$1,221   £620**

THOMAS WATERMAN WOOD (1823–1903) - His own doctor; Thinking it over; Thinking it over; and The day before election (L. of C. 2;6;6; and not in L. of C.) – etchings in dark brown – 1880s – on various papers signed in pencil – four
(Christie's)   **$825   £489**

ROBERT WOOD (1889–1979) – View through a meadow – signed and dated 41 – oil on canvas – 48 x 68.5cm.
(Butterfield & Butterfield)   **$2,475   £1,213**

THOMAS WATERMAN WOOD (1823–1903) – Uncle Ned and I – signed and dated 1882 – pen and black ink on board – 36.8 x 26.7cm.
(Christie's)   **$8,250   £4,896**

THOMAS WATERMAN WOOD (1823–1903) – A view from cliff side – watercolour and pencil on paper – 22.8 x 13.9cm.
(Christie's) $3,520   £2,089

MABEL WOODWARD (1877–1945) – Girl with doll on beach at Ogunquit, Maine – circa 1925 – oil on canvas – signed – 24 x 16in.
(Bruce D. Collins) $19,800   £10,703

DAVID WOODLOCK – Resting in the wood – signed – oil on paper – 22.9 x 14.6cm.
(Christie's) $1,052   £528

RICHARD CATON WOODVILLE (1825–1856) – Shrapnel bursting over the French infantry – signed R. Caton Woodville – gouache en grisaille on board – 30.5 x 53.3cm.
(Christie's) $990   £587

MABEL WOODWWARD (1877–1945) – Cottage by the sea, Provincetown – oil on board – signed – 6 x 8in.
(Bruce D. Collins) $3,750   £2,027

ALFRED JOSEPH WOOLMER (English, 1805–1895)
'Love's young dream' – oil on canvas, arched top –
91.4 x 71.1cm.
(Bonhams)   **$3,335   £1,900**

Follower of PHILIPS WOUWERMANS – A farmer
harnessing a horse before a farm building with horses
watering at a trough, a landscape beyond – oil on canvas –
34.3 x 44.4cm.
(Christie's)   **$2,200   £1,100**

Attributed to PIETER WOUWERMAN (1623–1682) –
Horses and horsemen outside a farrier's, an extensive
landscape beyond – oil on panel – 33 x 47.3cm.
(Christie's)   **$6,098   £3,080**

GEORGE WRIGHT – Polo – signed – oil on canvas –
31 x 46cm.
(Sotheby's)   **$20,906   £11,550**

CONSTANT WOUTERS (1826–1853) – The pangs of
love – signed and dated 1850 – on panel – 30 x 24cm.
(Christie's)   **$2,340   £1,322**

GEORGE WRIGHT (1860–1942) – Stormy weather –
signed – oil on canvas – 23 x 31cm.
(Christie's)   **$3,267   £1,650**

WTEWAEL

Studio of JOACHIM WTEWAEL (1566–1638) – Adam and Eve – oil on canvas – 156 x 115cm.
(Sotheby's)   **$171,380   £90,200**

ARNOUD WYDEVELD (American, fl. 1855–1862) – Striped Bass on the Shores of Cuttyhunk Island, Old Cuttyhunk Light in the Distance – signed – oil on canvas – 36 x 60in.
(Skinner Inc.)   **$4,250   £2,202**

PAUL WUNDERLICH (b. 1927) – Woman seated – signed and dated 1971 – pencil – 85 x 68cm.
(AB Stockholms Auktionsverk)   **$2,972   £1,532**

JAN WYNANTS (1630/35–1684) – A traveller with his pack horse talking to a woman seated outside the walls of a town – signed J. Wynants F. and dated 1668 – oil on canvas – 46 x 40cm.
(Phillips)   **$9,960   £5,000**

NEWELL CONVERS WYETH (1882–1945) – Checking
the traps – signed – oil on panel – 63.5 x 101.5cm.
(Christie's) $63,800 £33,814

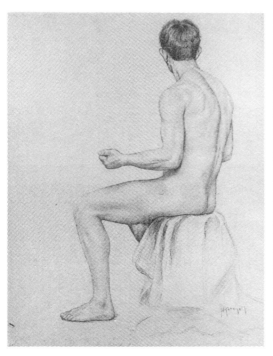

NEWELL CONVERS WYETH (1882–1945) – Nude
study – signed – charcoal on paper – 62.3 x 48.2cm.
(Christie's) $2,750 £1,458

NEWELL CONVERS WYETH (1882–1945) – Bucking
bronco – signed N.C. Wyeth and dated 03, l.c. – oil on
canvas laid down on masonite – 70.4 x 49.5cm.
(Christie's) $37,400 £19,822

WYNGAERDT

PETRUS THEODORUS VAN WYNGAERDT (Dutch 1816–93) – Interior with women – signed – oil on panel – 30 x 25cm.
(AB Stockholms Auktionsverk) **$2,239 £1,154**

RODOLPHE WYTSMAN (1860–1927) – The port of Delft – signed – oil on board – 32 x 24.5cm.
(Hôtel de Ventes Horta) **$1,905 £943**

RODOLPHE WYTSMAN (1860–1927) – Small farm at Linkebeek – oil on panel – signed and dated 1915 – 27 x 36cm.
(Hôtel de Ventes Horta) **$3,104 £1,600**

JACK BUTLER YEATS, R.H.A. (1871-1957) – Waiting for the Long Car – signed – oil on canvas – 34 x 45cm.
(Christie's) **$106,546 £63,800**

Follower of FRANS YKENS – Roses, narcissi, blackthorn blossom, periwinkle, daisies and other flowers in a basket with insects on a ledge – indistinctly signed – on panel – 40 x 60.9cm.
(Christie's) **$25,047 £12,650**

CHARLES M. YOUNG, A.N.A. (1869–1964) – Just west of Clairmont Hotel, Southwest Harbour – oil on canvas – signed and dated 1915 – 30½ x 40½in.
(Bruce D. Collins) $9,350 £5,054

FREDERICK COFFAY YOHN (1875–1933) – "Throw up your hands!" – signed – gouache, watercolour and chinese white en grisaille on board – 52.1 x 33cm.
(Christie's) $440 £261

WILLIAM BLAMIRE YOUNG (1862–1935) – Lake poets – signed twice – titled on a label on the frame – ink and watercolour – 48 x 61cm.
(Phillips) $9,978 £6,000

ART YOUNG (1866–1943) – Stranger welcome – signed – pen and brush and black ink on board – 44.4 x 65.4cm.
(Christie's) $605 £359

YUNKERS

ADJA YUNKERS – signed in red pen 'Shoemakers' – coloured woodcut on thin paper – 34.7 x 22.5cm.
(AB Stockholms Auktionsverket)   **$179**   **£94**

CHRISTIAN ZACHO – An extensive coastal landscape – signed and dated 1911 – 106.7 x 157.5cm.
(Christie's)   **$2,082**   **£1,045**

DOMENICO ZAMPIERI, called Il Domenichino (1581–1641), Circle of – The infant St. John the Baptist with a lamb, in a landscape – oil on copper – 25.5 x 19.5cm.
(Phillips)   **$1,584**   **£880**

EUGENIO ZAMPIGHI (1859–19144) – The centre of
attraction – signed – oil on canvas – 68.9 x 51.5cm.
(Christie's) $23,782 £12,650

EUGENIO EDUARDO ZAMPIGHI (Italian,
1859–1944) – A Private Moment – signed – oil on canvas
– 18 x 22³/₄in.
(Skinner) $7,500 £3,866

EUGENIO ZAMPIGHI (1859–1914) – In the kitchen –
signed - oil on canvas – 55.9 x 98.7cm.
(Christie's) $31,020 £16,500

JAN ADAM ZANDLEVEN (1868–1923) – African
marigolds in a ginger jar – signed and dated 1922 –
43.5 x 50.5cm.
(Christie's) $3,352 £1,676

JOSE VELA ZANETTI (b. 1913) – On the threshing
floor - oil on panel – signed and dated 77 – 101 x 69cm.
(Duran) $30,315 £15,707

JOHN J. ZANG (American, 19th century) – Rest Along
the Logging Trail, Winter – signed – oil on canvas –
framed – 30 x 40in.
(Skinner Inc.) $4,812 £2,750

ZARINA

VIJA ZARINA (b. 1961) – Duo – signed and dated 90 –
oil on canvas – 100 x 50cm.
(Jean-Claude Anaf)   **$1,572   £821**

HANS ZATZKA (Austrian, b. 1859) – Floral still life
with butterflies and parrot – signed and inscribed – oil on
canvas – 30 x 25in.
(Skinner Inc.)   **$4,750   £2,547**

FRANZ ANTON ZEILLER (1716–1793) – Sketch for a
ceiling fresco – The triumph of Virtue and damnation of
Vice – oil on canvas – 71.5 x 88cm.
(Lempertz)   **$56,788   £32,450**

RUDOLF ZENDER (Swiss, 1901–1988) – Place de la
Concorde, Paris, 1947 – signed and dated – oil on canvas –
50 x 92cm.
(Galerie Koller Zürich)   **$10,287   £5,372**

H. ZIEGER – The birches – signed – 73.6 x 55.8cm.
(Christie's)   **$2,090   £1,100**

HEINRICH ZILLE (1858–1929) – Children singing –
signed – original lithograph on light grey printing paper –
34.8 x 27.3cm.
(Lempertz)   **$2,829   £1,458**

DORIS ZINKEISEN – Café in the Champs Elysées – oil
on canvas – signed – 61 x 51cm.
(Bonhams)   **$6,000   £3,000**

CARL-FRIEDRICH ZIMMERMANN (1796–1820) –
The artist's studio – signed and dated 1818 – oil on canvas
– 41.3 x 62cm.
(Sotheby's)   **$29,284   £16,734**

DORIS ZINKEISEN – Bathing at Scarborough – signed
– 50.7 x 61cm.
(Christie's)   **$3,135   £1,650**

AURELIO ZINGONI (1853–1922) – Lo Spazzacamino –
signed and dated 1885 – oil on canvas – 72.6 x 51.3cm.
(Christie's)   **$11,994   £6,380**

ZOETELIEF-TROMP

JAN ZOETELIEF-TROMP (1872–1947) – Two children playing on a beach – signed – on panel – 19 x 26.5cm.
(Christie's)   **$21,057**   **£11,896**

RUFUS FAIRCHILD ZOGBAUM (1849–1925) – A memory of the war – signed and dated 92 – gouache en grisaille on board – 24.8 x 31.8cm.
(Christie's)   **$1,980**   **£1,175**

MARGUERITE ZORACH (1887–1968) – Maine fishing village – signed – oil on canvas – 66 x 81.5cm.
(Christie's)   **$20,900**   **£10,868**

ANDERS ZORN (1860–1920) – Little Morakulla with a basket on her arm – signed – watercolour – oval – 43 x 32.5cm.
(AB Stockholms Auktionsverk)   **$50,157**   **£25,854**

ANDERS ZORN (Swedish, 1860–1920) – Gerta Lundequist – signed – etching on paper – unframed – 7⁷/₈ x 5⁷/₈in.
(Skinner Inc.)   **$275**   **£147**

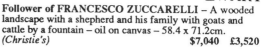

Follower of FRANCESCO ZUCCARELLI – A wooded landscape with a shepherd and his family with goats and cattle by a fountain – oil on canvas – 58.4 x 71.2cm.
(Christie's)   **$7,040**   **£3,520**

Follower of FRANCESCO ZUCCARELLI, R.A. – Saint Joseph and the Christ Child with Angels – 81.2 x 104.2cm.
(Christie's)   **$6,600**   **£3,300**

ANDERS ZORN – The torn shift, 1905 – signed – etching on laid paper – 19.5 x 14.5cm.
(AB Stockholms Auktionsverk)   **$1,167**   **£576**

JAN JACOB ZUIDEMA BROOS (1833–1882) – 'Uitspanning' – An elegant company merrymaking outside an inn – signed – on panel – 31 x 42cm.
(Christie's)   **$7,019**   **£3,965**

ANDERS ZORN (1860–1920) – Cousins, 1883 – etching on vellum – 44.4 x 27.8cm.
(AB Stockholms Auktionsverk)   **$15,311**   **£7,892**

WILLEM DE ZWART (1862–1931) – Summer: Elegant figures having tea in the park – signed – 26.5 x 47cm.
(Christie's)   **$15,207**   **£8,592**